Mastering API Architecture
Design, Operate, and Evolve API-Based Systems

James Gough, Daniel Bryant, and Matthew Auburn

Beijing · Boston · Farnham · Sebastopol · Tokyo

Mastering API Architecture

by James Gough, Daniel Bryant, and Matthew Auburn

Copyright © 2023 James Gough Ltd, Big Picture Tech Ltd, and Matthew Auburn Ltd. All rights reserved.

Published by O'Reilly Media, Inc., 1005 Gravenstein Highway North, Sebastopol, CA 95472.

O'Reilly books may be purchased for educational, business, or sales promotional use. Online editions are also available for most titles (*http://oreilly.com*). For more information, contact our corporate/institutional sales department: 800-998-9938 or *corporate@oreilly.com*.

Acquisitions Editor: Melissa Duffield	**Indexer:** nSight, Inc.
Development Editor: Virginia Wilson	**Interior Designer:** David Futato
Production Editor: Clare Laylock	**Cover Designer:** Karen Montgomery
Copyeditor: Kim Cofer	**Illustrator:** Kate Dullea
Proofreader: Amnet Systems LLC	

October 2022:   First Edition

Revision History for the First Edition
2022-10-17:   First Release

See *http://oreilly.com/catalog/errata.csp?isbn=9781492090632* for release details.

The O'Reilly logo is a registered trademark of O'Reilly Media, Inc. *Mastering API Architecture*, the cover image, and related trade dress are trademarks of O'Reilly Media, Inc.

While the publisher and the authors have used good faith efforts to ensure that the information and instructions contained in this work are accurate, the publisher and the authors disclaim all responsibility for errors or omissions, including without limitation responsibility for damages resulting from the use of or reliance on this work. Use of the information and instructions contained in this work is at your own risk. If any code samples or other technology this work contains or describes is subject to open source licenses or the intellectual property rights of others, it is your responsibility to ensure that your use thereof complies with such licenses and/or rights.

978-1-492-09063-2

[LSI]

This book is dedicated to Alex Blewitt, who unfortunately passed away before publication. We would like to thank Alex for his candid feedback, constant support, and warm friendship over the years.

—The Authors

Table of Contents

Part I.   Designing, Building, and Testing APIs

Part IV. Evolutionary Architecture with APIs

Foreword

When I built my first APIs at the *Financial Times*, over a decade ago, there weren't too many of them. We were building on a monolithic architecture, and the APIs were solely there for external third parties to get access to our content.

Now though, APIs are everywhere and they are core to your success when building a system.

That's because, over the last decade, a couple of things have combined to change the way many of us do software development.

Firstly, the technology available for us changed. The rise of cloud computing gave us self-service, on-demand provisioning. Automated build and deployment pipelines allowed us to do continuous integration and deployment, and containers and associated technologies like orchestration let us run large numbers of small, independent services as a distributed system.

Why are we doing that? Because of the second thing: the research showing that successful software development organizations have loosely coupled architectures and autonomous, empowered teams. Successful here is defined in terms of a positive impact on the business: increased market share, productivity, and profitability.

Our architectures now tend to be more loosely coupled, distributed, and built around APIs. You want your APIs to be discoverable, consistent, and unlikely to cause problems to the consumers even if they change unexpectedly or disappear. Anything else will couple work together and slow down your teams.

In this book, James, Daniel and Matthew provide a comprehensive and practical guide to building effective API architectures. They cover a lot of ground, from how to build and test an individual API, through the ecosystem you deploy them into, the ways to release and operate them effectively, and perhaps most importantly, how to use APIs to evolve your architecture. Those first APIs I built at the *Financial Times* don't exist anymore, and we built those systems again from scratch. That's costly. James, Daniel, and Matthew provide a template for how to deal with inevitable change and evolve your systems, using APIs as a key tool.

Software architecture has been defined as those decisions that are both important and hard to change. These are the decisions that will make your project succeed—or fail.

The authors' focus is not on architecture in the abstract, but on how you apply architecture within your own organizations. Deciding to adopt an API gateway or a service mesh, and which one, is exactly the kind of hard-to-undo decision that you should approach with caution and evaluate carefully. James, Daniel, and Matthew give strong, opinionated guidance where they feel it is appropriate, and where the options are less clearcut, they provide a framework to help you make the best choice for your circumstances.

They illustrate throughout with a practical and realistic case study that takes the concepts and shows how you actually make them work in practice. Their case study evolves throughout the book, in the same way real systems do. The authors show that you don't have to do everything upfront; you can evolve your architecture piece by piece, extracting services and adding tools like API gateways and service meshes as you find you need them.

When I built my first APIs, I made a lot of mistakes. I wish I'd had a book like this, to help me understand where I might trip up, and to guide me towards sensible decisions.

I recommend this book to anyone leading work on systems where APIs play a major role. With it, you should be able to develop a consistent set of tools and standards to support every team building APIs in your organization.

— Sarah Wells,
Co-Chair of the QCon London conference,
independent consultant, and former
Technical Director at the Financial Times,
Reading, UK, September 2022

Preface

Why Did We Write This Book?

In early 2020 we attended O'Reilly Software Architecture in New York, where Jim and Matt gave a workshop on APIs and a presentation on API gateways. Jim and Daniel know each other from the London Java Community, and like at many architecture events, we got together to talk about our thoughts and understanding around API architectures. As we were talking on the hallway track, several conference delegates came up to us and chatted about their experiences with APIs. People were asking for our thoughts and guidance on their API journey. It was at this point that we thought writing a book on the topic of APIs would help share our discussions from conferences with other architects.

Why Should You Read This Book?

This book has been designed to provide a complete picture on designing, operating, and evolving an API architecture. We have shared our experience and advice through both our writing and an accompanying case study that mimics a real-life event-management conference system that enables attendees to view and book presentation sessions. The case study runs throughout the book, with the goal of you exploring how abstract concepts sometimes translate into practical application. If you want a high-level overview of the evolution of the case study, you can find this in Chapter 10.

We also believe in allowing you to make your own decisions. To support this, we will:

- Be clear when we have a strong recommendation or guidance.
- Highlight areas of caution and problems that you may encounter.

- Supply an Architecture Decision Record (ADR) Guideline[1] to help inform the best possible decision given the circumstances of your architecture and provide guidance on what to consider (because sometimes the answer is "it depends").

- Highlight references and useful articles where you can find more in-depth content.

The book is not just a greenfield technology book. We felt that covering existing architectures with an evolutionary approach toward more suitable API architectures would provide the most benefit for you. We also tried to balance this with looking forward to newer technologies and developments in the API architecture domain.

Who This Book Is For

Although we had an initial persona in mind when creating this book, during the writing and reviewing process three key personas emerged: the developer, an accidental architect, and the solutions or enterprise architect. We have outlined these personas in the following sections, with the aim that you not only identify with at least one of them, but also so that you can look at each chapter through the different lens these personas provide.

Developer

You have most likely been coding professionally for several years and have a good understanding of common software development challenges, patterns, and best practices. You are increasingly realizing that the software industry's march toward building service-oriented architecture (SOA) and adopting cloud services means that building and operating APIs is fast becoming a core skill. You are keen to learn more about designing effective APIs and testing them. You want to explore the various implementation choices (e.g., synchronous versus asynchronous communication) and technologies and learn how to ask the right questions and evaluate which approach is best for a given context.

Accidental Architect

You have most likely been developing software for many years and have often operated as a team lead or resident software architect (even if you don't have the official titles). You understand core architectural concepts, such as designing for high cohesion and loose coupling, and apply these to all aspects of software development, including design, testing, and operating systems.

---

1 You will learn more about ADRs and their importance to making and documenting architectural decisions in the Introduction.

You realize that your role is increasingly focused on combining systems to meet customer requirements. This could include internally built applications and third-party SaaS-type offerings. APIs play a big part in successfully integrating your systems with external systems. You want to learn more about the supporting technologies (e.g., API gateway, service mesh, etc.) and also understand how to operate and secure API-based systems.

Solutions/Enterprise Architect

You have been designing and building enterprise software systems for several years and most likely have the word *architect* in your job title or role description. You are responsible for the big picture of software delivery and typically work within the context of a large organization or a series of large interconnected organizations.

You recognize the changes that the latest iteration of service-based architectural styles are having on the design, integration, and governance of software, and you see APIs are pivotal to the success of your organization's software strategy. You are keen to learn more about evolutionary patterns and understand how the choice of API design and implementation will impact this. You also want to focus on the cross-functional "ilities"—usability, maintainability, scalability, and availability—and understand how to build API-based systems that exhibit such properties, as well as provide security.

What You Will Learn

After reading this book you will understand:

- The fundamentals of REST APIs and how to best build, version, and test APIs
- The architectural patterns involved in building an API platform
- The differences in managing API traffic at ingress and within service-to-service communication, and how to apply patterns and technologies such as API gateways and service meshes
- Threat modeling and key security considerations for APIs, such as authentication, authorization, and encryption
- How to evolve existing systems toward APIs and different target deployments, such as the cloud

And you will be able to:

- Design, build, and test API-based systems
- Help to implement and drive an organization's API program from an architectural perspective
- Deploy, release, and configure key components of an API platform

- Deploy gateways and service meshes based on case studies
- Identify vulnerabilities in API architecture and implement measured security mitigations
- Contribute to emerging API trends and the associated communities

What This Book Is Not

We realize that APIs encompass a vast market space and we want to be clear what this book will not cover. That doesn't mean to say that we believe these topics are not important; however, if we tried to cover everything we wouldn't be able to share our knowledge effectively with you.

We will cover application patterns for migration and modernization that will include taking advantage of cloud platforms, but *the book is not wholly focused on cloud technologies*. Many of you will have hybrid architectures or even have all of your systems hosted in data centers. We want to ensure that we cover the design and operational factors of API architectures that support both approaches.

The book is not tied to a specific language but will use some lightweight examples to demonstrate approaches to building/designing APIs and their corresponding infrastructure. The book will focus more on the approach, and code examples will be available in the accompanying GitHub repository (*https://github.com/masteringapi*).

The book does not favor one style of architecture over another, however we will discuss situations in which architectural approaches may cause limitations to the API offering presented.

Conventions Used in This Book

The following typographical conventions are used in this book:

Italic
> Indicates new terms, URLs, email addresses, filenames, and file extensions.

`Constant width`
> Used for program listings, as well as within paragraphs to refer to program elements such as variable or function names, databases, data types, environment variables, statements, and keywords.

`Constant width bold`
> Shows commands or other text that should be typed literally by the user.

`Constant width italic`
> Shows text that should be replaced with user-supplied values or by values determined by context.

This element signifies a tip or suggestion.

This element signifies a general note.

This element indicates a warning or caution.

Using Code Examples

Supplemental material (code examples, exercises, etc.) is available for download at *https://github.com/masteringapi*.

If you have a technical question or a problem using the code examples, please send an email to *bookquestions@oreilly.com*.

This book is here to help you get your job done. In general, if example code is offered with this book, you may use it in your programs and documentation. You do not need to contact us for permission unless you're reproducing a significant portion of the code. For example, writing a program that uses several chunks of code from this book does not require permission. Selling or distributing examples from O'Reilly books does require permission. Answering a question by citing this book and quoting example code does not require permission. Incorporating a significant amount of example code from this book into your product's documentation does require permission.

We appreciate, but generally do not require, attribution. An attribution usually includes the title, author, publisher, and ISBN. For example: "*Mastering API Architecture* by James Gough, Daniel Bryant, and Matthew Auburn (O'Reilly). Copyright 2023 James Gough Ltd, Big Picture Tech Ltd, and Matthew Auburn Ltd, 978-1-492-09063-2."

If you feel your use of code examples falls outside fair use or the permission given above, feel free to contact us at *permissions@oreilly.com*.

O'Reilly Online Learning

 For more than 40 years, *O'Reilly Media* has provided technology and business training, knowledge, and insight to help companies succeed.

Our unique network of experts and innovators share their knowledge and expertise through books, articles, and our online learning platform. O'Reilly's online learning platform gives you on-demand access to live training courses, in-depth learning paths, interactive coding environments, and a vast collection of text and video from O'Reilly and 200+ other publishers. For more information, visit *https://oreilly.com*.

How to Contact Us

Please address comments and questions concerning this book to the publisher:

O'Reilly Media, Inc.
1005 Gravenstein Highway North
Sebastopol, CA 95472
800-998-9938 (in the United States or Canada)
707-829-0515 (international or local)
707-829-0104 (fax)

We have a web page for this book, where we list errata, examples, and any additional information. You can access this page at *https://oreil.ly/Mastering-API-Architecture*.

Email *bookquestions@oreilly.com* to comment or ask technical questions about this book.

For news and information about our books and courses, visit *https://oreilly.com*.

Find us on LinkedIn: *https://linkedin.com/company/oreilly-media*.

Follow us on Twitter: *https://twitter.com/oreillymedia*.

Watch us on YouTube: *https://www.youtube.com/oreillymedia*.

Acknowledgments

As with almost all technical books, only three names may be listed as authors on the front of this book, but the reality is that many people have contributed, either directly in the form of feedback as the book was written, or indirectly by their teaching and guidance over the years.

Although we can't possibly list everyone who has helped us during this journey, we would like to explicitly thank the people who took time out of their busy schedules to provide extensive discussions, feedback, and support.

Our technical reviewers: Sam Newman, Dov Katz, Sarah Wells, Antoine Cailliau, Stefania Chaplin, Matt McLarty, and Neal Ford.

For general detail, encouragement, advice, and introductions: Charles Humble, Richard Li, Simon Brown, Nick Ebbitt, Jason Morgan, Nic Jackson, Cliff Tiltman, Elspeth Minty, George Ball, Benjamin Evans, and Martijn Verberg.

The O'Reilly Team: Virginia Wilson, Melissa Duffield, and Nicole Tache.

James Gough

I would like to thank my incredible family: Megan, Emily, and Anna. Writing would not have been possible without their help and support. I'd also like to thank my parents, Heather and Paul, for encouraging me to learn and for their constant support.

I'd like to thank my coauthors Daniel and Matt; writing a book is a challenge and, like architecture, is never perfect. It has been a fun journey and we have all learned a lot from each other and our amazing reviewers. Finally, I'd like to thank Jon Daplyn, Ed Safo, David Halliwell, and Dov Katz for providing me support, opportunities, and encouragement throughout my career.

Daniel Bryant

I would like to thank my entire family for their love and support, both during the authoring process and throughout my career. I would also like to thank Jim and Matt for being great partners on this writing journey. We started this book in early 2020, just as the pandemic hit. Our weekly Wednesday morning calls were not only useful for collaboration but also a great source of fun and support as our worlds rapidly changed. Finally, I would like to thank everyone involved in the London Java Community (LJC), the InfoQ/QCon teams, and everyone at Ambassador Labs. These three communities have provided me with access to mentors, guidance, and so many opportunities. I hope to someday pay all of this forward.

Matthew Auburn

I would like to thank my amazing wife Hannah—without your support I would not have been able to write this book. Thank you to both of my parents; you have shown me that anything is possible and never stopped believing in me. This book has been such an amazing experience to go through, and Jim and Dan, you have both been excellent mentors. Both of you have taught me so much and helped me write the best material possible. An additional thanks to Jim—you introduced me to speaking and have helped me more than anyone else in my career. Finally and most importantly, I want to thank my son Joshi: you are an absolute joy.

Introduction

In this introduction, you will discover the basics of APIs and their potential to be part of the architecture journey. We will introduce a lightweight definition for APIs and their use in and out of process. In order to demonstrate the importance of APIs, we will introduce the conference system case study, a running example that will evolve throughout the book. Out-of-process APIs allow you to think beyond a simple three-tiered architecture; we will introduce traffic patterns and their importance to demonstrate this. We will outline a summary of the case study steps, allowing you to skip ahead if an area is of interest to you straight away.

In order to present APIs and their associated ecosystem, we will use a series of important artifacts. We will introduce the case study with C4 model diagrams (*https:// c4model.com*) and revisit the specifics and logic behind the approach. You will also learn about the use of Architecture Decision Records (ADRs) and the value of clearly defining decisions across the software lifecycle. As the introduction closes, we will outline ADR Guidelines—our approach to help you make decisions when the answer is "it depends."

The Architecture Journey

Anyone who has taken a long journey will no doubt have encountered the question (and possibly persistently) *"are we there yet?"* For the first few inquiries, you look at the GPS or a route planner and provide an estimate—hoping that you don't encounter any delays along the way. Similarly, the journey to building API-based architectures can be complex for developers and architects to navigate; even if there was an *Architecture GPS*, what would your destination be?

Architecture is a journey without a destination, and you cannot predict how technologies and architectural approaches will change. For example, you may not have been able to predict service mesh technology would become so widely used, but once you learn about its capabilities it may cause you to think about evolving your existing architecture. It is not only technologies that influence change in architecture; new business requirements and constraints also drive change in architectural direction.

The culminating effect of delivering incremental value combined with new emerging technologies leads to the concept of evolutionary architecture. Evolutionary architecture is an approach to incrementally changing an architecture, focusing on the ability to change with speed and reducing the risk of negative impacts. Along the way, we ask you to keep the following advice in approaching API architecture in mind:

> Though architects like to be able to strategically plan for the future, the constantly changing software development ecosystem makes that difficult. Since we can't avoid change, we need to exploit it.
>
> —*Building Evolutionary Architectures* by Neal Ford, Rebecca Parsons, and Patrick Kua (O'Reilly)

In many projects APIs themselves are evolutionary, requiring change as more systems and services are integrated. Most developers have built services that focus on a single function without considering the broader API reuse from a consumer perspective.

API-First design is an approach where developers and architects consider the functionality of their service and design an API in a consumer-centric manner. The API consumer could be a mobile application, another service, or even an external customer. In Chapter 1 we will review design techniques to support an API-First approach and discover how we build APIs that are durable to change and deliver value to a broad consumer base.

The good news is that you can start an API-driven architecture journey at any point. If you are responsible for preexisting technical inventory, we will show you techniques to evolve your architecture to promote the use of APIs in your platform. On the other hand, if you are lucky and have a blank canvas to work with, we will share with you the benefit of adopting API architectures based on our years of experience, while also highlighting key factors in decision making.

A Brief Introduction to APIs

In the field of software architecture, there are a handful of terms that are incredibly difficult to define. The term API, which stands for application programming interface, falls into this categorization, as the concept first surfaced as many as 80 years ago. Terms that have been around for a significant amount of time end up being overused and having multiple meanings in different problem spaces. We consider an API to mean the following:

- An API represents an abstraction of the underlying implementation.
- An API is represented by a specification that introduces types. Developers can understand the specifications and use tooling to generate code in multiple languages to implement an API consumer (software that consumes an API).
- An API has defined semantics or behavior to effectively model the exchange of information.
- Effective API design enables extension to customers or third parties for a business integration.

Broadly speaking, APIs can be broken into two general categories depending on whether the API invocation is *in process* or *out of process*. The *process* being referred to here is an operating system (OS) process. For example, a Java method invocation from one class to another is an *in-process* API invocation, as the call is handled by the same process from which the call was made. A .NET application invocating an external REST-like API using an HTTP library is an *out-of-process* API invocation, as the call is handled by an additional external process other than the process from which the call was made. Typically, an out-of-process API call will involve data traversing a network, potentially a local network, virtual private cloud (VPC) network, or the internet. We will focus on the latter style of APIs; however, architects will often encounter the requirement to remodel an in-process API to an out-of-process API. In order to demonstrate this concept (and others), we will create a running case study that will evolve throughout the book.

Running Example: Conference System Case Study

We have chosen to model a conference system for our case study because the domain is easily recognizable but also provides enough complexity for modeling an evolutionary architecture. Figure I-1 visualizes the conference system at the top level, allowing us to set the context of the architecture under discussion. The system is used by an external customer to create their attendee account, review the conference sessions available, and book their attendance.

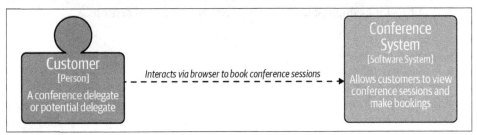

Figure I-1. C4 conference system context diagram

Let's zoom in to the conference system box in Figure I-2. Expanding the conference system provides us more detail about its major technical building blocks. The customer interacts with the web application, which invokes APIs on the conference application. The conference application uses SQL to query the backing datastore.

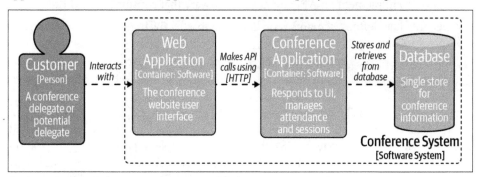

Figure I-2. C4 conference system container diagram

Figure I-2 reveals that from an API perspective the most interesting functionality is within the conference application container. Figure I-3 zooms in to this specific container, allowing you to explore the structure and interactions.

Four major components and the database are involved in the current system. The *API Controller* faces all incoming traffic from the UI and makes a decision about where to route the request in the system. This component would also be responsible for marshaling from the *on the wire* network-level representation to an object or representation in code. The API Controller component is intriguing from the perspective of *in-process* routing and acting as a junction point or *front controller* pattern. For API requests and processing, this is an important pattern; all requests pass through the controller, which makes a decision on where the request is directed. In Chapter 3 we will look at the potential for taking the controller out of process.

The *Attendee, Booking,* and *Session* components are involved in translating the requests into queries and execute SQL against the database out of process. In the existing architecture, the database is an important component, potentially enforcing relationships—for example, constraints between bookings and sessions.

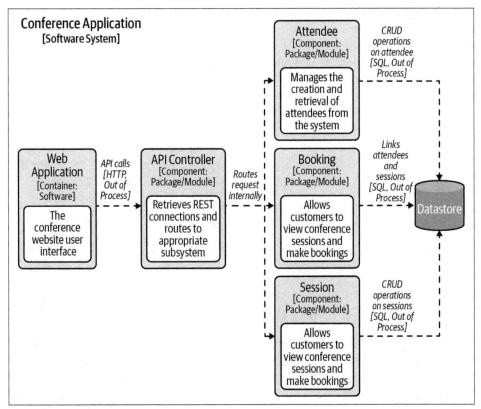

Figure I-3. C4 conference system component diagram

Now that we have drilled down to the appropriate level of detail, let's revisit the types of API interactions in the case study at this point.

Types of APIs in the Conference Case Study

In Figure I-3 the *Web Application* to *API Controller* arrow is an out-of-process call, whereas the *API Controller* to *Attendee Component* arrow is an example of an in-process call. All interactions within the Conference Application boundary are examples of in-process calls. The in-process invocation is well defined and restricted by the programming language used to implement the Conference Application. The invocation is compile-time safe (the conditions under which the exchange mechanism are enforced at the time of writing code).

Reasons for Changing the Conference System

The current architectural approach has worked for the conference system for many years, however the conference owner has asked for three improvements, which are driving architectural change:

- The conference organizers would like to build a mobile application.
- The conference organizers plan to go global with their system, running tens of conferences instead of one per year. In order to facilitate this expansion, they would like to integrate with an external Call for Papers (CFP) system for managing speakers and their application to present sessions at the conference.
- The conference organizers would like to decommission their private data center and instead run the conference system on a cloud platform with global reach.

Our goal is to migrate the conference system to be able to support the new requirements, without impacting the existing production system or rewriting everything in one go.

From Tiered Architecture to Modeling APIs

The starting point of the case study is a typical three-tier architecture, composed of a UI, a server-side processing tier, and a datastore. To begin to discuss an evolutionary architecture we need a model to think about the way API requests are processed by the components. We need a model/abstraction that will work for both the public cloud, virtual machines in a data center and a hybrid approach.

The abstraction of traffic will allow us to consider out-of-process interactions between an API consumer and an API service, sometimes referred to as the API producer. With architectural approaches like service-oriented architecture (SOA) and microservices-based architecture, the importance of modeling API interactions is critical. Learning about API traffic and the style of communication between components will be the difference between realizing the advantages of increased decoupling or creating a maintenance nightmare.

 Traffic patterns are used by data center engineers to describe network exchanges within data centers and between low-level applications. At the API level we are using traffic patterns to describe flows between groups of applications. For the purposes of this book, we are referring to application and API-level traffic patterns.

Case Study: An Evolutionary Step

To start to consider traffic pattern types, it will be useful to take a small evolutionary step in our case study architecture. In Figure I-4 a step has been taken to refactor the *Attendee* component into an independent service, as opposed to a package or module within the *legacy conference system*. The conference system now has two traffic flows: the interaction between the customer and the legacy conference system and the interaction between the legacy system and the attendee system.

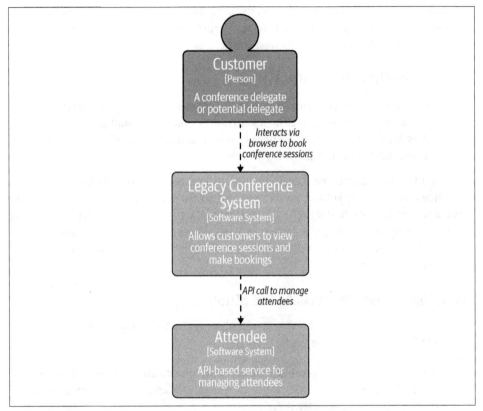

Figure I-4. C4 conference system context—evolutionary step

North–south traffic

In Figure I-4 interaction between the customer and the legacy conference system is referred to a north–south traffic, and it represents an ingress flow. The customer is using the UI, which is sending requests to the legacy conference system over the internet. This represents a point in our network that is exposed publicly and will be accessed by the UI.[1] This means that any component handling north–south traffic must make concrete checks about client identity and also include appropriate challenges before allowing traffic to progress through the system. Chapter 7 will go into detail about securing north–south API traffic.

---

1 The intention is it will be the UI accessing the ingress point. However, it is open for potential exploit.

East–west traffic

The new interaction between the legacy conference system and the Attendee service introduces an east–west traffic flow to our system. East–west traffic can be thought of as *service-to-service* style of communication within a group of applications. Most east–west traffic, particularly if the origin is within your wider infrastructure, can be trusted to some degree. Although we can trust the source of the traffic, it is still necessary to consider securing east–west traffic.

API Infrastructure and Traffic Patterns

There are two key infrastructure components present in API-based architectures, which are key to controlling traffic. Controlling and coordinating traffic is often described as *traffic management*. Generally north–south traffic will be controlled by API gateways, the key subject for Chapter 3.

East–west traffic will often be handled by infrastructure components like Kubernetes or service mesh, the key subject for Chapter 4. Infrastructure components like Kubernetes and service mesh use network abstractions to route to services, requiring services to run inside a managed environment. In some systems east–west traffic is managed by the application itself and service discovery techniques are implemented to locate other systems.

Roadmap for the Conference Case Study

Throughout the course of the book you will observe the following changes or applications of technology to the case study:

- In Chapter 1 you will explore the design and specification of the Attendee API. We will also present the importance of versioning and modeling exchanges for performance of the Attendee API.

- In Chapter 2 you will explore contract and component testing to verify behavior of the Attendee service. You will also see how Testcontainers can help with integration testing.

- In Chapter 3 you will look at exposing the Attendee service to consumers using an API gateway. We will also demonstrate how to evolve the conference system using an API gateway on Kubernetes.

- In Chapter 4 we will refactor the sessions functionality out of the legacy conference system using a service mesh. You will also learn about how service mesh helps with routing, observability, and security.

- In Chapter 5 we will discuss feature flagging and how this can help to evolve the conference system and avoid a coupled deployment and release. You will also explore approaches for modeling releases in the conference system and we will demonstrate the use of Argo Rollouts for the Attendee service.

- In Chapter 6 you will explore how to apply threat modeling and mitigate OWASP concerns in the Attendee service.

- In Chapter 7 you will look at authentication and authorization and how this is implemented for the Attendee service.

- In Chapter 8 you will look at establishing the Attendee service domain boundaries and how different service patterns can help.

- In Chapter 9 you will look at cloud adoption and how to move the Attendee service to the cloud and consider replatforming.

The case study and the planned roadmap require us to visualize architectural change and record decisions. These are important artifacts that help to explain and plan changes in software projects. We believe that C4 diagrams and Architecture Decision Records (ADRs) represent a clear way of recording change.

Using C4 Diagrams

As part of introducing the case study, we revealed three types of C4 diagrams from the C4 model (*https://c4model.com*). We believe C4 is the best documentation standard for communicating architecture, context, and interactions to a diverse set of stakeholders. You may be wondering what about UML? The Unified Modeling Language (UML) provides an extensive dialect for communicating software architectures. A major challenge is that the majority of what UML provides is not committed to memory by architects and developers, and people quickly revert to boxes/circles/diamonds. It becomes a real challenge to understand the structure of diagrams before getting into the technical content of the discussion. Many diagrams are only committed to a project history if someone accidentally uses a permanent marker instead of dry wipe marker by mistake. The C4 model provides a simplified set of diagrams that act as a guide to your project architecture at various levels of detail.

C4 Context Diagram

Figure I-1 is represented using a C4 context diagram from the C4 model. The intention of this diagram is to set context for both a technical and nontechnical audience. Many architecture conversations dive straight into the low-level details and miss setting the context of the high-level interactions. Consider the implications of getting a system context diagram wrong—the benefit of summarizing the approach may save months of work to correct a misunderstanding.

C4 Container Diagram

While Figure I-1 provides the big picture of the conference system, a container diagram helps describe the technical breakout of the major participants in the architecture. A container in C4 is defined as *"something that needs to be running in order for the overall system to work"* (for example, the conference database). Container diagrams are technical in nature and build on the higher-level system context diagram. Figure I-2, a container diagram, documents the detail of a customer interacting with the conference system.

 The conference application container in Figure I-2 is documented as simply *software*. Normally a C4 container would provide more detail into the type of container (e.g., *Java Spring Application*). However in this book we will be avoiding technology specifics, unless it helps to demonstrate a specific solution. The advantage of APIs and indeed modern applications is that there is a significant amount of flexibility in the solution space.

C4 Component Diagram

The C4 component diagram in Figure I-3 helps to define the roles and responsibilities within each container, along with the internal interactions. This diagram is useful if the detail of a container is queried, and it also provides a very useful map to the codebase. Think about the first time starting work on a new project: browsing a *self-documenting* codebase is one approach—but it can be difficult to piece everything together. A component diagram reveals the detail of the language/stack you are using to build your software. In order to remain technology agnostic, we have used the term *package/module*.

Using Architecture Decision Records

As developers, architects, and indeed humans, we have all been in the position where we ask the question *"what were they thinking??"* If you have ever driven on the M62 between Leeds and Manchester in the United Kingdom, you may have been baffled by the construction of the motorway. As you climb the hill on the three-lane highway, it starts to deviate away from the traffic contraflow, until eventually Scott Hall Farm emerges surrounded by around 15 acres of farming land nestled between the carriages. Local legend of what happened described the owner of the land as stubborn and refusing to move or hand over his land, so the engineers simply built around him.[2] Fifty years later a documentary surfaced revealing that the real reason

---

2 Local stubborn traits fueled this likely explanation.

for this was a geological fault beneath the land, meaning the motorway had to be built that way. When people guess why something was done in a particular way, expect rumor, humor, and criticism to emerge.

In software architecture there will be many constraints that we have to build around, so it is important to ensure our decisions are recorded and transparent. ADRs help make decisions clear in software architecture.

> One of the hardest things to track during the life of a project is the motivation behind certain decisions. A new person coming on to a project may be perplexed, baffled, delighted, or infuriated by some past decision.
>
> —Michael Nygard, creator of the ADR concept

There are four key sections in an ADR: status, context, decision, and consequences. An ADR is created in a proposed status and based on discussion will usually be either accepted or rejected. It is also possible that the decision may be superseded later by a new ADR. The context helps to set the scene and describe the problem or the bounds in which the decision will be made. Although creating a blog post ahead of the ADR and then linking from the ADR helps the community to follow your work, the context is not intended to be a blog post or detailed description. The decision clearly sets out what you plan to do and how you plan to do it. All decisions carry consequences or trade-offs in architecture, and these can sometimes be incredibly costly to get wrong.

When reviewing an ADR it is important to see if you agree with the decision in the ADR or if there is an alternative approach. An alternative approach that has not been considered may cause the ADR to be rejected. There is a lot of value in a rejected ADR and most teams choose to keep ADRs immutable to capture the change in perspective. ADRs work best when they are presented in a location where key participants can view them, comment, and help move the ADR to accepted.

A question we often get asked is at what point should the team create an ADR? It is useful to ensure that there has been discussion ahead of the ADR and the record is a result of collective thinking in the team. Publishing an ADR to the wider community allows the opportunity for feedback beyond the immediate team.

Attendees Evolution ADR

In Figure I-4 we made the decision to take an evolutionary step in the conference system architecture. This is a major change and would warrant an ADR. Table I-1 is an example ADR that might have been proposed by the engineering team owning the conference system.

Table I-1. ADR001 separating attendees from the legacy conference system

Status	Proposed
Context	The conference owners have requested two new major features to the current conference system that need to be implemented without disrupting the current system. The conference system will need to be evolved to support a mobile application and an integration with an external CFP system. Both the mobile application and the external CFP system need to be able to access attendees to log in users to the third-party service.
Decision	We will take an evolutionary step as documented in Figure I-4 to split out the Attendee component into a standalone service. This will allow API-First development against the Attendee service and allow the API to be invoked from the legacy conference service. This will also support the ability to design for direct access to the Attendee service to provide user information to the external CFP system.
Consequences	The call to the Attendee service will not be *out of process* and may introduce a latency that will need to be tested. The Attendee service could become a single point of failure in the architecture and we may need to take steps to mitigate the potential impact of running a single Attendee service. With the planned multiple consumer model for the Attendee service, we will need to ensure good design, versioning, and testing to reduce accidental breaking changes.

Some of the consequences in the ADR are fairly major and definitely require further discussion. We are going to defer some of the consequences to later chapters.

Mastering API: ADR Guidelines

Within *Mastering API Architecture* we will be supplying *ADR Guidelines* to help collect important questions to ask when making decisions on the topic we are covering. Making decisions about an API-based architecture can be really tough, and in a lot of situations the answer is "it depends." Rather than say it depends without context, the ADR Guidelines will help describe what it depends on and help inform your decisions. The ADR Guidelines can be used as a reference point to come back to or to read ahead to if you're facing a specific challenge. Table I-2 outlines the format for the ADR Guidelines and what you should expect from them.

Table I-2. ADR Guideline: Format

Decision	Describes a decision that you might need to make when considering an aspect of this book.
Discussion Points	This section helps to identify the key discussions that you should be having when making a decision about your API architecture.
	In this section we will reveal some of our experiences that may have influenced the decision. We will help you to identify the key information to inform your decision making process.
Recommendations	We will make specific recommendations that you should consider when creating your ADR, explaining the rationale behind why we are making a specific recommendation.

Summary

In this introduction we have provided a foundation with both the case study and the approach we will take to discussing API-driven architectures:

- Architecture is an endless journey and APIs can play a major part in helping it evolve.

- APIs are an abstraction of the implementation and can either be in process or out of process. Often architects find themselves in a position of evolving to out-of-process APIs, the onward focus of this book.

- The conference case study is to describe and explain concepts. In this introduction you have seen a small evolutionary step to break out the Attendee service to address the upcoming business requirements.

- You have seen the first three levels of C4 diagrams and their importance in sharing and communicating architecture.

- ADRs provide a valuable record for making decisions and have both present and historical value in the lifetime of a project.

- You have seen the structure for ADR Guidelines that will be used throughout the book to help facilitate decision making.

With the decision made to break the Attendee service out from the conference system, we will now explore the options for designing and specifying the Attendee API.

PART I

Designing, Building, and Testing APIs

This section provides the foundational building blocks for API-driven architectures.

In Chapter 1 you will learn about REST and Remote Procedure Call (RPC)–based APIs. We will explore specifications and schemas, recommended standards, strategies for versioning, and how to choose the right API for your system.

In Chapter 2 you will learn about testing APIs and how different test styles are best applied to API-driven architectures.

Design, Build, and Specify APIs

You will be presented with many options when designing and building APIs. It is incredibly fast to build a service with modern technologies and frameworks, but creating a durable approach requires careful thought and consideration. In this chapter we will explore REST and RPC to model the producer and consumer relationships in the case study.

You will discover how standards can help to shortcut design decisions and navigate away from potential compatibility issues. You will look at OpenAPI Specifications, the practical uses for teams, and the importance of versioning.

RPC-based interactions are specified using a schema; to compare and contrast with a REST approach, we will explore gRPC. With both REST and gRPC in mind, we will look at the different factors to consider in how we model exchanges. We will look at the possibility of providing both a REST and RPC API in the same service and whether this is the right thing to do.

Case Study: Designing the Attendee API

In the Introduction we decided to migrate our legacy conference system and move toward a more API-driven architecture. As a first step to making this change, we are going to create a new Attendee service, which will expose a matching Attendee API. We also provided a narrow definition of an API. In order to design effectively, we need to consider more broadly the exchange between the producer and consumer, and more importantly who the producer and consumer are. The producer is owned by the attendee team. This team maintains two key relationships:

- The attendee team owns the producer, and the legacy conference team owns the consumer. There is a close relationship between these two teams and any changes in structure are easily coordinated. A strong cohesion between the producer/consumer services is possible to achieve.

- The attendee team owns the producer, and the external CFP system team owns the consumer. There is a relationship between the teams, but any changes need to be coordinated to not break the integration. A loose coupling is required and breaking changes would need to be carefully managed.

We will compare and contrast the approaches to designing and building the Attendee API throughout this chapter.

Introduction to REST

REpresentation State Transfer (REST) is a set of architectural constraints, most commonly applied using HTTP as the underlying transport protocol. Roy Fielding's dissertation "Architectural Styles and the Design of Network-based Software Architectures" (*https://oreil.ly/VZ8VV*) provides a complete definition of REST. From a practical perspective, to be considered RESTful your API must ensure that:

- A producer-to-consumer interaction is modeled where the producer models resources the consumer can interact with.

- Requests from producer to consumer are stateless, meaning that the producer doesn't cache details of a previous request. In order to build up a chain of requests on a given resource, the consumer must send any required information to the producer for processing.

- Requests are cachable, meaning the producer can provide hints to the consumer where this is appropriate. In HTTP this is often provided in information contained in the header.

- A uniform interface is conveyed to the consumer. You will explore the use of verbs, resources, and other patterns shortly.

- It is a layered system, abstracting away the complexity of systems sitting behind the REST interface. For example, the consumer should not know or care if they're interacting with a database or other services.

Introduction to REST and HTTP by Example

Let's see an example of REST over HTTP. The following exchange is a *GET* request, where GET represents the method or verb. A verb such as GET describes the action to take on a particular resource; in this example, we consider the *attendees* resource.

An *Accept* header is passed to define the type of content the consumer would like to retrieve. REST defines the notion of a representation in the body and allows for representation *metadata* to be defined in the headers.

In the examples in this chapter, we represent a request above the - - - separator and a response below:

```
GET http://mastering-api.com/attendees
Accept: application/json
---
200 OK
Content-Type: application/json
{
    "displayName": "Jim",
    "id": 1
}
```

The response includes the status code and message from the server, which enables the consumer to interrogate the result of the operation on the server-side resource. The status code of this request was a 200 OK, meaning the request was successfully processed by the producer. In the response body a JSON representation containing the conference attendees is returned. Many content types are valid for return from a REST, however it is important to consider if the content type is parsable by the consumer. For example, returning `application/pdf` is valid but would not represent an exchange that could easily be used by another system. We will explore approaches to modeling content types, primarily looking at JSON, later in this chapter.

 REST is relatively straightforward to implement because the client and server relationship is stateless, meaning no client state is persisted by the server. The client must pass the context back to the server in subsequent requests; for example, a request for *http://mastering-api.com/attendees/1* would retrieve more information on a specific attendee.

The Richardson Maturity Model

Speaking at QCon (*https://oreil.ly/scjnV*) in 2008, Leonard Richardson presented his experiences of reviewing many REST APIs. Richardson found levels of adoption that teams apply to building APIs from a REST perspective. Martin Fowler also covered Richardson's maturity heuristics on his blog (*https://oreil.ly/j6U3s*). Table 1-1 explores the different levels represented by Richardson's maturity heuristics and their application to RESTful APIs.

Table 1-1. Richardson maturity heuristics

Level 0 - HTTP/RPC	Establishes that the API is built using HTTP and has the notion of a single URI. Taking our preceding example of /attendees and not applying a verb to specify intent, we would open up an endpoint for exchange. Essentially this represents an RPC implementation over the REST protocol.
Level 1 - Resources	Establishes the use of resources and starts to bring in the idea of modeling resources in the context of the URI. In our example, if we added GET /attendees/1 returning a specific attendee, it would start to look like a level 1 API. Martin Fowler draws an analogy to the classic object-oriented world of introducing identity.
Level 2 - Verbs (Methods)	Starts to introduce the correct modeling of multiple resource URIs accessed by different request methods (also known as HTTP verbs) based on the effect of the resources on the server. An API at level 2 can make guarantees around GET methods not impacting server state and presenting multiple operations on the same resource URI. In our example adding DELETE /attendees/1, PUT /attendees/1 would start to add the notion of a level 2–compliant API.
Level 3 - Hypermedia Controls	This is the epitome of REST design and involves navigable APIs by the use of HATEOAS (Hypertext As The Engine Of Application State) (*https://oreil.ly/7F18d*). In our example, when we call GET /attendees/1, the response would contain the actions that are possible on the object returned from the server. This would include the option to be able to update the attendee or delete the attendee and what the client is required to invoke in order to do so. In practical terms level 3 is rarely used in modern RESTful HTTP services, and although the navigation is a benefit in flexible UI style systems, it doesn't suit interservice API calls. Using HATEOAS would be a chatty experience and is often short-circuited by having a complete specification of possible interactions up front while programming against the producer.

When designing API exchanges, the different levels of Richardson Maturity are important to consider. Moving toward level 2 will enable you to project an understandable resource model to the consumer, with appropriate actions available against the model. In turn, this reduces coupling and hides the full detail of the backing service. Later we will also see how this abstraction is applied to versioning.

If the consumer is the CFP team, modeling an exchange with low coupling and projecting a RESTful model would be a good starting point. If the consumer is the legacy conference team, we may still choose to use a RESTful API, but there is also another option with RPC. In order to start to consider this type of traditionally east–west modeling, we will explore RPC.

Introduction to Remote Procedure Call (RPC) APIs

A Remote Procedure Call (RPC) involves calling a method in one process but having it execute code in another process. While REST can project a model of the domain and provides an abstraction from the underlying technology to the consumer, RPC involves exposing a method from one process and allows it to be called directly from another.

gRPC is a modern open source high-performance RPC. gRPC is under stewardship of the Linux Foundation and is the de facto standard for RPC across most platforms. Figure 1-1 describes an RPC call in gRPC, which involves the legacy conference service invoking the remote method on the Attendee service. The gRPC Attendee service starts and exposes a gRPC server on a specified port, allowing methods to be invoked remotely. On the client side (the legacy conference service), a stub is used to abstract the complexity of making the remote call into the library. gRPC requires a schema to fully cover the interaction between producer and consumer.

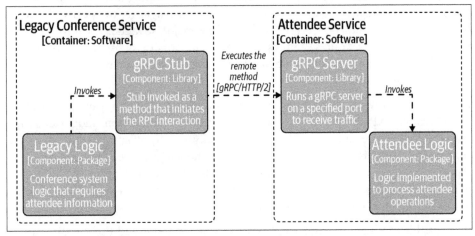

Figure 1-1. Example C4 component diagram using gRPC

A key difference between REST and RPC is state. REST is by definition stateless—with RPC state depends on the implementation. RPC-based integrations in certain situations can also build up state as part of the exchange. This buildup of state has the convenience of high performance at the potential cost of reliability and routing complexities. With RPC the model tends to convey the exact functionality at a method level that is required from a secondary service. This optionality in state can lead to an exchange that is potentially more coupled between producer and consumer. Coupling is not always a bad thing, especially in east–west services where performance is a key consideration.

A Brief Mention of GraphQL

Before we explore REST and RPC styles in detail, we would be remiss not to mention GraphQL and where it fits into the API world. RPC offers access to a series of individual functions provided by a producer but does not usually extend a model or abstraction to the consumer. REST, on the other hand, extends a resource model for a single API provided by the producer. It is possible to offer multiple APIs on the same base URL using API gateways. We will explore this notion further in Chapter 3. If we offer multiple APIs in this way, the consumer will need to query sequentially to build up state on the client side. The consumer also needs to understand the structure of all services involved in the query. This approach is wasteful if the consumer is only interested in a subset of fields on the response. Mobile devices are constrained by smaller screens and network availability, so GraphQL is excellent in this scenario.

GraphQL introduces a technology layer over existing services, datastores, and APIs that provides a query language to query across multiple sources. The query language allows the client to ask for exactly the fields required, including fields that span across multiple APIs. GraphQL uses the GraphQL schema language, to specify the types in individual APIs and how APIs combine. One major advantage of introducing a GraphQL schema in your system is the ability to provide a single version across all APIs, removing the need for potentially complex version management on the consumer side.

GraphQL excels when a consumer requires uniform API access over a wide range of interconnected services. The schema provides the connection and extends the domain model, allowing the customer to specify exactly what is required on the consumer side. This works extremely well for modeling a user interface and also reporting systems or data warehousing–style systems. In systems where vast amounts of data are stored across different subsystems, GraphQL can provide an ideal solution to abstracting away internal system complexity.

It is possible to place GraphQL over existing legacy systems and use this as a facade to hide away the complexity, though providing GraphQL over a layer of well-designed APIs often means the facade is simpler to implement and maintain. GraphQL can be thought of as a complementary technology and should be considered when designing and building APIs. GraphQL can also be thought of as a complete approach to building up an entire API ecosystem.

GraphQL shines in certain scenarios and we would encourage you to take a look at *Learning GraphQL* (O'Reilly) and *GraphQL in Action* (O'Reilly) for a deeper dive into this topic.

REST API Standards and Structure

REST has some very basic rules, but for the most part the implementation and design is left as an exercise for the developer. For example, what is the best way to convey errors? How should pagination be implemented? How do you accidentally avoid building an API where compatibility frequently breaks? At this point, it is useful to have a more practical definition around APIs to provide uniformity and expectations across different implementations. This is where standards or guidelines can help, however there are a variety of sources to choose from.

For the purposes of discussing design, we will use the Microsoft REST API Guidelines (*https://oreil.ly/H0lfH*), which represent a series of internal guidelines that have been open sourced. The guidelines use RFC-2119, which defines terminology for standards such as MUST, SHOULD, SHOULD NOT, MUST NOT, etc., allowing the developer to determine whether requirements are optional or mandatory.

As REST API standards are evolving, an open list of API standards are available on the book's Github page (*https://oreil.ly/jWx2x*). Please contribute via pull request any open standards you think would be useful for other readers to consider.

Let's consider the design of the *Attendee* API using the Microsoft REST API Guidelines and introduce an endpoint to create a new `attendee`. If you are familiar with REST, the thought will immediately be to use POST:

```
POST http://mastering-api.com/attendees
{
    "displayName": "Jim",
    "givenName": "James",
    "surname": "Gough",
    "email": "jim@mastering-api.com"
}
---
201 CREATED
Location: http://mastering-api.com/attendees/1
```

The *Location* header reveals the location of the new resource created on the server, and in this API we are modeling a unique ID for the user. It is possible to use the *email* field as a unique ID, however the Microsoft REST API Guidelines recommend in section 7.9 that personally identifiable information (PII) should *not* be part of the URL.

The reason for removing sensitive data from the URL is that paths or query parameters might be inadvertently cached in the network—for example, in server logs or elsewhere.

Another aspect of APIs that can be difficult is naming. As we will discuss in "API Versioning" on page 15, something as simple as changing a name can break compatibility. There is a short list of standard names that should be used in the Microsoft REST API Guidelines, however teams should expand this to have a common domain data dictionary to supplement the standards. In many organizations it is incredibly helpful to proactively investigate the requirements around data design and in some cases governance. Organizations that provide consistency across all APIs offered by a company present a uniformity that enables consumers to understand and connect responses. In some domains there may already be widely known terminology—use them!

Collections and Pagination

It seems reasonable to model the GET /attendees request as a response containing a raw array. The following source snippet shows an example of what that might look like as a response body:

```
GET http://mastering-api.com/attendees
---
200 OK
[
    {
        "displayName": "Jim",
        "givenName": "James",
        "surname": "Gough",
        "email": "jim@mastering-api.com",
        "id": 1,
    },
    ...
]
```

Let's consider an alternative model to the GET /attendees request that nests the array of attendees inside an object. It may seem strange that an array response is returned in an object, however the reason for this is that it allows for us to model bigger collections and pagination. Pagination involves returning a partial result, while providing instructions for how the consumer can request the next set of results. This is reaping the benefits of hindsight; adding pagination later and converting from an array to an object in order to add a @nextLink (as recommended by the standards) would break compatibility:

```
GET http://mastering-api.com/attendees
---
200 OK
{
    "value": [
        {
            "displayName": "Jim",
            "givenName": "James",
            "surname": "Gough",
            "email": "jim@mastering-api.com",
            "id": 1,
        }
    ],
    "@nextLink": "{opaqueUrl}"
}
```

Filtering Collections

Our conference is looking a little lonely with only one attendee, however when collections grow in size we may need to add filtering in addition to pagination. The filtering standard provides an expression language within REST to standardize how filter queries should behave, based upon the OData Standard. For example, we could find all attendees with the `displayName` Jim using:

```
GET http://mastering-api.com/attendees?$filter=displayName eq 'Jim'
```

It is not necessary to complete all filtering and searching features from the start. However, designing an API in line with the standards will allow the developer to support an evolving API architecture without breaking compatibility for consumers. Filtering and querying is a feature that GraphQL is really good at, especially if querying and filtering across many of your services becomes relevant.

Error Handling

An important consideration when extending APIs to consumers is defining what should happen in various error scenarios. Error standards (*https://oreil.ly/creK4*) are useful to define upfront and share with producers to provide consistency. It is important that errors describe to the consumer exactly what has gone wrong with the request, as this will avoid increasing the support required for the API.

The guidelines state *"For non-success conditions, developers SHOULD be able to write one piece of code that handles errors consistently."* An accurate status code must be provided to the consumer, because often consumers will build logic around the status code provided in the response. We have seen many APIs that return errors in the body along with a 2xx type of response, which is used to indicate success. 3xx status codes for redirects are actively followed by some consuming library implementations, enabling providers to relocate and access external sources. 4xx usually indicates a client-side error; at this point the content of the `message` field is extremely useful to the developer or end user. 5xx usually indicates a failure on the server side and some client libraries will retry on these types of failures. It is important to consider and document what happens in the service based on an unexpected failure—for example, in a payment system does a 500 mean the payment has gone through or not?

 Ensure that the error messages sent back to an external consumer do not contain stack traces and other sensitive information. This information can help a hacker aiming to compromise the system. The error structure in the Microsoft guidelines has the concept of an *InnerError*, which could be useful in which to place more detailed stack traces/descriptions of issues. This would be incredibly helpful for debugging but must be stripped prior to an external consumer.

We have just scratched the surface on building REST APIs, but clearly there are many important decisions to be made when beginning to build an API. If we combine the desire to present intuitive APIs that are consistent and allow for an evolving and compatible API, it is worth adopting an API standard early.

ADR Guideline: Choosing an API Standard

To make your decision on API standards, the guideline in Table 1-2 lists important topics to consider. There are a range of guidelines to choose from, including the Microsoft guidelines discussed in this section, and finding one that best matches the styles of APIs being produced is a key decision.

Table 1-2. API Standards Guideline

Decision	Which API standard should we adopt?
Discussion Points	Does the organization already have other standards within the company? Can we extend those standards to external consumers?
	Are we using any third-party APIs that we will need to expose to a consumer (e.g., Identity Services) that already have a standard?
	What does the impact of not having a standard look like for our consumers?
Recommendations	Pick an API standard that best matches the culture of the organization and formats of APIs you may already have in the inventory.
	Be prepared to evolve and add to a standard any domain/industry-specific amendments.
	Start with something early to avoid having to break compatibility later for consistency.
	Be critical of existing APIs. Are they in a format that consumers would understand or is more effort required to offer the content?

Specifying REST APIs Using OpenAPI

As we're beginning to see, the design of an API is fundamental to the success of an API platform. The next consideration we'll discuss is sharing the API with developers consuming our APIs.

API marketplaces provide a public or private listing of APIs available to a consumer. A developer can browse documentation and quickly try out an API in the browser to explore the API behavior and functionality. Public and private API marketplaces have placed REST APIs prominently into the consumer space. The success of REST APIs has been driven by both the technical landscape and the low barrier to entry for both the client and server.

As the number of APIs grew, it quickly became necessary to have a mechanism to share the *shape* and structure of APIs with consumers. This is why the OpenAPI Initiative was formed by API industry leaders to construct the OpenAPI Specification (OAS). Swagger was the original reference implementation of the OpenAPI Specifications, but most tooling has now converged on using OpenAPI.

The OpenAPI Specifications are JSON- or YAML-based representations of the API that describe the structure, the domain objects exchanged, and any security requirements of the API. In addition to the structure, they also convey metadata about the API, including any legal or licensing requirements, and also carry documentation and examples that are useful to developers consuming the API. OpenAPI Specifications are an important concept surrounding modern REST APIs, and many tools and products have been built around its usage.

Practical Application of OpenAPI Specifications

Once an OAS is shared, the power of the specification starts to become apparent. OpenAPI.Tools (*https://oreil.ly/8dFUS*) documents a full range of available open and closed source tools. In this section we will explore some of the practical applications of tools based on their interaction with the OpenAPI Specification.

In the situation where the CFP team is the consumer, sharing the OAS enables the team to understand the structure of the API. Using some of the following practical applications can help both improve the developer experience and ensure the health of the exchange.

Code Generation

Perhaps one of the most useful features of an OAS is allowing the generation of client-side code to consume the API. As discussed earlier, we can include the full details of the server, security, and of course the API structure itself. With all this information we can generate a series of model and service objects that represent and invoke the API. The OpenAPI Generator (*https://oreil.ly/wx0Ce*) project supports a wide range of languages and toolchains. For example, in Java you can choose to use Spring or JAX-RS and in TypeScript you can choose a combination of TypeScript with your favorite framework. It is also possible to generate the API implementation stubs from the OAS.

This raises an important question about what should come first—the specification or the server-side code? In Chapter 2, we discuss "contract tracing," which presents a behavior-driven approach to testing and building APIs. The challenge with OpenAPI Specifications is that alone they only convey the shape of the API. OpenAPI Specifications do not fully model the semantics (or expected behavior) of the API under different conditions. If you are going to present an API to external users, it is important that the range of behaviors is modeled and tested to help avoid having to drastically change the API later.

APIs should be designed from the perspective of the consumer and consider the requirement to abstract the underlying representation to reduce coupling. It is important to be able to freely refactor components behind the scenes without breaking API compatibility, otherwise the API abstraction loses value.

OpenAPI Validation

OpenAPI Specifications are useful for validating the content of an exchange to ensure the request and response match the expectations of the specification. At first it might not seem apparent where this would be useful—if code is generated, surely the exchange will always be right? One practical application of OpenAPI validation is in securing APIs and API infrastructure. In many organizations a zonal architecture is common, with a notion of a demilitarized zone (DMZ) used to shield a network from inbound traffic. A useful feature is to interrogate messages in the DMZ and terminate the traffic if the specification does not match. We will cover security in more detail in Chapter 6.

Atlassian, for example, open sourced a tool called the swagger-request-validator (*https://oreil.ly/HLCzT*), which is capable of validating JSON REST content. The project also has adapters that integrate with various mocking and testing frameworks to help ensure that API Specifications are conformed to as part of testing. The tool has an OpenApiInteractionValidator, which is used to create a ValidationReport on an exchange. The following code demonstrates building a validator from the specification, including any basePathOverrides—which may be necessary if deploying an API behind infrastructure that alters the path. The validation report is generated from analyzing the request and response at the point where validation is executed:

```
//Using the location of the specification create an interaction validator
//The base path override is useful if the validator will be used
//behind a gateway/proxy
final OpenApiInteractionValidator validator = OpenApiInteractionValidator
        .createForSpecificationUrl(specUrl)
        .withBasePathOverride(basePathOverride)
        .build;

//Requests and Response objects can be converted or created using a builder
final ValidationReport report = validator.validate(request, response);

if (report.hasErrors()) {
    // Capture or process error information
}
```

Examples and Mocking

The OAS can provide example responses for the paths in the specification. Examples, as we've discussed, are useful for documentation to help developers understand the expected API behavior. Some products have started to use examples to allow the user to query the API and return example responses from a mock service. This can be really useful in features such as a developer portal, which allows developers to explore documentation and invoke APIs. Another useful feature of mocks and examples is the ability to share ideas between the producer and consumer ahead of committing to build the service. Being able to "try out" the API is often more valuable than trying to review if a specification would meet your requirements.

Examples can potentially introduce an interesting problem, which is that this part of the specification is essentially a string (in order to model XML/JSON, etc.). openapi-examples-validator (*https://oreil.ly/bM9fp*) validates that an example matches the OAS for the corresponding request/response component of the API.

Detecting Changes

OpenAPI Specifications can also be helpful in detecting changes in an API. This can be incredibly useful as part of a DevOps pipeline. Detecting changes for backward compatibility is very important, but first we need to understand versioning of APIs in more detail.

API Versioning

We have explored the advantages of sharing an OAS with a consumer, including the speed of integration. Consider the case where multiple consumers start to operate against the API. What happens when there is a change to the API or one of the consumers requests the addition of new features to the API?

Let's take a step back and think about if this was a code library built into our application at compile time. Any changes to the library would be packaged as a new version and until the code is recompiled and tested against the new version, there would be no impact to production applications. As APIs are running services, we have a few upgrade options that are immediately available to us when changes are requested:

Release a new version and deploy in a new location.
> Older applications continue to operate against the older version of the APIs. This is fine from a consumer perspective, as the consumer only upgrades to the new location and API if they need the new features. However, the owner of the API needs to maintain and manage multiple versions of the API, including any patching and bug fixing that might be necessary.

Release a new version of the API that is backward compatible with the previous version of the API.
> This allows additive changes without impacting existing users of the API. There are no changes required by the consumer, but we may need to consider downtime or availability of both old and new versions during the upgrade. If there is a small bug fix that changes something as small as an incorrect field name, this would break compatibility.

Break compatibility with the previous API and all consumers must upgrade code to use the new API.

This seems like an awful idea at first, as that would result in things breaking unexpectedly in production.[1] However, a situation may present itself where we cannot avoid breaking compatibility with older versions. This type of change can trigger a whole-system lockstep change that requires coordination of downtime.

The challenge is that all of these different upgrade options offer advantages but also drawbacks either to the consumer or the producer. The reality is that we want to be able to support a combination of all three options. In order to do this we need to introduce rules around versioning and how versions are exposed to the consumer.

Semantic Versioning

Semantic versioning (*https://semver.org*) offers an approach that we can apply to REST APIs to give us a combination of the preceding upgrade options. Semantic versioning defines a numerical representation attributed to an API release. That number is based on the change in behavior in comparison to the previous version, using the following rules:

- A *major* version introduces noncompatible changes with previous versions of the API. In an API platform, upgrading to a new major version is an active decision by the consumer. There is likely going to be a migration guide and tracking as consumers upgrade to the new API.

- A *minor* version introduces a backward compatible change with the previous version of the API. In an API service platform, it is acceptable for consumers to receive minor versions without making an active change on the client side.

- A *patch* version does not change or introduce new functionality but is used for bug fixes on an existing `Major.Minor` version of functionality.

Formatting for semantic versioning can be represented as `Major.Minor.Patch`. For example, 1.5.1 would represent major version 1, minor version 5, with patch upgrade of 1. In Chapter 5 you will explore how semantic versioning connects with the concept of API lifecycle and releases.

OpenAPI Specification and Versioning

Now that we have explored versioning we can look at examples of breaking changes and nonbreaking changes using the Attendee API specification. There are several tools to choose from to compare specifications, and in this example we will use openapi-diff from OpenAPITools (*https://oreil.ly/QrgTf*).

---

[1] We have been in this situation many times, usually first thing on a Monday!

We will start with a breaking change: we will change the name of the givenName field to firstName. This is a breaking change because consumers will be expecting to parse givenName, not firstName. We can run the diff tool from a docker container using the following command:

```
$docker run --rm -t \
  -v $(pwd):/specs:ro \
  openapitools/openapi-diff:latest /specs/original.json /specs/first-name.json
========================================================================
...
- GET    /attendees
  Return Type:
    - Changed 200 OK
      Media types:
        - Changed */*
          Schema: Broken compatibility
          Missing property: [n].givenName (string)
--------------------------------------------------------------------
--                            Result                            --
--------------------------------------------------------------------
            API changes broke backward compatibility
--------------------------------------------------------------------
```

We can try to add a new attribute to the /attendees return type to add an additional field called age. Adding new fields does not break existing behavior and therefore does not break compatibility:

```
$ docker run --rm -t \
  -v $(pwd):/specs:ro \
openapitools/openapi-diff:latest --info /specs/original.json /specs/age.json
========================================================================
...
- GET    /attendees
  Return Type:
    - Changed 200 OK
      Media types:
        - Changed */*
          Schema: Backward compatible
--------------------------------------------------------------------
--                            Result                            --
--------------------------------------------------------------------
            API changes are backward compatible
--------------------------------------------------------------------
```

It is worth trying this out to see which changes would be compatible and which would not. Introducing this type of tooling as part of the API pipeline is going to help avoid unexpected noncompatible changes for consumers. OpenAPI Specifications are an important part of an API program, and when combined with tooling, versioning, and lifecycle, they are invaluable.

Tools are often OpenAPI version–specific, so it is important to check whether the tool supports the specification you are working with. In the preceding example we tried the diff tool with an earlier version of a spec and no breaking changes were detected.

Implementing RPC with gRPC

East–west services such as Attendee tend to be higher traffic and can be implemented as microservices used across the architecture. gRPC may be a more suitable tool than REST for east–west services, owing to the smaller data transmission and speed within the ecosystem. Any performance decisions should always be measured in order to be informed.

Let's explore using a Spring Boot Starter (*https://oreil.ly/opOij*) to rapidly create a gRPC server. The following *.proto* file models the same `attendee` object that we explored in our OpenAPI Specification example. As with OpenAPI Specifications, generating code from a schema is quick and supported in multiple languages.

The attendees *.proto* file defines an empty request and returns a repeated Attendee response. In protocols used for binary representations, it is important to note that the position and order of fields is critical, as they govern the layout of the message. Adding a new service or new method is backward compatible as is adding a field to a message, but care is required. Any new fields that are added must not be mandatory fields, otherwise backward compatibility would break.

Removing a field or renaming a field will break compatibility, as will changing the data type of a field. Changing the field number is also an issue as field numbers are used to identify fields on the wire. The restrictions of encoding with gRPC mean the definition must be very specific. REST and OpenAPI are quite forgiving as the specification is only a guide.[2] Extra fields and ordering do not matter in OpenAPI, and therefore versioning and compatibility is even more important when it comes to gRPC:

```
syntax = "proto3";
option java_multiple_files = true;
package com.masteringapi.attendees.grpc.server;

message AttendeesRequest {
}

message Attendee {
  int32 id = 1;
  string givenName = 2;
```

---

2 Validation of OpenAPI Specifications at runtime helps enforce a greater strictness.

```
    string surname = 3;
    string email = 4;

}

message AttendeeResponse {
  repeated Attendee attendees = 1;
}

service AttendeesService {
  rpc getAttendees(AttendeesRequest) returns (AttendeeResponse);
}
```

The following Java code demonstrates a simple structure for implementing the behavior on the generated gRPC server classes:

```java
@GrpcService
public class AttendeesServiceImpl extends
    AttendeesServiceGrpc.AttendeesServiceImplBase {

    @Override
    public void getAttendees(AttendeesRequest request,
        StreamObserver<AttendeeResponse> responseObserver) {
            AttendeeResponse.Builder responseBuilder
                = AttendeeResponse.newBuilder();

            //populate response
            responseObserver.onNext(responseBuilder.build());
            responseObserver.onCompleted();
    }
}
```

You can find the Java service modeling this example on this book's GitHub page (*https://oreil.ly/GMy9m*). gRPC cannot be queried directly from a browser without additional libraries, however you can install gRPC UI (*https://oreil.ly/F4C78*) to use the browser for testing. grpcurl also provides a command-line tool:

```
$ grpcurl -plaintext localhost:9090 \
    com.masteringapi.attendees.grpc.server.AttendeesService/getAttendees
{
  "attendees": [
    {
      "id": 1,
      "givenName": "Jim",
      "surname": "Gough",
      "email": "gough@mail.com"
    }
  ]
}
```

gRPC gives us another option for querying our service and defines a specification for the consumer to generate code. gRPC has a more strict specification than OpenAPI and requires methods/internals to be understood by the consumer.

Modeling Exchanges and Choosing an API Format

In the Introduction we discussed the concept of traffic patterns and the difference between requests originating from outside the ecosystem and requests within the ecosystem. Traffic patterns are an important factor in determining the appropriate format of API for the problem at hand. When we have full control over the services and exchanges within our microservices-based architecture, we can start to make compromises that we would not be able to make with external consumers.

It is important to recognize that the performance characteristics of an east–west service are likely to be more applicable than a north–south service. In a north–south exchange, traffic originating from outside the producer's environment will generally involve the exchange using the internet. The internet introduces a high degree of latency, and an API architecture should always consider the compounding effects of each service. In a microservices-based architecture it is likely that one north–south request will involve multiple east–west exchanges. High east–west traffic exchange needs to be efficient to avoid cascading slow-downs propagating back to the consumer.

High-Traffic Services

In our example, Attendees is a central service. In a microservices-based architecture, components will keep track of an `attendeeId`. APIs offered to consumers will potentially retrieve data stored in the Attendee service, and at scale it will be a high-traffic component. If the exchange frequency is high between services, the cost of network transfer due to payload size and limitations of one protocol versus another will be more profound as usage increases. The cost can present itself in either monetary costs of each transfer or the total time taken for the message to reach the destination.

Large Exchange Payloads

Large payload sizes may also become a challenge in API exchanges and are susceptible to decreasing transfer performance across the wire. JSON over REST is human readable and will often be more verbose than a fixed or binary representation fuelling an increase in payload sizes.

A common misconception is that "human readability" is quoted as a primary reason to use JSON in data transfers. The number of times a developer will need to read a message versus the performance consideration is not a strong case with modern tracing tools. It is also rare that large JSON files will be read from beginning to end. Better logging and error handling can mitigate the human-readable argument.

Another factor in large payload exchanges is the time it takes components to parse the message content into language-level domain objects. Performance time of parsing data formats varies vastly depending on the language a service is implemented in. Many traditional server-side languages can struggle with JSON compared to a binary representation, for example. It is worth exploring the impact of parsing and include that consideration when choosing an exchange format.

HTTP/2 Performance Benefits

Using HTTP/2-based services can help to improve performance of exchanges by supporting binary compression and framing. The binary framing layer (*https://oreil.ly/5Ql7R*) is transparent to the developer, but behind the scenes will split and compress the message into smaller chunks. The advantage of binary framing is that it allows for a full request and response multiplexing over a single connection. Consider processing a list in another service and the requirement is to retrieve 20 different attendees; if we retrieved these as individual HTTP/1 requests it would require the overhead of creating 20 new TCP connections. Multiplexing allows us to perform 20 individual requests over a single HTTP/2 connection.

gRPC uses HTTP/2 by default and reduces the size of exchange by using a binary protocol. If bandwidth is a concern or cost, then gRPC will provide an advantage, in particular as content payloads increase significantly in size. gRPC may be beneficial compared to REST if payload bandwidth is a cumulative concern or the service exchanges large volumes of data. If large volumes of data exchanges are frequent, it is also worth considering some of the asynchronous capabilities of gRPC.

HTTP/3 is on the way and it will change everything. HTTP/3 uses QUIC, a transport protocol built on UDP. You can find out more in HTTP/3 explained (*https://oreil.ly/DM1j9*).

Vintage Formats

Not all services in an architecture will be based on a modern design. In Chapter 8 we will look at how to isolate and evolve vintage components, as older components will be an active consideration for evolving architectures. It is important that those involved with an API architecture understand the overall performance impact of introducing vintage components.

Guideline: Modeling Exchanges

When the consumer is the legacy conference system team, the exchange is typically an east–west relationship. When the consumer is the CFP team, the exchange is typically a north–south relationship. The difference in coupling and performance requirements will require the teams to consider how the exchange is modeled. You will see some aspects for consideration in the guideline shown in Table 1-3.

Table 1-3. Modeling exchanges guideline

Decision	What format should we use to model the API for our service?
Discussion Points	Is the exchange a north–south or east–west exchange? Are we in control of the consumer code?
	Is there a strong business domain across multiple services or do we want to allow consumers to construct their own queries?
	What versioning considerations do we need to have?
	What is the deployment/change frequency of the underlying data model?
	Is this a high-traffic service where bandwidth or performance concerns have been raised?
Recommendations	If the API is consumed by external users, REST is a low barrier to entry and provides a strong domain model. External users also usually means that a service with loose coupling and low dependency is desirable.
	If the API is interacting between two services under close control of the producer or the service is proven to be high traffic, consider gRPC.

Multiple Specifications

In this chapter we have explored a variety of API formats to consider in an API architecture, and perhaps the final question is *"Can we provide all formats?"* The answer is yes, we can support an API that has a RESTful presentation, a gRPC service, and connections into a GraphQL schema. However, it is not going to be easy and may not be the right thing to do. In this final section, we will explore some of the options available for a multiformat API and the challenges it can present.

Does the Golden Specification Exist?

The *.proto* file for attendees and the OpenAPI Specification do not look too dissimilar; they contain the same fields and both have data types. Is it possible to generate a *.proto* file from an OAS using the openapi2proto tool (*https://oreil.ly/f11XL*)? Running `openapi2proto --spec spec-v2.json` will output the *.proto* file with fields ordered alphabetically by default. This is fine until we add a new field to the OAS that is backward compatible and suddenly the ID of all fields changes, breaking backward compatibility.

The following sample *.proto* file shows that adding `a_new_field` would be alphabetically added to the beginning, changing the binary format and breaking existing services:

```
message Attendee {
    string a_new_field = 1;
    string email = 2;
    string givenName = 3;
    int32 id = 4;
    string surname = 5;
}
```

 Other tools are available to solve the specification conversion problem, however it is worth noting that some tools only support OpenAPI Specification version 2. The time taken to move between versions 2 and 3 in some of the tools built around OpenAPI has led to many products needing to support both versions of the OAS.

An alternative option is grpc-gateway (*https://oreil.ly/u2Em7*), which generates a reverse proxy providing a REST facade in front of the gRPC service. The reverse proxy is generated at build time against the *.proto* file and will produce a best-effort mapping to REST, similar to `openapi2proto`. You can also supply extensions within the *.proto* file to map the RPC methods to a nice representation in the OAS:

```
import "google/api/annotations.proto";
//...
service AttendeesService {
  rpc getAttendees(AttendeesRequest) returns (AttendeeResponse) {
      option(google.api.http) = {
              get: "/attendees"
      };
}
```

Using grpc-gateway gives us another option for presenting both a REST and gRPC service. However, grpc-gateway involves several commands and a setup that would only be familiar to developers who work with the Go language or build environment.

Challenges of Combined Specifications

It's important to take a step back here and consider what we are trying to do. When converting from OpenAPI we are effectively trying to convert our RESTful representation into a gRPC series of calls. We are trying to convert an extended hypermedia domain model into a lower-level function-to-function call. This is a potential conflation of the difference between RPC and APIs and is likely going to result in wrestling with compatibility.

With converting gRPC to OpenAPI we have a similar issue; the objective is trying to take gRPC and make it look like a REST API. This is likely going to create a difficult series of issues when evolving the service.

Once specifications are combined or generated from one another, versioning becomes a challenge. It is important to be mindful of how both the gRPC and OpenAPI Specifications maintain their individual compatibility requirements. An active decision should be made as to whether coupling the REST domain to an RPC domain makes sense and adds overall value.

Rather than generate RPC for east–west from north–south, what makes more sense is to carefully design the microservices-based architecture (RPC) communication independently from the REST representation, allowing both APIs to evolve freely. This is the choice we have made for the conference case study and would be recorded as an ADR in the project.

Summary

In this chapter we have covered how to design, build, and specify APIs and the different circumstances under which you may choose REST or gRPC. It is important to remember that it is not REST versus gRPC, but rather given the situations, which is the most appropriate choice for modeling the exchange. The key takeaways are:

- The barrier to building REST- and RPC-based APIs is low in most technologies. Carefully considering the design and structure is an important architectural decision.

- When choosing between REST and RPC models, consider the Richardson Maturity Model and the degree of coupling between the producer and consumer.

- REST is a fairly loose standard. When building APIs, conforming to an agreed API standard ensures your APIs are consistent and have the expected behavior for your consumers. API standards can also help to short-circuit potential design decisions that could lead to an incompatible API.

- OpenAPI Specifications are a useful way of sharing API structure and automating many coding-related activities. You should actively select OpenAPI features and choose what tooling or generation features will be applied to projects.

- Versioning is an important topic that adds complexity for the producer but is necessary to ease API usage for the consumer. Not planning for versioning in APIs exposed to consumers is dangerous. Versioning should be an active decision in the product feature set and a mechanism to convey versioning to consumers should be part of the discussion.

- gRPC performs incredibly well in high-bandwidth exchanges and is an ideal option for east–west exchanges. Tooling for gRPC is powerful and provides another option when modeling exchanges.
- Modeling multiple specifications starts to become quite tricky, especially when generating from one type of specification to another. Versioning complicates matters further but is an important factor to avoid breaking changes. Teams should think carefully before combining RPC representations with RESTful API representations, as there are fundamental differences in terms of usage and control over the consumer code.

The challenge for an API architecture is to meet the requirements from a consumer business perspective, to create a great developer experience around APIs, and to avoid unexpected compatibility issues. In Chapter 2 you will explore testing, which is essential in ensuring services meet these objectives.

Testing APIs

Chapter 1 covered the different types of APIs and the value that they provide to your architecture. This chapter closes out the Designing, Building, and Testing APIs section of this book by reviewing approaches to testing APIs. The new Attendee API that was extracted within the Introduction should obviously be tested and validated. We believe that testing is core to building APIs. It helps provide a high level of confidence to you that your service is working as expected, which will help you deliver a quality product to consumers of your API. It is only by testing your API under varying conditions that you will gain the confidence that it is operating correctly.

When building APIs, as with creating any product, the only way to verify that the product works as expected is to test it. In the case of a mouthguard, this can mean stretching, hitting, pushing, and pulling the product, or even running simulations.[1]

As discussed in "Specifying REST APIs Using OpenAPI" on page 12, an API should not return anything that differs from what is documented. It is also frustrating when an API introduces breaking changes or causes network timeouts due to the large duration of time to retrieve a result. These types of issues drive customers away and are entirely preventable by creating quality tests around the API service. Any API built should be ready to fulfill a variety of requirements, including sending useful feedback to users who provide a bad input, being secure, and returning results within a specified service-level objective (SLO) based on our service-level indicators (SLIs) that are agreed.[2]

---

[1] Matthew's friend owns a mouthguard company and was on the receiving end of hearing about the arduous process for testing the integrity of the product. No one wants a mouthguard where the only testing takes place during the match!

[2] SLOs and SLIs will be discussed in more detail in Chapter 5.

In this chapter we will introduce the different types of testing that you can apply to your API to help avoid these issues from occurring.

We will highlight the positives and the negatives of each type of testing, so you can decide where best to invest your time. We are going to focus on testing APIs and where we believe that you will gain the most value; we will not be covering generic testing of services. The chapter will contain additional resources for those readers seeking to gain a significantly more in-depth and specialist knowledge about testing.

Conference System Scenario for This Chapter

In "Attendees Evolution ADR" on page xxxiii, we explained the reasons to separate the Attendee API from the rest of the conference system. The separation of the Attendee API introduces new interactions. The Attendee API will be used by the external CFP system and legacy conference system, as is shown in Figure 2-1. You will spend this chapter covering the testing needed for the Attendee service and how testing can help verify the interactions between the legacy conference system and the Attendee API. As a collective we have seen enough APIs that become inconsistent or produce accidental breaking changes as new releases are made, and this is primarily due to a lack of testing. For the new Attendee API it is important to ensure that it avoids these pitfalls by providing confidence that the correct results will always be returned, and the only way this can happen is by investing in the right levels of testing.

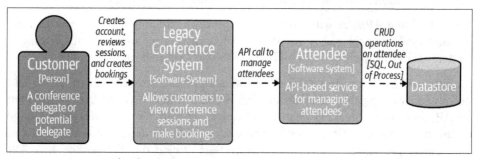

Figure 2-1. Scenario for the chapter

Testing can be applied at different levels of an API, starting with the individual building blocks that make up the service, going all the way to verifying that it works as part of the entire ecosystem. Before showing you some tools and frameworks that are available for API testing, it is important to understand the strategies that can be used.

Testing Strategies

Testing is important; it ensures that you are building a working application. However, you don't want something that just works, you want something that also has the right behavior. Realistically, though, you have limited time and resources to write tests, so you will want to ensure that you are not wasting cycles writing tests that provide little to no value. After all, the value for customers is when you are running in production. Therefore, you need to be smart about deciding upon the coverage and proportions of the types of tests you should be using. Avoid creating irrelevant tests, duplicating tests, and any tests that are going to take more time and resources than the value they provide (i.e., flaky tests). Not all the testing that is introduced needs to be implemented to be able to release an API, as it may not be feasible due to time constraints and business demands.

To guide you to getting the right balance and the right tests for your case, we will introduce the test quadrant and test pyramid. These will give you focus on identifying the testing you should be implementing.

Test Quadrant

The test quadrant was first introduced by Brian Marick in his blog series on agile testing (*https://oreil.ly/JAg7C*). This became popularized in the book *Agile Testing* (*https://agiletester.ca*) by Lisa Crispin and Janet Gregory (Addison-Wesley). The technology side of building an API cares that it has been built correctly, that its pieces (e.g., functions or endpoints) respond as expected, and that it is resilient and continues to behave under abnormal circumstances. The business cares that the right service is being developed (i.e., in our case, that the Attendee API provides the right functionality). To clarify, the term "the business" means someone who has a clear understanding of the product and the features and the functionality that should be developed; they need not have a technical understanding.

The test quadrant brings together tests that help technology and business stakeholders alike—each perspective will have different opinions on priorities. The popular image of the test quadrant is shown in Figure 2-2.

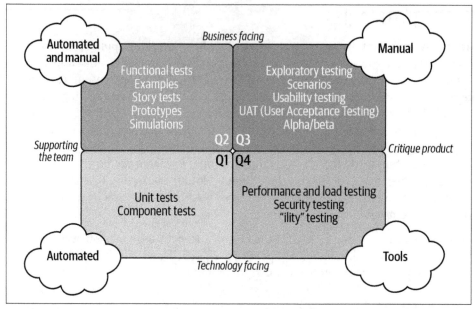

Figure 2-2. Agile Test Quadrants from Agile Testing *(Addison-Wesley) by Lisa Crispin and Janet Gregory*

The test quadrant does *not* depict any order. The quadrants are labeled for convenience and this is a common source of confusion that Lisa describes in one of her blog posts (*https://oreil.ly/n2lwu*). The four quadrants can be generally described as follows:

Q1

Unit and component tests for technology. These should verify that the service that has been created works, and this verification should be performed using automated testing.

Q2

Tests with the business. These ensure what is being built is serving a purpose. This is verified with automated testing and can also include manual testing.

Q3

Testing for the business. This is about ensuring that functional requirements are met and also includes exploratory testing. When Figure 2-2 was originally created, this type of testing was manual; now it is possible to perform automated testing in this area as well.

Q4

Ensuring that what exists works from a technical standpoint. From Q1 you know that what has been built works; however, when the product is being used, is it performing as expected? Examples of performing correctly from a technical standpoint could include security enforcement, SLA integrity, and autoscaling.

The left side of quadrant (Q1, Q2) is all about supporting the product. It helps guide the product and prevent defects. The right side (Q3, Q4) is about critiquing the product and finding defects. The top of the quadrant (Q2, Q3) is the external quality of your product, making sure that it meets your users' expectations. This is what the business finds important. The bottom of the quadrant (Q1, Q4) is the technology-facing tests to maintain the internal quality of your application.[3]

The test quadrant does not say where you should start testing; it helps guide you on the tests that you might want. This is something that you must decide and should be based on the factors important to you. For example, a ticketing system must handle large traffic spikes, so it may be best to start with ensuring that your ticket system is resilient (e.g., performance testing). This would be part of Q4.

Test Pyramid

In addition to the test quadrants, the test pyramid (also known as the test automation pyramid) can be used as part of your strategy for test automation. The test pyramid was first introduced in the book *Succeeding with Agile* (*https://oreil.ly/iHOra*) by Mike Cohn. This pyramid illustrates a notion of how much time should be spent on a given test area, its corresponding difficulty to maintain, and the value it provides in terms of additional confidence. The test pyramid at its core has remained unchanged. It has unit tests as its foundation, service tests in the middle block, and UI tests at the peak of the pyramid. Figure 2-3 shows the areas of the test pyramid you will explore.

---

3 To learn more on agile testing, check out the books *Agile Testing* (O'Reilly), *More Agile Testing* (O'Reilly), or the video series Agile Testing Essentials.

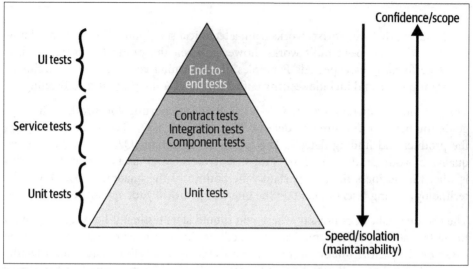

Figure 2-3. The test pyramid, showing the proportion of tests desired

The test automation pyramid shows the trade-offs that exist in terms of confidence, isolation, and scope. By testing small parts of the codebase, you have better isolation and faster tests; however, this does not give confidence that the whole application is working. By testing the entire application in its ecosystem, the opposite is true. The tests give you more confidence that the application is working, but the scope of the test will be large as many pieces will be interacting together. This also makes it more difficult to maintain and slow. The following defines each of the core elements of the test pyramid:

- Unit tests are at the bottom of the pyramid; they form the foundation of your testing. They test small, isolated units of your code to ensure that your defined unit is running as expected.[4] If your test is going to escape the boundaries of your unit, you can use test doubles. Test doubles are objects that look like real versions of an external entity; however, they are under your control.[5] Because unit tests form the foundation of your pyramid, there should be more unit tests than any other type of test; we recommend using TDD as a practice.[6] TDD is about writing tests before you write the logic. Unit tests fit into Q1 of the test quadrant and are

---

4 The typical example of a unit in object-oriented (OO) languages is a class.

5 Test doubles include stubs, which look like real implementations of an external entity, except they return hardcoded responses. Mocks look like real implementations of preprogrammed objects, but instead are used to verify behavior.

6 Kent Beck's book *Test Driven Development: By Example* (*https://oreil.ly/u3COo*) (Addison-Wesley) is a fantastic resource for learning more about TDD.

used to provide quality to the internals of the application. Unit testing will not be covered further as we will be focusing on tests that verify your API from an external consumer standpoint as opposed to the internals of an API.

- Service tests make up the middle tier of the pyramid. They will provide you with more confidence that your API is working correctly than unit tests, though they are more expensive. The expense comes from the tests having a larger scope and less isolation, which incurs a higher maintenance and development cost. Service tests include some of the following cases: the verification that multiple units are working together, that behavior is as expected, and that the application itself is resilient. Therefore, service tests fit into Q1, Q2, and Q4 of the test quadrant.

- UI tests sit at the top of the test pyramid. In the old days a majority of applications being built for the web were LAMP stacks (*https://oreil.ly/dtgJF*), and the only way to test your application from the front to the backend was through the Web UI. There is a UI with APIs: it is just not graphical, so these tests will now be referred to as end-to-end tests. They cover the same ground of a request flowing from a start to an end point but do not necessarily imply or assume that traffic originates from a Web UI. End-to-end tests are the most complex. They have the largest scope and are slow to run; however, they will verify entire modules are working together so they provide lots of confidence. End-to-end tests will generally sit in Q2, Q3, Q4 of the quadrant. Tooling for testing has improved and become more advanced, and it is now making more and more of Q3 available for automation.

One type of test is not better than another—the test pyramid is a guide to the proportions of each type of testing you should aim to implement. It can be tempting to ignore the test pyramid and concentrate on end-to-end testing as this gives a high degree of confidence. However, this is a fallacy and instead gives a false sense of security that these higher-level tests are of higher quality/value than unit tests. The fallacy gives rise to the ice cream cone representation of testing, which is the opposite of a test pyramid. For a robust argument on this topic, please read Steve Smith's blog post "End-to-End Testing considered harmful" (*https://oreil.ly/Iv1Yd*). You may also consider implementing other proportions of tests, though it is not recommended. Martin Fowler (*https://oreil.ly/2DdPE*) wrote an updated piece on testing shapes and covered why he feels that testing that is guided by any shape other than the test pyramid is incorrect.

ADR Guideline for Testing Strategies

To help you decide on the testing strategy that you should use, the ADR Guideline in Table 2-1 should help you make an informed decision.

Table 2-1. ADR Guideline: Testing strategies

Decision	When building your API, which testing strategy should be made part of the development process?
Discussion Points	Do all parties that have a stake in the API have the time and the availability to regularly discuss how the API should be working? If you are unable to effectively communicate with the stakeholders, you could end up stalling your product waiting for a decision to be made.
	Are the skills and experience available to effectively use these testing strategies? Not everyone has used these practices before, so you need to weigh if you have the time resources to train everyone on them.
	Are there other practices within your workplace that are recommended and should be used? Sometimes there can be internal strategies to building software that work for an organization or are required due to the nature of the business.
Recommendations	We recommend using test quadrants and the test pyramid.
	The test quadrant is very valuable to ensure that your customers are getting the right product. The test quadrant coupled with the test pyramid will help you build a great API.
	We do recognize that using the test quadrant in its truest form by having someone readily available from the business to help guide your testing is not always possible. However, at a minimum, use the test pyramid as this concentrates the automated side of the test quadrant. This at the very least will ensure that you find bugs early in your development cycle.
	Whatever the case, you will always need someone to help guide the product direction.

Contract Testing

Contract testing has two entities: a consumer and a producer. A consumer requests data from an API (e.g., web client, terminal shell), and a producer (also known as a provider) responds to the API requests, i.e., it is producing data, such as a RESTful web service. A contract is a definition of an interaction between the consumer and producer. It is a statement to say if a consumer makes a request that matches the contract request definition, then the producer will return a response that matches the contract response definition. In the case of the Attendee API, it is a producer and the consumer is the legacy conference system. The legacy conference system is a consumer as it is calling the Attendee API.[7] So why use contracts? What do they offer you?

Why Contract Testing Is Often Preferable

As you learned in "Specifying REST APIs Using OpenAPI" on page 12, APIs should have a specification, and it is important that your API responses conform to the API specification that you have laid out. Having a written definition of these interactions

---

[7] To clarify, it is also possible that a service can be both a producer and consumer.

that must be adhered to by the producer ensures that consumers can keep using your API and makes it possible to generate tests. The contract defines what a request and response should look like and these can be used to verify that the producer (the API) is fulfilling the contract. If you break a contract test, then it means that the producer is not fulfilling the contract anymore, which means that consumers will be broken.

As the contract has the response definition, it is also possible to generate a stub server.[8] This stub server can be used by consumers to verify that they can call the producer correctly and parse the response from the producer. Contract testing can be performed locally—it is not required to launch additional services, which makes it part of your service tests. Contracts will evolve and the consumers and producers pick up these changes as they are made available, which ensures that they are able to continually integrate with the latest contract.

There is already a lot of value here about why you would want to use contracts. Additionally, contract testing has a well-developed ecosystem. There are established methodologies that guide what the contract should be, as well as frameworks and test integrations to generate contracts and provide effective ways to distribute them. We believe that contracts are the best way to define interactions between the service you implement and a consumer. Other tests are important and should be implemented as well, but these offer the most bang for the buck.

It is important to note that contract testing is not the same as saying that an API conforms to a schema. A system is either compatible with a schema (like OpenAPI Spec) or it is not; a contract is about a defined interaction between parties and provides examples. Matt Fellows has an excellent piece on this titled "Schema-based contract testing with JSON schemas and Open API (Part 1)" (*https://oreil.ly/QTbbZ*).

How a Contract Is Implemented

As mentioned, a contract is a shared definition of how a producer and consumer interact. The following example shows a contract for a GET request to the endpoint /conference/{conference-id}/attendees. It states that the expected response has a property called value that contains an array of values about the attendees. In this sample definition of a contract, you can see that it is defining an interaction, which is used to generate the tests and stub server:

```
Contract.make {
  request {
    description('Get a list of all the attendees at a conference')
```

---

8 A stub server is a service that can be run locally and will return canned responses.

```
    method GET()
    url '/conference/1234/attendees'
    headers {
      contentType('application/json')
    }
  }
  response {
    status OK()
    headers {
      contentType('application/json')
    }
    body(
        value: [
            $(
                id: 123456,
                givenName: 'James',
                familyName: 'Gough'
            ),
            $(
                id: 123457,
                givenName: 'Matthew',
                familyName: 'Auburn'
            )
        ]
    )
  }
}
```

In Figure 2-4 you see how the generated tests are used by the consumer and producer.

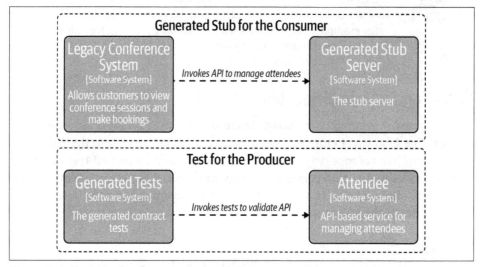

Figure 2-4. Generated stub server and tests from a contract

It is tempting to use contracts for scenario tests. For example:

Step 1: add an attendee to a conference.
Step 2: get the list of attendees of the conference and check that the attendee was added correctly.

Frameworks do support this but also discourage it. Contracts are about defining interaction; if you wish to test this type of behavior, then use component tests.

A key benefit of using contracts is that once the producer agrees to implement a contract, this decouples the dependency of building the consumer and producer.

We have used generated stub servers to run demos for stakeholders. This was useful as the producer was still implementing the logic; however, they had agreed to the contracts.

The consumer has a stub server to develop against and the producer has tests to ensure that they are building the right interaction. The contract test process saves time, as when both the consumer and producer are deployed, they should integrate seamlessly.

The generated tests need to be executed against your running API (producer). When your API launches, you should use test doubles for external dependencies. You do not want to be testing integrations with other services as part of your generated contract tests against the consumer.

To understand how contracts are agreed upon, let's look at the two main contract methodologies.

Producer contracts

Producer contract testing is when a producer defines its own contracts. This practice is commonly utilized when your API is being used outside your immediate organization (i.e., external third parties). When you're developing an API for an external audience, the API needs to maintain its integrity, because the interface cannot make breaking changes without a migration plan, as you learned in "API Versioning" on page 15. Though interactions will be updated and improved, no individual consumer is likely to be able to ask for changes that affect the whole API and receive a quick change, because these changes need to be carefully orchestrated.

A real-world example of such an API is the Microsoft Graph API. Microsoft has thousands of consumers of this API from companies all over the world. Having companies or individuals adjust contracts for the Graph API with what they believe the contract should look like isn't feasible. That is not to say that changes should not be suggested to Microsoft, as they definitely are. However, even if a change is agreed to it will not be made quickly as the change will need to be verified and tested carefully.

If the Attendee API is going to be made available for public consumption, then the same concerns occur. What is important for the Attendee API is to use contracts to ensure that the interactions do not diverge and that the data returned is consistent.

Another reason to use producer contracts is that it is easier to get started. It is a good way to introduce contracts to your APIs. Having contracts is far more beneficial than not having them. However, when consumers and producers are both in the same organization, we suggest that you use the consumer-driven contracts methodology.

Consumer-driven contracts

Consumer-driven contracts (CDCs), by definition, are implemented by a consumer driving the functionality that they wish to see in an interaction. Consumers submit contracts, or changes to a contract, to the producer for new or additional API functionality. When the new/updated contract is submitted to the producer, a discussion about the change will begin, which will result in accepting or rejecting this change.

CDC is very much an interactive and social process. The owners of the applications that are consumers and producers should be within reach (e.g., in the same organization as one another). When a consumer would like a new interaction (e.g., API call) or have an interaction updated (e.g., a new property added), then they submit a request for that feature.

Case study: Applying CDC

In our case, this may mean that a pull request is submitted from the legacy conference system to the new Attendee API service. The request for the new interaction is then reviewed and a discussion takes place about this new functionality. This discussion is to ensure that this is something that the Attendee service should and will fulfill. For example, if a contract is suggested for a PUT request, a discussion can take place, as it may be preferable to have this as a PATCH request.

This is where a good part of the value of contracts comes from: this discussion for both parties about what the problem is, and using a contract to assert that this is what the two parties accept and agree to. Once the contract is agreed to, the producer (Attendee service) accepts the contract as part of the project and can start fulfilling it.

Contracts methodology overview

These methodologies should hopefully give an overview of how to use contracts as part of the development process. This should not be taken as gospel, as variations do exist on the exact steps. For example, one process may request that the consumer—when writing the contract—also creates a basic implementation of producer code to fulfill the contract. In another example, the consumer should TDD the functionality they require and then create the contract before submitting the pull request. The exact process that is put in place may vary by team. Once you understand the core concepts and patterns of CDC, the exact process that is used is just an implementation detail.

If you are starting out on a journey to add contracts, you should note that there is a cost—the setup time to incorporate contracts into a project and also the cost of writing the contracts. It is worth looking at tooling that can create contracts for you based on an OpenAPI Specification.[9]

Contract testing frameworks

It is likely that when it comes to contract testing frameworks for HTTP, you will want to look at Pact (*https://pact.io*). Pact has evolved into the default contract testing framework due to the ecosystem that has been built around it and the sheer number of languages it supports. Other contract testing frameworks are available, and they can be opinionated. Pact is opinionated; it enforces that you should perform CDC and is specifically designed for that. A test is written by a consumer and that test generates a contract, which takes the form of an intermediate representation of the interaction. This language-agnostic intermediate representation is why Pact has such wide language usage. Other frameworks have differing opinions; for example, Spring Cloud Contracts does not have a strong opinion on CDC or producer contracts, and either can be achieved. This is possible as with Spring Cloud Contracts you write the contracts by hand as opposed to having them generated. Though Spring Cloud Contracts is language agnostic by using a containerized version of the product, to get the most out of it you need to be using the Spring and JVM ecosystem.[10]

There are options for contract testing for other protocols; it is not exclusively for HTTP communications.

---

9 At the time of writing, there are a few projects that are available, though none are actively maintained, so it is difficult to recommend any.

10 Pact does a good job of comparing itself to other contract frameworks (*https://oreil.ly/h8WrT*).

API contracts storage and publishing

Having seen how contracts work and methodologies of incorporating them into the development process, the next consideration becomes where contracts are stored and how they should be published.

There are a few options for storing and publishing contracts and these again depend on the setup that is available to you and your organization.

Contracts can be stored alongside the producer code in version control (e.g., Git). They can also be published alongside your build into an artifact repository such as Artifactory (*https://oreil.ly/jXuCS*).

Ultimately the contracts need to be obtainable by the producer and the consumer. The storage point also needs to allow for the submission of new contracts. The producer should have control over which contracts are accepted in the project and can ensure that undesired changes aren't made or additional contracts are added. The downside to this approach is that in a large organization it can be difficult to find all the API services that use contracts.

Another option is to store all the contracts in a centralized location to enable visibility into other API interactions that are available. This central location could be a Git repository, but the downside to this approach is that unless organized and set up correctly, it is possible and likely that contracts get pushed into a module that the producer has no intention of fulfilling.

Yet another option for storing contracts is to use a broker. The Pact contract framework has a broker product (*https://oreil.ly/PIThd*) that can be used as a central location to host contracts. A broker can show all contracts that have been validated by the producer as the producer will publish those contracts that have been fulfilled. A broker can also see who is using a contract to produce a network diagram, integrate with CI/CD pipelines, and provide even more valuable information. This is the most comprehensive solution available and if you use a framework that is compatible with the Pact Broker, then it is recommended.

ADR Guideline: Contract Testing

To understand if applying contract testing is valid for your case and weighing the pros and cons of using contracts, the ADR Guideline in Table 2-2 should help guide you to a decision.

Table 2-2. ADR Guideline: Contract testing

Decision	When building an API should you use contract testing and, if so, should you use consumer-driven contracts or producer contracts?
Discussion Points	Determine whether you are ready to include contract testing as part of your API testing.

Discussion Points continued:

- Do you want to add an extra layer of testing to your API that developers will be required to learn about?

If contracts have not been used before, then it requires time to decide how you will use them.

- Should contracts be centralized or in a project?
- Do additional tools and training need to be provided to help people with contracts?

If deciding to use contracts, then which methodology should be used—CDC or producer contracts?

- Do you know who will use this API?
- Will this API be used just within your organization?
- Does the API have consumers that are willing to engage with you to help drive your functionality?

Recommendations	We recommend using contract testing when building an API. Even if there is a developer learning curve and you are deciding how you are going to set up your contracts for the first time, we believe it is worth the effort. Defined interactions that are tested save so much time when integrating services together.

If you are exposing your API to a large external audience, it is important to use producer contracts. Again, having defined interactions that help ensure that your API does not break backward compatibility is crucial.

If you're building an internal API, the ideal is to work toward CDC, even if you have to start with producer contracts and evolve over to CDC.

If contract testing is not feasible, then for a producer you need alternatives to ensure that your API is conforming your agreed interactions and provide a way that consumers can test. This means that you have to be very careful with your tests that the responses and requests match with what is expected, which can be tricky and time-consuming.

API Component Testing

Component testing can be used to validate that multiple units work together and should be used to validate behavior—they are service tests in the test pyramid in Figure 2-3. An example of a component test is sending a request to your API and verifying the response. At a high level it will require that your application can read the request, perform authentication and authorization, deserialize a payload, perform the business logic, serialize the payload, and respond. That is a lot of units being tested, and it would be difficult to point to exactly where a bug could be. Where this example differs from a contract test is that you should be checking that the service had the correct behavior; for example, if this was creating a new attendee, you want to verify that the service made a call to the (mocked) database. You are not just checking the shape of the response like contract tests do. As component tests verify multiple units together, they are (normally) slower running than unit tests. Component tests should not call out to external dependencies. Like contract testing, you are not using these tests to verify external integration points. The type of tests that you want to trigger in this scope varies based on the business case; however, for APIs you would be looking to validate cases such as:

- Is the correct status code returned when a request is made?

- Does the response contain the correct data?

- Is an incoming payload rejected if a null or empty parameter is passed in?

- When I send a request where the accepted content type is XML, will the data return the expected format?

- If a request is made by a user who does not have the correct entitlements, what will the response be?

- What will happen if an empty dataset is returned? Is this a 404 or is it an empty array?

- When creating a resource, does the location header point to the new asset created?

From this selection of tests, you can see how these bleed into two areas of the test quadrant. This includes Q1, where you are confirming that the API being built works (i.e., it is producing results), and Q2, where you test to verify that the responses of the Attendee API are correct.

Contract Testing Versus Component Testing

If contract testing is not available, you should use API component tests to verify that your API conforms to your agreed interactions, i.e., your API specification. Using API component tests to verify that your API conforms to an interaction is not ideal—for a start, it is much more likely to be error-prone and is tedious to write. You should make contracts your golden source of agreed interactions, as the generated tests ensure that the shape of your API is accurate.

Case Study: Component Test to Verify Behavior

Let's look at an example of a case for our Attendee API for the endpoint /confer ence/{conference-id}/attendees. This endpoint returns a list of the attendees at a conference event. For this component test, a mock is used to represent our external database dependency, and as seen in Figure 2-5, in this case that is the DAO.

Some things to test this endpoint for are:

- Requests that are successful have response of 200 (OK)

- Users without the right level of access will return a status of 403 (Forbidden)

- When a conference has no attendees, an empty array will be returned

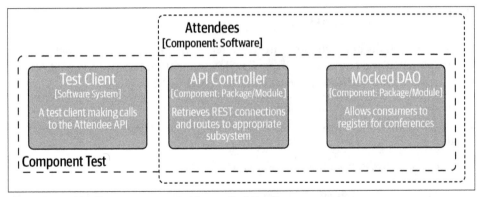

Figure 2-5. API Component test with mocked DAO

A library or testing framework that wraps a request client can be really useful. Here REST-Assured (*https://oreil.ly/aaJ77*) is used to call the Attendee API endpoint and to verify these test cases:[11]

```
@Test
void response_for_attendees_should_be_200() {
    given()
        .header("Authorization", VALID_CREDENTIAL)
    .when()
        .get("/conference/conf-1/attendees")
    .then()
        .statusCode(HttpStatus.OK.value());
}
@Test
void response_for_attendees_should_be_403() {
    given()
        .header("Authorization", INVALID_CREDENTIAL)
    .when()
        .get("/conference/conf-1/attendees")
    .then()
        .statusCode(HttpStatus.FORBIDDEN.value());
...
}
```

Running this type of test gives us confidence that our API is behaving correctly.

---

11 These testing libraries usually have a Domain Specific Language (DSL) and make it easy to analyze responses from the API. RestAssured is one such REST testing framework in Java, and the `httptest` package comes out of the box with Golang. Depending on the language or framework that you use, there should be something available; otherwise, creating a small wrapper around a standard client can make things considerably easier to integrate responses when writing tests.

API Integration Testing

Integration tests in our definition are tests across boundaries between the module being developed and any external dependencies. Integration tests are a type of service test and can be seen in the test pyramid image in Figure 2-3.

When performing integration testing, you want to confirm that the communication across the boundary is correct; i.e., your service can correctly communicate with another service that is external to it.

The types of things you want to verify are the following:

- Ensuring that an interaction is being made correctly; e.g., for a RESTful service, this may be specifying the correct URL or that the payload body is correct.

- Can the unit that is interacting with an external service handle the responses that are being returned?

In our case the legacy conference system needs to verify that it can make a request to the new Attendee API and can interpret the response.

Using Stub Servers: Why and How

If you are using contract tests, the generated stub servers can be used to verify that the consumer can communicate with the producer. The legacy conference system has a generated stub server and can use this to test against. This will keep testing local, and the stub server will be accurate. This is the preferred option for testing an external boundary.

However, a generated stub server from a contract is not always available and other options are required, as in the case of testing with an external API, such as the Microsoft Graph API, or within your organization when contracts are not used. The simplest one is to hand roll a stub server that mimics the requests and responses of the service you interact with. This is certainly a viable option, as in your chosen language and framework it is usually very easy for a developer to create a stub server with canned responses that integrate with tests.

The key considerations when hand rolling a stub server is to make sure that the stub is accurate. It can be very easy to make mistakes, such as inaccurately portraying the URL or making mistakes in the response property names and values. Can you see the errors in this handtyped response?[12]

---

12 Duplicate value for id and misspelled familyNane (sic).

```
{
    "values": [
        {
            "id":  123456,
            "givenName": "James",
            "familyName": "Gough"
        },
        {
            "id":  123457,
            "givenName": "Matthew",
            "familyNane": "Auburn"
        },
        {
            "id":  123456,
            "givenName": "Daniel",
            "familyName": "Bryant"
        }
    ]
}
```

This should still not put you off as this is a good solution. One of the authors had great success with this approach after a requirement for a project meant he had to hand roll a stub server for a login service.

A way to avoid these inaccuracies and to ensure that requests to URLs are accurately captured along with the responses is to use a recorder. It is possible to use a tool that will record the requests and responses to an endpoint and generate files that can be used for stubbing. Figure 2-6 shows how this works.

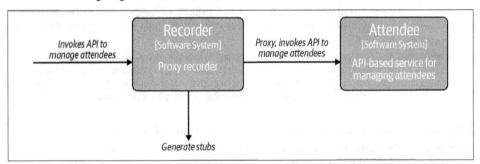

Figure 2-6. How a consumer of the Attendee API would use a recorder to capture a request/response for test data

These generated files are mappings that can then be used for tests to accurately portray requests and responses, and as they are not hand rolled they are guaranteed to be accurate at the point of generation. To use these generated files, a stub server is launched that is capable of reading in the mappings files. When a request is made to the stub server, it checks to see if the request matches any of the expected requests in the mappings file. If it matches, then the mapped response will be returned.[13] Recording calls to APIs will produce more accurate stubs than that of hand rolling a stub. If you do use recordings, then you need to make sure they stay updated and in sync; also, if you make recordings against production, you need to watch that no PII is saved into the mapping files.

ADR Guideline: Integration Testing

Integration testing is important, so to help you understand what types of integration testing you need, see the ADR Guideline in Table 2-3.

Table 2-3. ADR Guideline: Integration testing

Decision	Should integration testing be added to API testing?
Discussion Points	If your API is integrating with any other service, what level of integration test should you use?
	• Do you feel confident that you can just mock responses and do not need to perform integration tests?
	• For creating a stub server to test against, are you able to accurately craft the request and responses or should they be recorded?
	• Will you be able to keep stub servers up-to-date and recognize if an interaction is incorrect?
	If your stubs are incorrect or become out of date, this means it is possible to have tests that pass against your stub server, but when you deploy to production, your service fails to interact with the other API as it has changed.
Recommendations	We do recommend using the generated stub servers from contract tests. However, if this is not available, then having integration testing using recordings of interactions is the next best option. Having integration tests that can be run locally gives confidence that an integration will work, especially when refactoring an integration; it will help to ensure that any changes have not broken anything.

Integration testing is a really useful tool; however, definitions of these interactions have issues. The main issue is that they are point-in-time snapshots. These bespoke setups do not get updated with changes.

We have been using stub servers for the integrations we have looked at; however, it is possible to use a real instance of the external service to verify an integration.

---

13 Wiremock (*http://wiremock.org*) is a tool that can be used as a standalone service, making it language agnostic, although since it is written in Java there are some specific Java integrations that you can take advantage of. There are many other tools available that have a similar capability in other languages such as camouflage (*https://oreil.ly/mzL1u*), which is written in TypeScript.

Containerizing Test Components: Testcontainers

It is common to build applications as containerized images, which means that many applications that your service will integrate with are also available as containerized solutions. These images can be run on your local machine as part of your testing. Not only does using local containers allow for testing communication with the external services, but also you can run the same image that is run in production.

Testcontainers (*https://www.testcontainers.org*) is a library that integrates with your testing framework to orchestrate containers. Testcontainers will start and stop and generally organize the lifecycle of containers you use with your tests.

Case Study: Applying Testcontainers to Verify Integrations

Let's take a look at two use cases where this is helpful for the Attendee API. The first case is that the Attendee API service will support a gRPC interface as well as the RESTful interface. The gRPC interface is to be developed after the RESTful interface, but there are eager developers who want to start testing against a gRPC interface. The decision is made to provide a stub server for the gRPC interface, which will be a stub that provides a few canned responses. To achieve this goal, a bare-bones application is made that fulfills this objective. This gRPC stub is then packaged up, containerized, and published. This stub can be now used by the developers for testing across a boundary; i.e., they can make real calls to this stub server in their tests, and this containerized stub server can run locally on their machine.

The second use case is that the Attendee API service has a connection to an external database, which is an integration to test. The options for testing integration boundaries for a database would be to mock out the database, use an in-memory database (e.g., H2 (*https://oreil.ly/s7mGq*)), or run a local version of the database using Testcontainers. Using a real instance of the database in your test provides a lot of value because with mocks you can mock the wrong return value or make an incorrect assumption. With an in-memory DB you are assuming that the implementation matches the real DB. Using a real instance of the dependency and it being the same version that you run in production means that you get reliable testing across a boundary, which ensures that the integration will work when going to production. In Figure 2-7 you see the structure of the test to confirm a successful integration across a boundary with a database.

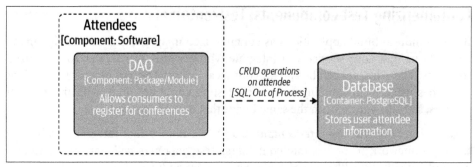

Figure 2-7. Testcontainers DAO test

Testcontainers is a powerful tool and should be considered when testing boundaries between any external services. Other common external services that benefit from using Testcontainers include Kafka, Redis, and NGINX. Adding this type of solution will increase the time it takes for your tests to run; however, integration tests are usually fewer and the additional confidence that is provided more often than not is a worthwhile trade-off for additional time.

Using Testcontainers raises a couple of questions. First, is this type of testing considered integration testing or is it end-to-end testing as a real instance of another service is being tested against? Second, why not just use this instead of contracts?

Using Testcontainers does not make the tests end-to-end if it stays within the integration boundary. We suggest that you use Testcontainers to test integrations; ensuring that the container has the right behavior is not your job (assuming that the owner of the image is outside your domain). For example, if I issue a statement to publish a message to a Kafka broker, I should not then subscribe to the topic to check that the item published was correct. I should trust that Kafka is doing its job and subscribers would be getting the message. If you want to verify this behavior, make it part of your end-to-end tests. That is why the boundary of what you are testing matters, so the case of the DAO to the database is not end-to-end testing, because only the interactions across the boundary are validated.

Testcontainers and integrating with a real service is a real boon and can add a lot of value to your testing, though they are not a replacement for contracts just because you can use a real version of a service. Working with a real instance is nice; however, contracts provide so much more than just a stub server—they provide all the testing, integration, and collaboration.

End-to-End Testing

The essence of end-to-end testing is to test services and their dependencies together to verify they work as expected. It is important to validate that when a request is made, and it reaches the front door (i.e., the request reaches your infrastructure), the request flows all the way through and the consumer gets the correct response. This validation gives confidence that all these systems work together as expected. For our case this is testing the legacy conference system, the new Attendee service, and the database all together.

Automating End-to-End Validation

This section concentrates on automated end-to-end tests. Automation is intended to save you time, so we will present automated testing that we believe gives you the best value. You will always need to verify that your systems work together—however, you can do this manually in a testing environment before releasing software into production.

 If you are building an external-facing API and you have multiple third parties that are consuming it, don't try to copy the third-party UI and replicate how it works. Doing so will mean that you spend huge amounts of time trying to replicate something out of your domain.

For end-to-end testing it is ideal is to have real versions of *your* services running and interacting together; however, sometimes this is not always feasible. Therefore, it is okay to stub out some entities of a system that are outside your organization's domain and are provided by an external party. A hypothetical case would be if the Attendee service required the use of AWS S3 (*https://oreil.ly/pzeua*). Relying on an external entity opens up concerns such as network issues or even the external provider being unavailable. Also, if your tests are not going to use an entity, there is no need to make it available for your test. For an end-to-end test of the Attendee service, the database and the Attendee service need to be launched, but this does not require the legacy conference system, as it is superfluous. This is why end-to-end tests sometimes require boundaries. The boundary for this end-to-end test is shown in Figure 2-8.

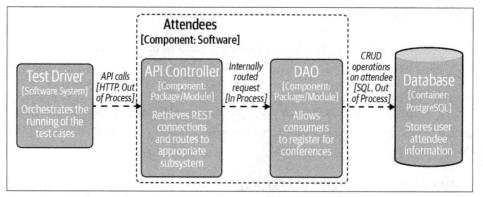

Figure 2-8. End-to-end test scope

Managing and coordinating multiple systems together is not easy to automate and end-to-end tests can be brittle. However, running end-to-end tests locally is becoming easier. As you have just seen in "Containerizing Test Components: Testcontainers" on page 47, containerization allows you to spin up multiple systems locally. Even though this is getting easier, you should still follow the test pyramid guidelines—end-to-end tests are at the top of the test pyramid for a reason.

When writing your end-to-end tests, you should use realistic payloads. We have seen cases where tests use small and concise payloads, then when investigating why APIs are breaking it is found that the consumers are regularly sending very large payloads—larger than the buffers support. This is why your end-to-end testing needs to be representative of the way that a consumer uses your API.

Types of End-to-End Tests

The end-to-end tests that you write should be driven off the requirements that are most important, as you saw in "Test Quadrant" on page 29.

Within Q3 of the test quadrant, you see scenario testing. Scenario tests are a common form of end-to-end testing. They are for testing out typical user journeys and provide confidence that your service is performing correctly. A scenario test can be based around a single action or multiple actions. It is important that you are only testing core user journeys and not testing edge cases or exception testing. To help you write your tests, you can use Behavior Driven Development (BDD) (*https://oreil.ly/qs7nY*). This is a nice way to write your user stories as part of your business-facing tests. An example for the conference system would be that when an attendee is registered for a conference talk, the attendee count should have increased when the conference talk information is retrieved.

The nice thing with scenario tests and validating these core user journeys is that you are not going to be concerned if a component is slower than in production. What is being interrogated is the correct behavior and expected results. However, you need to be more careful when running performance end-to-end tests. Performance testing, Q4 in the testing quadrant, should be deployed to a like-for-like environment of your production environment. If the two differ, you will not get results indicative of how your services are working. This does mean that you are going to need to deploy your services to this representative hardware, and depending on your resources and environment, that can be tricky. You should take this into consideration if it is going to make your tests flaky or is going to cost more development time than the return of confidence. However, this should not put you off because we have seen this type of end-to-end testing be successful.

The performance tests that you write as part of your end-to-end testing should be focused on ensuring that you are still serving requests within your targeted SLOs. You want these performance tests to show you have not introduced any sudden lag to your services (e.g., accidentally adding in some blocking code). If volume is important, you want to verify that your service is able to handle the loads you expect. Some great tools are available for performance testing, such as Gatling, JMeter, Locust, and K6. Even if none of these appeal to you, others are available and in many different languages that you should be familiar with. The performance figures that you want should be driven from your business requirements.

As part of your end-to-end testing, you should also ensure that your security is in place (i.e., TLS is turned on and the appropriate authentication mechanisms are in place). Security should not be turned off for these tests as it does not make it representative of a user journey, or it misrepresents metrics.

End-to-end testing is more complex than any other type of testing as it takes resources to create and maintain. Though it can be a time saver over doing end-to-end manual testing, it provides confidence in the application and evidence that services were working from a technical standpoint to meet service agreements.

ADR Guideline: End-to-End Testing

Knowing what to include, and whether end-to-end testing is worthwhile for your case, are important considerations. The ADR Guidelines in Table 2-4 should help you make a decision.

Table 2-4. ADR Guideline: End-to-End Testing

Decision	As part of your testing setup, should you use automated end-to-end tests?
Discussion Points	Determine how complex your setup is to enable end-to-end testing. Do you have a good idea of end-to-end tests that you require and will provide value? Are there any specific requirements or more advanced end-to-end tests that you should add?
Recommendations	We recommend that you do perform at a minimum end-to-end testing on core user journeys. This is going to give feedback as early as possible in your development cycle that a user could be impacted with the changes that have been made. Ideally you can run these end-to-end tests locally; however, if not, then it should be part of your build pipeline.
	End-to-end testing is valuable but must be balanced against the time investment you need to get it running. If it is not possible to do automated end-to-end testing, then you need to have a run book of manual tests that you can use. This run book should be used against a testing environment before a production release. This type of manual testing will considerably slow down your production releases and ability to deliver value to customers.

Summary

In this chapter you have learned about the core types of testing for APIs, including what should be tested and where time should be dedicated. The key takeaways are:

- Stick to the fundamentals of testing and make unit testing a core of your API.
- Contract testing can help you develop a consistent API and test with other APIs.
- Perform service tests on your component and isolate the integrations to validate incoming and outgoing traffic.
- Use end-to-end tests to replicate core user journeys to help validate that your APIs all integrate correctly.
- Use the ADR Guidelines as a way to work out if you should add different tests to your API.

While we've given you lots of information, ideas, and techniques for testing your API, this is by no means an exhaustive list of tools available. We encourage you to do some research on testing frameworks and libraries that you may want to use, to ensure you are making an informed decision.

However, no matter how much testing is done upfront, nothing is as good as seeing how an application actually runs in production. You will learn more about testing in production in Chapter 5. The next chapter will focus on exposing and managing APIs in a production setting using API gateways.

PART II

API Traffic Management

This section explores how API traffic is managed. This includes both traffic originating externally from end users that is entering (ingressing) into your system and traffic originating internally from services that is traveling across (service-to-service) your system.

In Chapter 3, where we recommend you begin your journey, you will explore using API gateway technology to manage ingress, or north–south traffic.

In Chapter 4, you will learn about managing east–west traffic using the service mesh pattern.

API Gateways: Ingress Traffic Management

Now that you have a good understanding of defining and testing an API, we can turn our attention to platforms and tooling that are responsible for delivering APIs to consumers in production. An API gateway is a critical part of any modern technology stack, sitting at the network "edge" of systems and acting as a management tool that mediates between a consumer and a collection of backend services.

In this chapter you will learn about the "why," "what," and "where" of API gateways and explore the history of the API gateway and other edge technologies. You will also explore the taxonomy of API gateways and learn how these fit into the bigger picture of system architecture and deployment models, all while avoiding common pitfalls.

Building on all of these topics, you will conclude the chapter by learning how to select an appropriate API gateway based on your requirements, constraints, and use cases.

Is an API Gateway the Only Solution?

We have frequently been asked, "Is an API gateway the only solution to getting user traffic to backend systems?" The short answer is no. But there is a bit more nuance here.

Many software systems need to route consumer API requests or ingress traffic from an external origin to an internal backend application. With web-based software systems, often the consumer's API requests originate from an end user interacting with a backend system via a web browser or mobile app. A consumer's requests may also originate from an external system (often third-party) making requests to an API via an application deployed elsewhere on the internet. In addition to providing a mechanism of routing traffic from a URL to a backend system, a solution that provides ingress will typically also be required to provide reliability, observability, and security.

As you will learn throughout this chapter, an API gateway isn't the only technology that can provide these requirements. For example, you can use a simple proxy or load balancer implementation. However, we believe it is the most commonly used solution, particularly within an enterprise context, and as the number of consumers and providers increases, it is often the most scalable, maintainable, and secure option.

As shown in Table 3-1, you will want to match your current requirements to the capabilities of each solution. Don't worry if you don't understand all of these requirements, as you will learn more about them throughout the chapter.

Table 3-1. Comparing reverse proxies, load balancers, and API gateways

Feature	Reverse proxy	Load balancer	API gateway
Single Backend	*	*	*
TIS/SSL	*	*	*
Multiple Backends		*	*
Service Discovery		*	*
API Composition			*
Authorization			*
Retry Logic			*
Rate Limiting			*
Logging and Tracing			*
Circuit Breaking			*

Guideline: Proxy, Load Balancer, or API Gateway

Table 3-2 provides a series of ADR Guidelines to help you decide the best ingress solution for your organization's system or current project.

Table 3-2. ADR Guideline: Proxy, load balancer, or API gateway

Decision	Should you use a proxy, load balancer, or API gateways for routing ingress traffic?
Discussion Points	Do you want simple routing, for example, from a single endpoint to a single backend service?
	Do you have cross-functional requirements that will require more advanced features, such as authentication, authorization, or rate limiting?
	Do you require API management functionality, such as API keys/tokens or monetization/chargeback?
	Do you already have a solution in place, or is there an organization-wide mandate that all traffic must be routed through certain components at the edge of your network?
Recommendations	Always use the simplest solution for your requirements, with an eye to the immediate future and known requirements.
	If you have advanced cross-functional requirements, an API gateway is typically the best choice.
	If your organization is an enterprise, an API gateway that supports API Management (APIM) features is recommended.
	Always perform due diligence within your organization for existing mandates, solutions, and components.

Case Study: Exposing the Attendee Service to Consumers

As the conference system has seen considerable uptake since its launch, the owners would like to enable conference attendees to be able to view their details via a new mobile application. This will require that the Attendee service API be exposed externally in order for the mobile app to query this data. As the Attendee service contains personally identifiable information (PII), this will mean that the API must be secure in addition to being reliable and observable. You could simply expose the API using a proxy or load balancer and implement any additional requirements using language- or framework-specific features. However, you must ask yourself if this solution would scale, would it be reusable (potentially supporting additional APIs using different languages and frameworks), and have these challenges already been solved within existing technologies or products? In this case study, we know that additional APIs are planned to be exposed in the future, and that additional languages and frameworks may be used in their implementation. It therefore makes sense to implement an API gateway-based solution.

As this chapter develops, you will add an API gateway to the existing conference system case study to expose the Attendee API in a manner that meets all of these requirements listed. Figure 3-1 shows what the conference system architecture will look like with the addition of an API gateway.

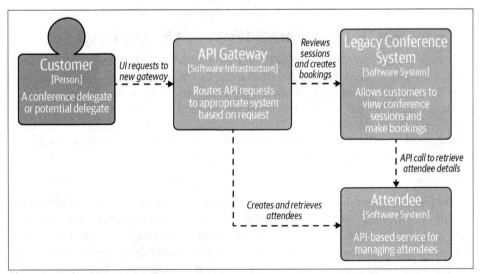

Figure 3-1. Using an API gateway to route to the Attendee service running independently from the monolith

What Is an API Gateway?

In a nutshell, an API gateway is a management tool that sits at the edge of a system between a consumer and a collection of backend services and acts as a single point of entry for a defined group of APIs. The consumer can be an end-user application or device, such as a single page web application or a mobile app, or another internal system, or third-party application or system.

An API gateway is implemented with two high-level fundamental components: a control plane and data plane. These components can typically be packaged together or deployed separately. The control plane is where operators interact with the gateway and define routes, policies, and required telemetry. The data plane is the location where all of the work specified in the control plane occurs, the network packets are routed, the policies enforced, and telemetry emitted.

What Functionality Does an API Gateway Provide?

At a network level an API gateway typically acts as a reverse proxy to accept all of the API requests from a consumer, calls and aggregates the various application-level backend services (and potentially external services) required to fulfill them, and returns the appropriate result.

What Is a Proxy, Forward Proxy, and Reverse Proxy?

A proxy server, sometimes referred to as a forward proxy, is an intermediary server that forwards requests for content from multiple clients to different servers across the internet. A forward proxy is used to protect clients. For instance, a business may have a proxy that routes and filters employee traffic to the public internet. A reverse proxy server, on the other hand, is a type of proxy server that typically sits behind the firewall in a private network and routes client requests to the appropriate backend server. A reverse proxy is designed to protect servers.

An API gateway provides cross-cutting requirements such as user authentication, request rate limiting, and timeouts/retries, and can provide metrics, logs, and trace data in order to support the implementation of observability within the system. Many API gateways provide additional features that enable developers to manage the lifecycle of an API, assist with the onboarding and management of developers using the APIs (such as providing a developer portal and related account administration and access control), and provide enterprise governance.

Where Is an API Gateway Deployed?

An API gateway is typically deployed at the edge of a system, but the definition of "system" in this case can be quite flexible. For startups and many small-medium businesses (SMBs), an API gateway will often be deployed at the edge of the data center or the cloud. In these situations there may only be a single API gateway (deployed and running via multiple instances for high availability) that acts as the front door for the entire backend estate, and the API gateway will provide all of the edge functionality discussed in this chapter via this single component.

Figure 3-2 shows how clients interact with an API gateway and backend systems over the internet.

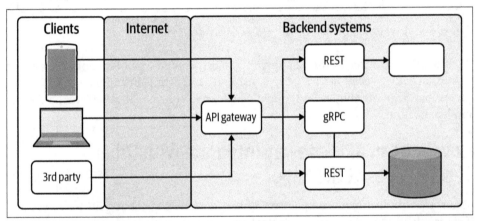

Figure 3-2. A typical startup/SMB API gateway deployment

For large organizations and enterprises, an API gateway will typically be deployed in multiple locations, often as part of the initial edge stack at the perimeter of a data center, and additional gateways may be deployed as part of each product, line of business, or organizational department. In this context these gateways would more typically be separate implementations and may offer differing functionality depending on geographical location (e.g., required governance) or infrastructure capabilities (e.g., running on low-powered edge compute resources).

Figure 3-3 shows how an API gateway often sits between the public internet and the demilitarized zone (DMZ) of a private network.

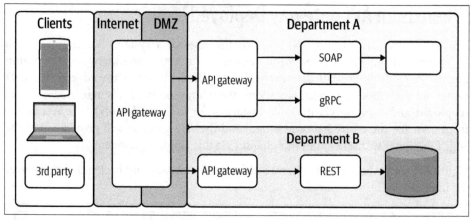

Figure 3-3. A typical large/enterprise API gateway deployment

As you will learn later in this chapter, the definition and exact functionality offered within an API gateway isn't always consistent across implementations, and so the preceding diagrams should be thought of as more conceptual rather than an exact implementation.

How Does an API Gateway Integrate with Other Technologies at the Edge?

There are typically many components deployed at the edge of an API-based system. This is where the consumers and users first interact with the backend, and hence many cross-cutting concerns are best addressed here. Therefore, a modern edge technology stack or "edge stack" provides a range of functionality that meets essential cross-functional requirements for API-based applications. In some edge stacks each piece of functionality is provided by a separately deployed and operated component, and in others the functionality and/or components are combined. You will learn more about the individual requirements in the next section of the chapter, but for the moment Figure 3-4 should highlight the key layers of a modern edge stack.

These layers should not be treated as a monolithic component. They are typically deployed separately and may be owned and operated by individual teams or third-party service providers. Several API gateways provide all of the functionality within an edge stack. Others simply focus on the API gateway functionality and API management. It is also common within cloud environments that the cloud vendor will provide a load balancer that can be integrated with an API gateway.

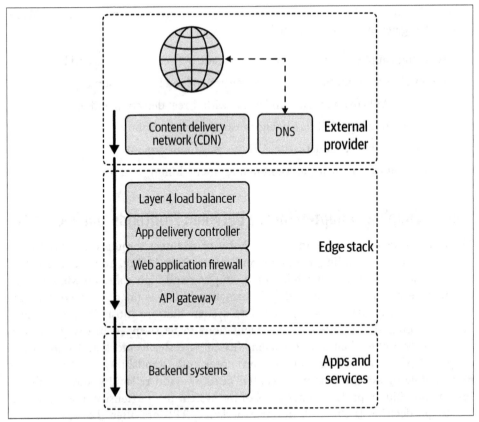

Figure 3-4. A modern edge stack

Now that you have a good idea about the "what" and "where" of an API gateway, let's now look at why an organization would use an API gateway.

Why Use an API Gateway?

A big part of the modern software architect's role is asking the hard questions about design and implementation. This is no different when dealing with APIs and traffic management and related technologies. You need to balance both short-term implementation and long-term maintainability. There are many API-related cross-cutting concerns that you might have, including maintainability, extensibility, security, observability, product lifecycle management, and monetization. An API gateway can help with all of these!

This section of the chapter will provide you with an overview of the key problems that an API gateway can address, such as:

- Reducing coupling by using an adapter/facade between frontends and backends
- Simplifying consumption by aggregating/translating backend services
- Protecting APIs from overuse and abuse with threat detection and mitigation
- Understanding how APIs are being consumed (observability)
- Managing APIs as products with API lifecycle management
- Monetizing APIs by using account management, billing, and pay

Reduce Coupling: Adapter/Facade Between Frontends and Backends

Three fundamental concepts that every software architect should learn about early in their career are coupling, cohesion, and information hiding. You are taught that systems that are designed to exhibit loose coupling and high cohesion will be easier to understand, maintain, and modify. Information hiding is the principle of segregation of the design decisions in a software system that are most likely to change. Loose coupling allows different implementations to be swapped in easily, and can be especially useful when testing systems (e.g., it is easier to mock and stub loosely coupled dependencies). High cohesion promotes understandability—that is, all code in a module or system supports a central purpose—and reliability and reusability. Information hiding protects other parts of the system from extensive modification if the design decision is changed. In our experience, APIs are often the locations in a system in which the architectural theory meets the reality; an API is quite literally and figuratively an interface that other engineers integrate with.

An API gateway can act as a single entry point and a facade or an adapter, and hence promote loose coupling and cohesion. A facade defines a new simpler interface for a system, whereas an adapter reuses an old interface with the goals of supporting interoperability between two existing interfaces. Clients integrate with the API exposed at the gateway, which, providing the agreed upon contract is maintained, allows components at the backend to change location, architecture, and implementation (language, framework, etc.) with minimal impact. Figure 3-5 demonstrates how an API gateway can act as a single entry point for client requests to the backend APIs and services.

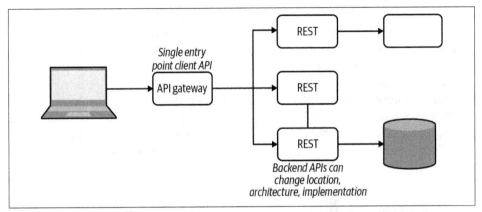

Figure 3-5. An API gateway providing a facade between frontends and backends

Simplify Consumption: Aggregating/Translating Backend Services

Building on the discussion of coupling in the previous section, it is often the case that the API you want to expose to the frontend systems is different than the current interface provided by a backend or composition of backend systems. For example, you may want to aggregate the APIs of several backend services that are owned by multiple owners into a single consumer-facing API in order to simplify the mental model for frontend engineers, streamline data management, or hide the backend architecture. GraphQL (*https://graphql.org*) is often used for exactly these reasons. Of course, there are trade-offs with implementing this type of functionality here, and it can be all too easy to highly couple logic within an API gateway with backend service business logic.

Orchestrating Concurrent API Calls

A popular simplification approach implemented in API gateways is orchestrating concurrent backend API calls. This is where the gateway orchestrates and coordinates the concurrent calling of multiple independent backend APIs. Typically you want to call multiple independent and noncoupled APIs in parallel rather than sequentially in order to save time when gathering results for the consumer. Providing this in the gateway removes the need to independently implement this functionality in each of the consumers. Once again the trade-off is that business logic can become spread across the API gateway and backend systems. There are also operation coupling issues to consider. An implementation change in an API gateway that alters the ordering of API calls can impact the expected results, particularly if the backend calls are not idempotent.

It is also a common requirement within an enterprise context that protocol translation is required. For example, you may have several "heritage" systems that provide only SOAP-based APIs, but you only want to expose REST-like APIs to consumers. An API gateway can provide this aggregation and translation functionality, although care should be taken with this usage. There is a design, implementation, and testing cost for making sure the translation has the correct fidelity. There is also a computational resource cost for implementing the translation, which can be costly when dealing within a large number of requests. Figure 3-6 shows how an API gateway can provide aggregation of backend service calls and translation of protocols.

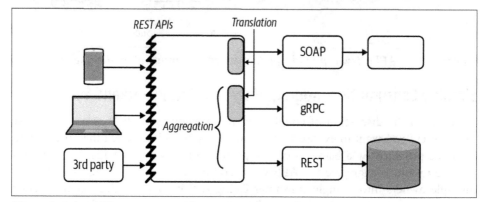

Figure 3-6. An API gateway providing aggregation and translation

Protect APIs from Overuse and Abuse: Threat Detection and Mitigation

The edge of a system is where your users first interact with your applications. It is also often the the point where bad actors and hackers first encounter your systems. Although the vast majority of enterprise organizations will have multiple security-focused layers to their edge stack, such as a content delivery network (CDN) and web application firewall (WAF), and even a perimeter network and dedicated demilitarized zone (DMZ), for many smaller organizations the API gateway can be the first line of defense. For this reason, many API gateways include security-focused functionality, such as TLS termination, authentication/authorization, IP allow/deny lists, WAFs (either inbuilt or via external integration), rate limiting and load shedding, and API contract validation. Figure 3-7 highlights how an allow/deny list and rate-limiting can be used to mitigate abuse of APIs.

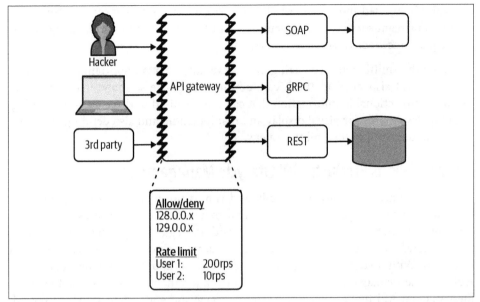

Figure 3-7. API gateway overuse and abuse

A big part of this functionality is the capability to detect API abuse, either accidental or deliberate, and for this you will need to implement a comprehensive observability strategy.

Understand How APIs Are Being Consumed: Observability

Understanding how systems and applications are performing is vitally important for ensuring business goals are being met and that customer requirements are being satisfied.[1] It is increasingly common to measure business objectives via key performance indicators (KPIs), such as customer conversion, revenue per hour, stream starts per second, and more. Infrastructure and platforms are typically observed through the lens of service-level indicators (SLIs) (*https://oreil.ly/S0ltZ*), such as latency, errors, queue depth, and the like.

As the vast majority (if not all) of user requests flow through the edge of a system, this is a vital point for observability. It is an ideal location to capture top-line ingress metrics, such as the number of errors, throughput, and latency, and it is also a key location for identifying and annotating requests (potentially with application-specific metadata) that flow throughout the system further upstream. Correlation identifiers[2]

---

1 Cindy Sridharan's O'Reilly book *Distributed Systems Observability* (*https://oreil.ly/pImte*) is a great primer for learning more about the topic of observability.

2 See, for example, OpenZipkin b3 headers (*https://oreil.ly/UOghv*).

are typically injected into a request via the API gateway and then can be propagated by each upstream service. These identifiers can then be used to correlate log entries and request traces across services and systems.

Although the emitting and collecting of observability data is important at the system level, you will also need to think carefully how to process, analyze, and interpret this data into actionable information that can then be used to drive decision making. Creating dashboards for visual display and manipulation, and also defining alerts, are vital for a successful observability strategy.

Manage APIs as Products: API Lifecycle Management

Modern APIs are often designed, built, and run as products that are consumed by both internal systems and third parties, and they must be managed as such. Many large organizations see APIs as a critical and strategic component and, as such, will create an API program strategy and set clear business goals, constraints, and resources. With a strategy set, the day-to-day tactical approach is often focused on API lifecycle management. Full lifecycle API Management (APIM) spans the entire lifespan of an API that begins at the planning stage and ends when an API is retired. Many of the stages within the lifecycle are heavily coupled to the implementation provided by an API gateway. For these reasons, choosing an appropriate API gateway is a critical decision if you are supporting APIM.

There are multiple definitions for key API lifecycle stages, and we believe that the Axway team strikes a good balance with defining 3 key components—create, control, and consume—and 10 top stages of an API lifecycle (*https://oreil.ly/2F8mV*):

Building
    Designing and building your API.

Testing
    Verifying functionality, performance, and security expectations.

Publishing
    Exposing your APIs to developers.

Securing
    Mitigating security risks and concerns.

Managing
    Maintaining and managing APIs to ensure they are functional, up-to-date, and meeting business requirements.

Onboarding

Enabling developers to quickly learn how to consume the APIs exposed. For example, offering OpenAPI or AsyncAPI documentation and providing a portal and sandbox.

Analyzing

Enabling observability and analyzing monitoring data to understand usage and detect issues.

Promoting

Advertising APIs to developers—for example, listing in an API marketplace.

Monetizing

Enabling the charging for and collection of revenue for use of an API. We cover this aspect of API lifecycle management as a separate stage in the next section.

Retirement

Supporting the deprecation and removal of APIs, which happens for a variety of reasons, including business priority shifts, technology changes, and security concerns.

Figure 3-8 demonstrates how API lifecycle management integrates with an API gateway and backend services.

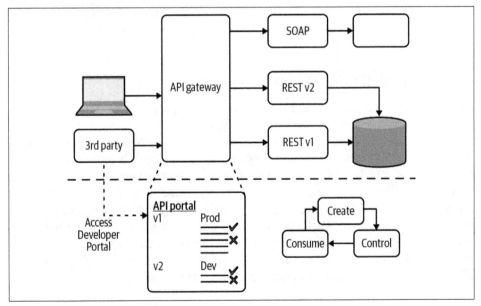

Figure 3-8. API gateway lifecycle management

Monetize APIs: Account Management, Billing, and Payment

The topic of billing-monetized APIs is closely related to API lifecycle management. The APIs being exposed to customers typically have to be designed as a product and offered via a developer portal that also includes account management and payment options. Many of the enterprise API gateways include monetization.[3] These payment portals often integrate with payment solutions, such as PayPal or Stripe, and enable the configuration of developer plans, rate limits, and other API consumption options.

A Modern History of API Gateways

Now that you have a good understanding of the "what," "where," and "why" of API gateways, it is time to take a glance backward through history before looking forward to current API gateway technology. As Mark Twain was alleged to have said, "history doesn't repeat itself, but it often rhymes," and anyone who has worked in technology for more than a few years will definitely appreciate the relevance this quote has to the general approach seen in the industry. Architecture style and patterns repeat in various "cycles" throughout the history of software development, as do operational approaches. There is typically progress made between these cycles, but we collectively need to be careful not to miss the teachings that history has to offer.

This is why it is important to understand the historical context of API gateways and traffic management at the edge of systems. By looking backward we can build on firm foundations, understand fundamental requirements, and also try to avoid repeating the same mistakes.

1990s Onward: Hardware Load Balancers

The concept of the World Wide Web (WWW) was proposed by Tim Berners-Lee in the late 1980s, but this didn't enter the consciousness of the general public until the mid-1990s, where the initial hype culminated in the dot-com boom and bust of the late '90s. This "Web 1.0" period drove the evolution of web browsers (Netscape Navigator was launched late 1994), the web server (Apache Web Server was released in 1995), and hardware load balancers (F5 was founded in 1996). The Web 1.0 experience consisted of users visiting websites via making HTTP requests using their browser, and the entire HTML document for each target page being returned in the response. Dynamic aspects of a website were implemented via Common Gateway Interface (CGI) in combination with scripts written in languages like Perl or C. This was arguably the first incantation of what we would call "function as a service (FaaS)" today.

---

3 Examples include Apigee Edge (*https://oreil.ly/1xrMi*) and 3Scale (*https://oreil.ly/kVrdp*).

As an increasing number of users accessed each website, this strained the underlying web servers. This added the requirement to design systems that supported spreading the increased load and also provide fault tolerance. Hardware load balancers were deployed at the edge of the data center, with the goal of allowing infrastructure engineers, networking specialists, and sysadmins to spread user requests over a number of web server instances. These early load balancer implementations typically supported basic health checks, and if a web server failed or began responding with increased latency, then user requests could be routed elsewhere accordingly. Hardware load balancers are still very much in use today. The technology may have improved alongside transistor technology and chip architecture, but the core functionality remains the same.

Early 2000s Onward: Software Load Balancers

As the web overcame the early business stumbles from the dot-com bust, the demand for supporting a range of activities, such as users sharing content, ecommerce and online shopping, and businesses collaborating and integrating systems, continued to increase. In reaction, web-based software architectures began to take a number of forms. Smaller organizations were building on their early work with CGI and were also creating monolithic applications in the emerging web-friendly languages such as Java and .NET. Larger enterprises began to embrace service-oriented architecture (SOA), and the associated "Web Service" specifications (WS-*) enjoyed a brief moment in the sun.

The requirements for high availability and scalability of websites were increasing, and the expense and inflexibility of early hardware load balancers was beginning to become a constraining factor. Enter software load balancers and general-purpose proxies that could be used to implement this functionality, with HAProxy being launched in 2001 and NGINX in 2002. The target users were still operations teams, but the skills required meant that sysadmins comfortable with configuring software-based web servers were increasingly happy to take responsibility for what used to be a hardware concern.

Software Load Balancers: Still a Popular Choice Today

Although they have both evolved from initial launches, NGINX and HAProxy are still widely in use, and they are still very useful for small organizations and simple API gateway use cases (both also offer commercial variants more suitable for enterprise deployment). The rise of the cloud (and virtualization) cemented the role of software load balancers, and we recommend learning about the basics of this technology.

This time frame also saw the rise of other edge technologies that still required specialized hardware implementation. Content delivery networks (CDNs), primarily driven by the need to eliminate performance bottlenecks of the internet, began to be increasingly adopted in order to offload requests from origin web servers. Web application firewalls (WAFs) also began to see increasing adoption, first implemented using specialized hardware, and later via software. The open source ModSecurity project, and the integration of this with the Apache Web Server, arguably drove mass adoption of WAFs.

Mid-2000s: Application Delivery Controllers (ADCs)

The mid-2000s continued to see the increasing pervasiveness of the web in everyday life. The emergence of internet-capable phones only accelerated this, with BlackBerry initially leading the field, and everything kicking into a higher gear with the launch of the first iPhone in 2007. The PC-based web browser was still the de facto method of accessing the web, and the mid-2000s saw the emergence of "Web 2.0" alongside widespread adoption in browsers of the XMLHttpRequest API and the corresponding technique named *Asynchronous JavaScript and XML* (Ajax). At the time, this technology was revolutionary. The asynchronous nature of the API meant that no longer did an entire HTML page have to be returned, parsed, and the display completely refreshed with each request. By decoupling the data interchange layer from the presentation layer, Ajax allowed web pages to change content dynamically without the need to reload the entire page.

All of these changes placed new demands on web servers and load balancers for yet again handling more load but also supporting more secure (SSL) traffic, increasingly large (media rich) data payloads, and different priority requests. This led to the emergence of *application delivery controllers* (ADCs), a term coined by the existing networking players like F5 Networks, Citrix, and Cisco. ADCs provided support for compression, caching, connection multiplexing, traffic shaping, and SSL offload, combined with load balancing. The target users were once again infrastructure engineers, networking specialists, and sysadmins.

By the mid-2000s nearly all of the components of a modern traffic management edge stack were widely adopted across the industry. However, the implementation and operation of many of the components was increasingly being siloed between teams. If a developer wanted to expose a new application within a large organization, this typically meant many separate meetings with the CDN vendors, the load balancing teams, the InfoSec and WAF teams, and the web/application server team. Movements like DevOps emerged, partly driven by a motivation to remove the friction imposed by these silos. If you still have a large number of layers in your edge stack and are migrating to the cloud or a new platform, now is the time to potentially think about the trade-offs with multiple layers and specialist teams.

Early 2010s: First-Generation API Gateways

The late 2000s and early 2010s saw the emergence of the API economy and associated technologies. Organizations like Twilio were disrupting telecommunications, with their founder, Jeff Lawson (*https://oreil.ly/jQsob*), pitching that "We have taken the entire messy and complex world of telephony and reduced it to five API calls." The Google Ads API was enabling content creators to monetize their websites, and Stripe was enabling larger organizations to easily charge for access to services. Founded in late 2007, Mashape was one of the early pioneers in attempting to create an API marketplace for developers. Although this exact vision didn't pan out (arguably it was ahead of its time, looking now to the rise of "no code"/"low code" solutions), a byproduct of the Mashape business model was the creation of the Kong API Gateway, built upon OpenResty (*https://openresty.org/en*) and the open source NGINX implementation. Other implementations included WSO2 with Cloud Services Gateway, Sonoa Systems with Apigee, and Red Hat with 3Scale Connect.

These were the first edge technologies that were targeted at developers in addition to platform teams and sysadmins. A big focus was on managing the software development lifecycle (SDLC) of an API and providing system integration functionality, such as endpoints and protocol connectors, and translation modules. Due to the range of functionality offered, the vast majority of first-generation API gateways were implemented in software. Developer portals sprang up in many products, which allowed engineers to document and share their APIs in a structured way. These portals also provided access controls, user/developer account management, and publishing controls and analytics. The theory was that this would enable the easy monetization of APIs and the management of "APIs as a product."

During this evolution of developer interaction at the edge, there was increasing focus on the HTTP part of the application layer (layer 7) of the OSI Networking model. The previous generations of edge technologies often focused on IP addresses and ports, which primarily operate at the transport layer (layer 4) of the OSI model. Allowing developers to make routing decisions in an API gateway based on HTTP metadata such as path-based routing or header-based routing provided the opportunity for richer functionality.

There was also an emerging trend toward creating smaller service-based architectures that took some of the ideas present in the original SOA, but recast using more lightweight implementation technologies and protocols. Organizations were extracting single-purpose standalone applications from their existing monolithic codebases, and some of these monoliths acted as an API gateway, or provided API gateway–like functionality, such as routing and authentication. With the first generation of API gateways it was often the case that both functional and cross-functional concerns, such as routing, security, and resilience, were performed both at the edge and also within the applications and services.

2015 Onward: Second-Generation API Gateways

The mid-2010s saw the rise of the next generation of modular and service-oriented architectures, with the concept of "microservices" firmly entering the zeitgeist by 2015. This was largely thanks to "unicorn" organizations like Netflix, AWS, and Spotify sharing their experiences of working with these architectural patterns. In addition to backend systems being decomposed into more numerous and smaller services, developers were also adopting container technologies based on Linux LXC. Docker was released in March of 2013, and Kubernetes followed hot on its heels with a v1.0 release in July of 2015. This shift in architectural style and changing runtimes drove new requirements at the edge. Netflix released its bespoke JVM-based API gateway, Zuul (*https://oreil.ly/rdN4q*), in mid-2013. Zuul supported service discovery for dynamic backend services and also allowed Groovy scripts to be injected at runtime in order to dynamically modify behavior. This gateway also consolidated many cross-cutting concerns into a single edge component, such as authentication, testing (canary releases), rate limiting and load shedding, and observability. Zuul was a revolutionary API gateway in the microservices space, and it has since evolved into a second version, and Spring Cloud Gateway has been built on top of this.

With the increasing adoption of Kubernetes and the open source release of the Envoy Proxy in 2016 by the Lyft Engineering team, many API gateways were created around this technology, including Ambassador Edge Stack (built upon the CNCF Emissary-ingress), Contour, and Gloo Edge. This drove further innovation across the API gateway space, with Kong mirroring functionality offered by the next generation of gateways and other gateways being launched, such as Traefik, Tyk, and others.

Confusion in the Cloud: API Gateways, Edge Proxies, and Ingress Controllers

As Christian Posta noted in his blog post "API Gateways Are Going Through an Identity Crisis" (*https://oreil.ly/Qkufv*), there is some confusion around what an API gateway is in relation to proxy technologies being adopted within the cloud computing domain. Generally speaking, in this context an API gateway enables some form of management of APIs, ranging from simple adaptor-style functionality operating at the application layer (OSI layer 7) that provides fundamental cross-cutting concerns, all the way to full lifecycle API management. Edge proxies are more general-purpose traffic proxies or reverse proxies that operate at the network and transport layers (OSI layers 3 and 4, respectively), provide basic cross-cutting concerns, and tend not to offer API-specific functionality. "Ingress Controllers" are a Kubernetes-specific technology that controls what traffic enters a cluster and how this traffic is handled.

The target users for the second generation of API gateways were largely the same as the cohort for the first generation but with a clearer separation of concerns and a stronger focus on developer self-service. The move from the first to second generation of API gateways saw increased consolidation of both functional and cross-functional requirements being implemented in the gateway. Although it became widely accepted that microservices should be built around the idea espoused by James Lewis and Martin Fowler (*https://oreil.ly/LySYe*) of "smart endpoints and dumb pipes," the uptake of polyglot language stacks means that "microservice gateways" emerged (more detail in the next section) that offered cross-cutting functionality in a language-agnostic way.

Current API Gateway Taxonomy

As can be the case with terminology in the software development industry, there often isn't an exact agreement on what defines or classifies an API gateway. There is broad agreement in regards to the functionality this technology should provide, but different segments of the industry have different requirements, and hence different views, for an API gateway. This has led to several subtypes of API gateway emerging and being discussed. In this section of the chapter, you will explore the emerging taxonomy of API gateways and learn about their respective use cases, strengths, and weaknesses.

Traditional Enterprise Gateways

The traditional enterprise API gateway is typically aimed at the use case of exposing and managing business-focused APIs. This gateway is also often integrated with a full API lifecycle management solution, as this is an essential requirement when releasing, operating, and monetizing APIs at scale. The majority of gateways in this space may offer an open source edition, but there is typically a strong usage bias toward the open core/commercial version of the gateway.

These gateways typically require the deployment and operation of dependent services, such as data stores. These external dependencies have to be run with high availability to maintain the correct operation of the gateway, and this must be factored into running costs and DR/BC plans.

Microservices/Micro Gateways

The primary use case of a microservices API gateway, or micro API gateway, is to route ingress traffic to backend APIs and services. In comparison with traditional enterprise gateways, there are typically not many features provided for the management of API lifecycles. These types of gateways are often available and fully featured as open source or are offered as a lightweight version of a traditional enterprise gateway.

They tend to be deployed and operated as standalone components and often make use of the underlying platform (e.g., Kubernetes) for the management of any internal state, such as API lifecycle data, rate limiting counts, and API consumer account management. As microservices gateways are typically built using modern proxy technology like Envoy, the integration capabilities with service meshes (especially those built using the same proxy technology) are typically good.

Service Mesh Gateways

The ingress or API gateway included with a service mesh is typically designed to provide only the core functionality of routing external traffic into the mesh. For this reason they often lack some of the typical enterprise features, such as comprehensive integration with authentication and identity provider solutions, and also integration with other security features, such as a WAF.

The service mesh gateway typically manages state using its own internal implementation or that provided by the platform (e.g., Kubernetes). This type of gateway is also implicitly coupled with the associated service mesh (and operational requirements), and so if you are not yet planning to deploy a service mesh, then this is most likely not a good first choice of API gateway.

Comparing API Gateway Types

Table 3-3 highlights the difference between the three most widely deployed API gateway types across six important criteria.

Table 3-3. Comparison of enterprise, microservices, and service mesh API gateway

Use case	Traditional enterprise API gateway	Microservices API gateway	Service mesh gateway
Primary Purpose	Expose, compose, and manage internal business APIs and associated services.	Expose, compose, and manage internal business services.	Expose internal services within the mesh.
Publishing Functionality	API management team or service team registers/updates gateway via admin API (in mature organizations this is achieved through delivery pipelines).	Service team registers/ updates gateway via declarative code as part of the deployment process.	Service team registers/ updates mesh and gateway via declarative code as part of the deployment process.
Monitoring	Admin and operations focused, e.g., meter API calls per consumer, report errors (e.g., internal 5XX).	Developer focused, e.g., latency, traffic, errors, saturation.	Platform focused, e.g., utilization, saturation, errors.

Use case	Traditional enterprise API gateway	Microservices API gateway	Service mesh gateway
Handling and Debugging Issues	L7 error-handling (e.g., custom error page). For troubleshooting, run gateway/API with additional logging and debug issue in staging environment.	L7 error-handling (e.g., custom error page, failover, or payload). For debugging issues configure more detailed monitoring, and enable traffic shadowing and/or canarying to re-create the problem.	L7 error-handling (e.g., custom error page or payload). For troubleshooting, configure more detailed monitoring and/or utilize traffic "tapping" to view and debug specific service-to-service communication.
Testing	Operate multiple environments for QA, staging, and production. Automated integration testing, and gated API deployment. Use consumer-driven API versioning for compatibility and stability (e.g., semver).	Enables canary routing and dark launching for dynamic testing. Use contract testing for upgrade management.	Facilitate canary routing for dynamic testing.
Local Development	Deploy gateway locally (via installation script, Vagrant, or Docker), and attempt to mitigate infrastructure differences with production. Use language-specific gateway mocking and stubbing frameworks.	Deploy gateway locally via service orchestration platform (e.g., container, or Kubernetes).	Deploy service mesh locally via service orchestration platform (e.g., Kubernetes).
User Experience	Web-based administration UI, developer portal, and service catalog.	IaC or CLI-driven, with simple developer portal and service catalog.	IaC or CLI-driven, with limited service catalog.

Case Study: Evolving the Conference System Using an API Gateway

In this section of the chapter, you will learn how to install and configure an API gateway to route traffic directly to the Attendee service that has been extracted from the monolithic conference system. This will demonstrate how you can use the popular "strangler fig" pattern,[4] which is covered in more detail under "Strangler Fig" on page 203, to evolve your system from a monolith to a microservices-based architecture over time by gradually extracting pieces of an existing system into independently deployable and runnable services. Figure 3-9 provides an overview of the conference system architecture with the addition of an API gateway.

---

4 Martin Fowler's take on StranglerFigApplication (*https://oreil.ly/KUxU3*).

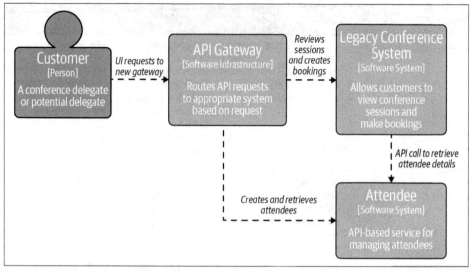

Figure 3-9. Using an API gateway to route to a new Attendee service running independently from the monolith

Many organizations often start such a migration by extracting services but have the monolithic application perform the routing and other cross-cutting concerns for the externally running services. This is often the easy choice, as the monolith already has to provide this functionality for internal functions. However, this leads to tight coupling between the monolith and services, with all traffic flowing through the monolithic application and the configuration cadence determined by the frequency of deployment of the monolith. From a traffic management perspective, both the increased load on the monolithic application and increased blast radius if this does fail mean the operational cost can be high. And being limited in updating routing information or cross-cutting configuration due to a slow release train or a failed deployment can prevent you from iterating at speed. Because of this, we generally do not recommend using the monolith to route traffic in this fashion, particularly if you plan to extract many services within a relatively short time scale.

As long as the gateway is deployed to be highly available and developers have direct (self-service) access to manage routing and configuration, extracting and centralizing application routing and cross-cutting concerns to an API gateway provide both safety and speed. Let's now walk through a practical example of deploying an API gateway within the conference system and using this to route to the new Attendee service.

Installing Ambassador Edge Stack in Kubernetes

As you are deploying the conference system into a Kubernetes cluster, you can easily install an API gateway using the standard Kubernetes-native approaches, such as applying YAML config or using Helm, in addition to using command-line utilities. For example, the Ambassador Edge Stack API gateway (*https://oreil.ly/4rakU*) can be installed using Helm. Once you have deployed and configured this API gateway, you can easily acquire a TLS certification from LetsEncrypt by following the Host configuration tutorial (*https://oreil.ly/TtthW*).

With the API gateway up and running and providing an HTTPS connection, the conference system application no longer needs to be concerned with terminating TLS connections or listening to multiple ports. Similarly, authentication and rate limiting can also be easily configured without having to reconfigure or deploy your application.

Configuring Mappings from URL Paths to Backend Services

You can now use an Ambassador Edge Stack Mapping Custom Resource (*https://oreil.ly/1Be0g*) to map the root of your domain to the "conferencesystem" service listening on port 8080 and running in the "legacy" namespace within the Kubernetes cluster. This Mapping should be familiar to anyone who has configured a web application or reverse proxy to listen for user requests. The metadata provides a name for the Mapping, and the prefix determines the path (the "/" root in this case) that is mapped to the target service (with the format `service-name.namespace:port`). Here is an example:

```
---
apiVersion: getambassador.io/v3alpha1
kind: Mapping
metadata:
  name: legacy-conference
spec:
  hostname: "*"
  prefix: /
  rewrite: /
  service: conferencesystem.legacy:8080
```

Another Mapping can be added to route any traffic sent to the "/attendees" path to the new ("nextgen") attendees microservice that has been extracted from the monolith. The information included in the Mapping should look familiar from the previous example. Here a `rewrite` is specified that "rewrites" the matching `prefix` path in the URL metadata before making the call to the target Attendee service. This makes it appear to the Attendee service that the request originated with the "/" path, effectively stripping out the "/attendees" part of the path.

```
---
apiVersion: getambassador.io/v3alpha1
kind: Mapping
metadata:
  name: legacy-conference
spec:
```

```
hostname: "*"
prefix: /attendees
rewrite: /
service: attendees.nextgen:8080
```

This pattern of creating additional Mappings as each new microservice is extracted from the legacy application can continue. Matching prefixes can be nested (e.g., /attendees/affiliation), or use regular expressions (e.g., /attendees/^[a-z].*"). Eventually the legacy application becomes a small shell with only a handful of functions, and all of the other functionality is handled by microservices, each with their own Mapping.

Configuring Mappings Using Host-based Routing

Most API gateways will also let you perform host-based routing (e.g., host: attend ees.conferencesystem.com). This can be useful if you need to create a new domain or subdomain to host the new services. An example of this using Ambassador Edge Stack Mappings is shown here:

```
---
apiVersion: getambassador.io/v3alpha1
kind: Mapping
metadata:
  name: attendees-host
spec:
  hostname: "attendees.conferencesystem.com"
  prefix: /
  service: attendees.nextgen:8080
```

Many modern API gateways will also support routing based on paths or query strings. Whatever your requirements, and whatever the limitations of your current infrastructure, you should be able to easily route to both your existing application and new services.

Avoid Routing on Request Payloads

Some API gateways will enable routing based on the payload or body of a request, but this should generally be avoided for two reasons. First, this often leaks highly coupled domain-specific information into the API gateway config (e.g., a payload often conforms to a schema/contract that may change in the application, which the gateway will now need to be synchronized with). And second, it can be computationally expensive (and time-consuming) to deserialize and parse a large payload in order to extract the required information for routing.

Deploying API Gateways: Understanding and Managing Failure

Regardless of the deployment pattern and number of gateways involved within a system, an API gateway is typically on the critical path of many, if not all, user requests entering into your system. An outage of a gateway deployed at the edge typically results in the unavailability of the entire system. And an outage of a gateway deployed further upstream typically results in the unavailability of some core subsystem. For this reason the topics of understanding and managing failure of an API gateway are vitally important to learn.

API Gateway as a Single Point of Failure

In a standard web-based system, the first obvious single point of failure is typically DNS. Although this is often externally managed, there is no escaping the fact that if this fails, then your site will be unavailable. The next single points of failure will typically then be the global and regional layer 4 load balancers, and depending on the deployment location and configuration, the security edge components, such as the firewall or WAF.

After these core edge components, the next layer is typically the API gateway. The more functionality you are relying on within the gateway, the bigger the risk involved and the bigger the impact of an outage. As an API gateway is often involved in a software release, the configuration is also continually being updated. It is critical to be able to detect and resolve issues and mitigate any risks.

Challenge Assumptions with Security Single Points of Failure

Depending on the product, deployment, and configuration, some security components may "fail open," i.e., if the component fails then traffic will simply be passed through to upstream components or the backend. For some scenarios where availability is the most important goal, this is desired, but for others (e.g., financial or government systems), this is most likely not. Be sure to challenge assumptions in your current security configuration.

Detecting and Owning Problems

The first stage in detecting issues is ensuring that you are collecting and have access to appropriate signals from your monitoring system—i.e., data from metrics, logs, and traces. Any critical system should have a clearly defined team that owns it and is accountable for any issues. Teams should communicate service-level objectives (SLOs), which can be codified into service-level agreements (SLAs) for both internal and external customers.

Additional Reading: Observability, Alerting, and SRE

If you are new to the concept of observability, then we recommend learning more about Brendan Gregg's utilization, saturation, and errors (USE) method (*https://oreil.ly/SgSSQ*), Tom Wilkie's rate, errors, and duration (RED) method (*https://oreil.ly/yFnDt*), and Google's four golden signals of monitoring (*https://oreil.ly/tESfc*). If you want to learn more about associated organizational goals and processes, the *Google Site Reliability Engineering (SRE)* book (*https://oreil.ly/rMBW3*) is highly recommended.

Resolving Incidents and Issues

First and foremost, each API gateway operating within your system needs an owner that is accountable if anything goes wrong with the component. In a smaller organization this may be the developers or SRE team who are also responsible for the underlying services. In a larger organization this may be a dedicated infrastructure team. As an API gateway is on the critical path of requests, some portion of this owning team should be on call as appropriate (this may be 24/7/365). The on-call team will then face the tricky task of fixing the issue as rapidly as possible, but also gathering enough information (or locating and quarantining systems and configuration) to learn what went wrong.

After any incident, the organization should strive to conduct a blameless postmortem and document and share all learning. Not only can this information be used to prevent this issue from reoccurring, but this knowledge can be very useful for engineers learning the system and for external teams dealing with similar technologies or challenges.[5]

Mitigating Risks

Any component that is on the critical path for handling user requests should be made as highly available as is practical in relation to cost and operational complexity. Software architects and technical leaders deal with trade-offs; this type is one of the most challenging. In the world of API gateways, high availability typically starts with running multiple instances. With on-premise/co-lo instances, this translates into operating multiple (redundant) hardware appliances, ideally spread across separate locations. In the cloud, this translates into designing and running the API gateway instance in multiple availability zones/data centers and regions. If a (global) load balancer is deployed in front of the API gateway instances, then this must be configured appropriately with health checks and failover processes that must be tested regularly.

---

5 If you are new to this space, then the Learning from Incidents (*https://oreil.ly/4aFqy*) website is a fantastic jumping-off point.

This is especially important if the API gateway instances run in active/passive or leader/node modes of operation.

You must ensure that your load balancer to API gateway failover process meets all of your requirements in relation to continuity of service. Common problems experienced during failover events include:

- User client state management issues, such as backend state not being migrated correctly, which causes the failure of sticky sessions

- Poor performance, as clients are not redirected based on geographical considerations (e.g., European users being redirected to the US west coast when an east coast data center is available)

- Unintentional cascading failure, such as a faulty leader election component that results in deadlock, which causes all backend systems to become unavailable

Common API Gateway Implementation Pitfalls

You've already seen that no technology is a silver bullet, but, continuing on the theme of technology cliches, it can be the case that when you have a technology hammer, everything tends to look like a nail. This can be the case with an API gateway "hammer," and there are several common API gateway pitfalls or antipatterns that you should always aim to avoid.

API Gateway Loopback

As with all common pitfalls, the implementation of this pattern often begins with good intentions. When an organization has only a few services, this typically doesn't warrant the installation of a service mesh. However, a subset of service mesh functionality is often required, particularly service discovery. An easy implementation is to route all traffic through the edge or API gateway, which maintains the official directory of all service locations. At this stage the pattern looks somewhat like a "hub and spoke" networking diagram. The challenges present themselves in two forms: first, when all of the service-to-service traffic is leaving the network before reentering via the gateway, this can present performance, security, and cost concerns (cloud vendors often charge for egress and inter-availability zone traffic); and second, this pattern doesn't scale beyond a handful of services, as the gateway becomes overloaded and a bottleneck, and it becomes a true single point of failure. This pattern can also add complexity to observability, as multiple cycles can make it challenging to understand what has happened with each call.

Looking at the current state of the conference system with the two Mappings that you have configured, you can see the emergence of this issue. Any external traffic, such as user requests, are correctly being routed to their target services by the API gateway. However, how does the legacy application discover the location of the Attendee service? Often the first approach is to route all requests back through the publicly addressable gateway (e.g., the legacy application makes calls to `www.conferencesystems.com/attendees`). Instead, the legacy application should use some form of internal service discovery mechanism and keep all of the internal requests within the internal network. You will learn more about how to use a service mesh to implement this in the next chapter.

API Gateway as an ESB

The vast majority of API gateways support the extension of their out-of-the-box functionality via the creation of plug-ins or modules. NGINX supported Lua modules, which OpenResty and Kong capitalized on. Envoy Proxy originally supported extensions in C, and now WebAssembly filters. And we've already discussed how the original implementation of Netflix's Zuul API gateway supported extension via Groovy scripts in "2015 Onward: Second-Generation API Gateways" on page 72. Many of the use cases realized by these plug-ins are extremely useful, such as authn/z, filtering, and logging. However, it can be tempting to put business logic into these plug-ins, which is a way to highly couple your gateway with your service or application. This leads to a potentially fragile system, where a change in a single plug-in ripples throughout the organization or adds additional friction during release where the target service and plug-in have to be deployed in lockstep.

Turtles (API Gateways) All the Way Down

If one API gateway is good, more must be better, right? It is common to find multiple API gateways deployed within the context of large organization, often in a hierarchical fashion, or in an attempt to segment networks or departments. The intentions are typically good: either for providing encapsulation for internal lines of business, or for a separation of concerns with each gateway (e.g., "this is the transport security gateway, this is the auth gateway, this is the logging gateway..."). The common pitfall rears its head when the cost of change is too high—e.g., you have to coordinate with a large number of gateway teams to release a simple service upgrade, there are understandability issues ("who owns the tracing functionality?"), or performance is impacted as every network hop naturally incurs a cost.

Selecting an API Gateway

Now that you learned about the functionality provided by an API gateway, the history of the technology, and how an API gateway fits into the overall system architecture, next is the $1M question: how do you select an API gateway to include in your stack?

Identifying Requirements

One of the first steps with any new software delivery or infrastructure project is identifying the related requirements. This may appear obvious, but it is all too easy to get distracted by shiny technology, magical marketing, or good sales documentation!

You can look back to the earlier section "Why Use an API Gateway?" on page 61 of this chapter to explore in more detail the high-level requirements you should be considering during the selection process. It is important to ask questions that are both focused on current pain points and also your future roadmap.

Build Versus Buy

A common discussion when selecting an API gateway is the "build versus buy" dilemma. This is not unique to this component of a software system, but the functionality offered via an API gateway does lead to some engineers gravitating to this—that they could build this "better" than existing vendors, or that their organization is somehow "special" and would benefit from a custom implementation. In general, we believe that the API gateway component is sufficiently well-established that it is typically best to adopt an open source implementation or commercial solution rather than build your own. Presenting the case for build versus buy with software delivery technology could take an entire book, and so in this section we only want to highlight some common challenges:

Underestimating the total cost of ownership (TCO)
> Many engineers discount the cost of engineering a solution, the continued maintenance costs, and the ongoing operational costs.

Not thinking about opportunity cost
> Unless you are a cloud or platform vendor, it is highly unlikely that a custom API gateway will provide you with a competitive advantage. You can deliver more value to your customers by building some functionality closer to your overall value proposition.

Not being aware of current technical solutions of products
> Both the open source and commercial platform component space move fast, and it can be challenging to keep up-to-date. This, however, is a core part of the role of being a technical leader.

ADR Guideline: Selecting an API Gateway

Table 3-4 provides a series of key ADR Guidelines that can be used to help you decide which API gateway to implement within your current organization or project.

Table 3-4. ADR Guideline: Selecting an API gateway checklist

Decision	How should we approach selecting an API gateway for our organization?
Discussion Points	Have we identified and prioritized all of our requirements associated with selecting an API gateway?
	Have we identified current technology solutions that have been deployed in this space within the organization?
	Do we know all of our team and organizational constraints?
	Have we explored our future roadmap in relation to this decision?
	Have we honestly calculated the "build versus buy" costs?
	Have we explored the current technology landscape and are we aware of all of the available solutions?
	Have we consulted and informed all involved stakeholders in our analysis and decision making?
Recommendations	Focus particularly on your requirement to reduce API/system coupling, simplify consumption, protect APIs from overuse and abuse, understand how APIs are being consumed, manage APIs as products, and monetize APIs.
	Key questions to ask include: is there an existing API gateway in use? Has a collection of technologies been assembled to provide similar functionality (e.g., hardware load balancer combined with a monolithic app that performs authentication and application-level routing)? How many components currently make up your edge stack (e.g., WAF, LB, edge cache, etc.)?
	Focus on technology skill levels within your team, availability of people to work on an API gateway project, and available resources and budget, etc.
	It is important to identify all planning changes, new features, and current goals that could impact traffic management and the other functionality that an API gateway provides.
	Calculate the total cost of ownership (TCO) of all of the current API gateway-like implementations and potential future solutions.
	Consult with well-known analysts, trend reports, and product reviews in order to understand all of the current solutions available.
	Selecting and deploying an API gateway will impact many teams and individuals. Be sure to consult with the developers, QA, the architecture review board, the platform team, InfoSec, etc.

Summary

In this chapter, you have learned what an API gateway is and also explored the historical context that led to the evolution of the features currently provided by this essential component in any web-based software stack:

- You have learned how an API gateway is a very useful tool for migrating and evolving systems and have gotten hands-on with how to use an API gateway to route to the Attendee service that was extracted from the conference system use case.

- You have explored the current taxonomy of API gateways and their deployment models, which has equipped you to think about how to manage potential single points of failure in an architecture where all user traffic is routed through an edge gateway.

- Building on the concepts of managing traffic at the (ingress) edge of systems, you have learned about service-to-service communication and how to avoid common pitfalls such as deploying an API gateway as a less-functional enterprise service bus (ESB).

- The combination of all of this knowledge has equipped you with the key thinking points, constraints, and requirements necessary to make an effective choice when selecting an API gateway for your current use cases.

- As with most decisions a software architect or technical leader has to make, there is no distinct correct answer, but there often can be quite a few bad solutions to avoid.

Now that you have explored the functionality that API gateways provide for managing north–south ingress traffic and related APIs, the next chapter will explore the role of service meshes for managing east–west, service-to-service traffic.

CHAPTER 4

Service Mesh: Service-to-Service Traffic Management

In the previous chapter you explored how to expose your APIs and manage associated ingress traffic from end users and other external systems in a reliable, observable, and secure way using an API gateway. Now you will learn about managing traffic for internal APIs, i.e., service-to-service communication, with similar goals.

At a fundamental level, service mesh implementations provide functionality for routing, observing, and securing traffic for service-to-service communication. It is worth saying that even this choice of technology is not a slam dunk; as with all architectural decisions, there are trade-offs; there is no such thing as a free lunch when you are performing the role of architect!

In this chapter you will evolve the case study by extracting the sessions-handling functionality from the legacy conference system into a new internally facing Session service. As you do this you will learn about the communication challenges introduced by creating or extracting new services and APIs that are deployed and run alongside the existing monolithic conference system. All of the API and traffic management techniques you explored in the previous chapter will apply here, and so your natural inclination may be to use an API gateway to expose the new Session service. However, given the requirements, this would most likely result in a suboptimal solution. This is where the service mesh pattern and associated technologies can provide an alternative approach.

Is Service Mesh the Only Solution?

Practically every web-based software application needs to make service-to-service-like calls, even if this is simply a monolithic application interacting with a database.

Because of this, solutions to manage this type of communication have long existed. The most common approach is to use a language-specific library, such as a software development kit (SDK) library or database driver. These libraries map application-based calls to service API requests and also manage the corresponding traffic, typically via the use of HTTP or TCP/IP protocols. As the design of modern applications has embraced service-oriented architectures, the problem space of service-to-service calls has expanded. It is a very common requirement for a service to need to call another service's API to satisfy a user's request. In addition to providing a mechanism of routing traffic, you will typically also require reliability, observability, and security.

As you will learn throughout this chapter, both a library and service mesh–based solution can often satisfy your service-to-service communication requirements. We have seen a rapid adoption of service meshes, particularly within an enterprise context, and as the number of consumers and providers increases, it is often the most scalable, maintainable, and secure option. Because of this, we have primarily focused this chapter on the service mesh pattern.

Guideline: Should You Adopt Service Mesh?

Table 4-1 provides a series of ADR Guidelines to help you decide whether you should adopt service mesh technology in your organization.

Table 4-1. ADR Guideline: Service mesh or libraries guidelines

Decision	Should you use a service mesh or a library for routing service traffic?
Discussion Points	Do you use a single programming language within your organization?
	Do you only require simple service-to-service routing for REST or RPC-like communication?
	Do you have cross-functional requirements that will require more advanced features, such as authentication, authorization, or rate limiting?
	Do you already have a solution in place, or is there an organization-wide mandate that all traffic must be routed through certain components within your network?
Recommendations	If your organization mandates the use of a single programming language or framework, you can typically take advantage of the language-specific libraries or mechanisms for service-to-service communication.
	Always use the simplest solution for your requirements, with an eye to the immediate future and known requirements.
	If you have advanced cross-functional requirements, particularly across services that use different programming languages or technology stacks, a service mesh may be the best choice.
	Always perform due diligence within your organization for existing mandates, solutions, and components.

Case Study: Extracting Sessions Functionality to a Service

For the next evolution of our conference system case study you will focus on the conference owners' requests to support a core new feature: *View and manage an attendee's conference sessions via the mobile application.*

This is a major change that would warrant the creation of an ADR. Table 4-2 is an example ADR that might have been proposed by the engineering team owning the conference system.

Table 4-2. ADR501 Separating sessions from the legacy conference system

Status	Proposed
Context	The conference owners have requested another new feature to the current conference system. The marketing team believes that conference attendee engagement will increase if an attendee can view details of and indicate their interest in conference sessions via the mobile application. The marketing team also wants to be able to see how many attendees are interested in each session.
Decision	We will take an evolutionary step to split out the Session component into a standalone service. This will allow API-first development against the Session service and allow the API to be invoked from the legacy conference service. This will also allow the Attendee service to call the API of the Session service directly in order to provide session information to the mobile application.
Consequences	The legacy application will call the new Session service when handling all session-related queries, both for existing and new functionality. When a user wants to view, add, or remove sessions they are interested in at a conference, the Attendee service will need to call the Session service. When a conference admin wants to see who is attending each session, the Session service will need to call the Attendee service in order to determine who is attending each session. The Session service could become a single point of failure in the architecture and we may need to take steps to mitigate the potential impact of running a single Session service. Because the viewing and managing of sessions by attendees increases dramatically during a live conference event, we will also need to account for large traffic spikes and potentially one or more Session services becoming overloaded or acting in a degraded fashion.

The C4 Model showing the proposed architectural change is shown in Figure 4-1.

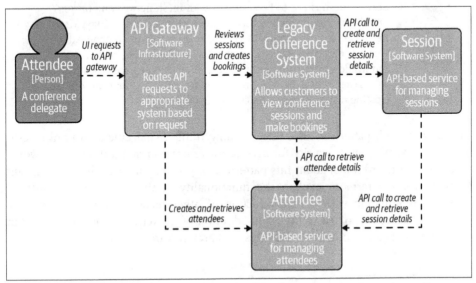

Figure 4-1. C4 Model showing the extraction of the Session service from the conference system

Note that even though the new Session service does not need to be exposed externally, you could easily meet the routing and reliability requirements stated in the preceding ADR by exposing this service via the API gateway and configuring both the legacy system and Attendee service to call this new service via the gateway's external address. However, this would be an example of the "API gateway loopback" antipattern you learned about in "Common API Gateway Implementation Pitfalls" on page 81. This antipattern can lead to internally destined traffic potentially leaving your network, which has performance, security, and (cloud vendor) cost implications. Let's now explore how a service mesh can help you meet your new requirements while avoiding this antipattern.

What Is Service Mesh?

Fundamentally, "service mesh" is a pattern for managing all service-to-service (or application-to-application) communication within a distributed software system. There is a lot of overlap between the service mesh and API gateway patterns, with the primary differences being twofold. First, service mesh implementations are optimized to handle service-to-service, or east–west, traffic within a cluster or data center. Second, following from this, the originator of the communication is typically a (somewhat) known internal service, rather than a user's device or a system running external to your applications.

Service Mesh Is Not Mesh Networking

Service mesh is not to be confused with mesh networking (*https:// oreil.ly/BbWJm*), which is a lower-level networking topology. Mesh networking is becoming increasingly prevalent in the context of Internet of Things (IoT) and also for implementing mobile communication infrastructure in remote or challenging scenarios (such as disaster relief). Service mesh implementations build on top of existing networking protocols and topologies.

The service mesh pattern focuses on providing traffic management (routing), resilience, observability, and security for service-to-service communication. Don't worry if you haven't heard much about this pattern, as it was only in 2016 that the Buoyant team coined the term to explain the functionality of their Linkerd technology.[1] This, in combination with the introduction of other related technologies like the Google-sponsored Istio, led to the rapid adoption of the term "service mesh" within the domains of cloud computing, DevOps, and architecture.

---

1 The Linkerd project emerged from Twitter's Finagle technology that was built to provide a communication framework for developers building Twitter's distributed applications. Linkerd has now evolved into a graduated Cloud Native Computing Foundation (CNCF) project.

Much like an API gateway, a service mesh is implemented with two high-level fundamental components: a control plane and data plane. In a service mesh these components are always deployed separately. The control plane is where operators interact with the service mesh and define routes, policies, and required telemetry. The data plane is the location where all of the work specified in the control plane occurs and where the network packets are routed, the policies enforced, and telemetry emitted.

If we take configuring service-to-service traffic within a Kubernetes cluster as an example, a human operator will first define routing and policy using Custom Resource configuration—for example, in our case study, specifying that the Attendee service can call the Session service—and then "apply" this to the cluster via a command-line tool, like kubectl, or continuous delivery pipeline. A service mesh controller application running within the Kubernetes cluster acts as the control plane, parsing this configuration and instructing the data plane—typically a series of "sidecar" proxies running alongside each of the Attendee and Session services—to enact this.

Service Mesh Sidecars and Proxies

Within the context of a service mesh you will often see the terms "sidecars" and "proxies" used interchangeably. However, this is not technically correct, as "sidecar" is a general-purpose pattern that is typically implemented using a proxy within a service mesh. Therefore any use of the word "sidecar" should also include the postfix "proxy" (e.g., "sidecar proxy"). The sidecar pattern is inspired from the motorcycle sidecar and consists of segregating the functionalities of an application or service into a series of separate processes that are run within the same network and process namespace. In software architecture a sidecar is attached to a parent application and extends/ enhances its functionalities in a loosely coupled fashion. This patterns allows you to add a number of capabilities to your application without using language-specific libraries or other techniques. You will learn more about the evolution of this pattern within service mesh implementations in "Evolution of Service Mesh" on page 102.

All service-to-service traffic within the Kubernetes cluster is routed via the sidecar proxies, typically transparently (without the underlying applications recognizing that a proxy is involved), which enables all of this traffic to be routed, observed, and secured as required. An example topology of the services and service mesh control plane and data plane is shown in Figure 4-2.

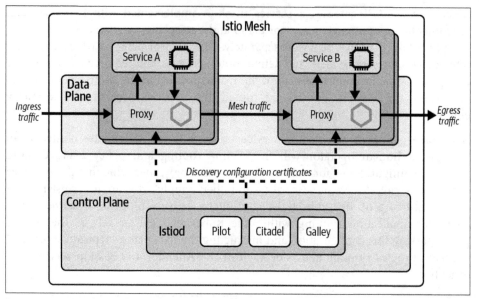

Figure 4-2. Topology of services and control plane and data plane of a service mesh (using Istio as an example)

What Functionality Does a Service Mesh Provide?

At a network level, a service mesh proxy acts as a full proxy, accepting all inbound traffic from other services and also initiating all outbound requests to other services. This includes all API calls and other requests and responses. Unlike an API gateway, the mapping from a service mesh data plane to a service is typically one-to-one, meaning that a service mesh proxy does not aggregate calls across multiple services. A service mesh provides cross-cutting functionality such as user verification, request rate limiting, and timeouts/retries, and can provide metrics, logs, and trace data in order to support the implementation of observability within the system. This is exactly the functionality that we require for evolving our case study by extracting the Session service and calling this from both the legacy conference system and the Attendee service.

Service Meshes Use Full Proxies to Intercept All Service Traffic

It is typical for all service mesh proxies to operate as "full proxies," as they need to observe and manipulate all of the traffic flowing through the mesh. In contrast with a half proxy, a full proxy handles all the communication between the client and server. A fundamental difference is that a full proxy maintains two distinct network stacks—one on the client side and one on the server side—and fully proxies both sides. With the proxy in the middle of all communications, it is possible to manipulate, drop, observe, and do what is required to the traffic on both sides and in both directions. This power and flexibility does, of course, come with a trade-off in that a full proxy requires more resources and potentially introduces more overhead/latency on communications.

Although less common in comparison with an API gateway, some service meshes provide additional features that enable developers to manage the lifecycle of an API. For example, an associated service catalog may assist with the onboarding and management of developers using the service APIs, or a developer portal will provide account administration and access control. Some service meshes also provide auditing of policies and traffic management in order to meet enterprise governance requirements.

Where Is a Service Mesh Deployed?

A service mesh is deployed within an internal network or cluster. Large systems or networks are typically managed by deploying several instances of a service mesh, often with each single mesh spanning a network segment or business domain.

Is a Service Mesh Deployed at the Edge?

Although deployed within a cluster, a service mesh may expose endpoints within a network demilitarized zone (DMZ), or to external systems, or additional networks or clusters. This is frequently implemented by using a proxy that is referred to as a "mesh gateway," "terminating gateway," or "transit gateway." These types of external gateways do not typically provide the level of functionality commonly found within an externally facing API gateway. There is some debate as to whether traffic management involving these service mesh gateways is north–south or east–west, and this can impact requirements and the required security policies, etc.

An example service mesh networking topology is shown in Figure 4-3.

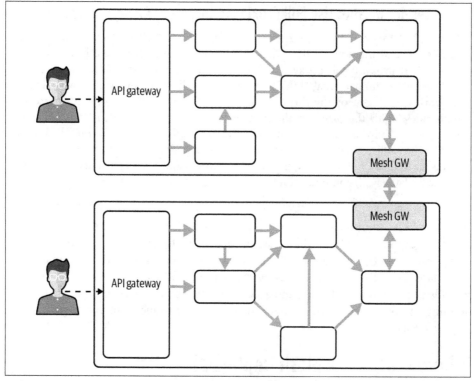

Figure 4-3. A typical service mesh topology, deployed across two clusters (with solid arrows showing service mesh traffic)

How Does a Service Mesh Integrate with Other Networking Technologies?

A modern networking stack can have many layers, particularly when working with cloud technologies where virtualization and sandboxing occur at multiple levels. A service mesh should work in harmony with these other networking layers, but developers and operators also need to be aware of potential interactions and conflict. Figure 4-4 shows the interaction between physical (and virtualized) networking infrastructure, a typical networking stack, and a service mesh.

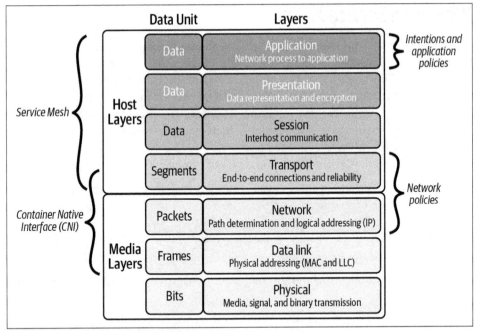

Data Unit | **Layers**

Data	Application — Network process to application	Intentions and application policies
Data	Presentation — Data representation and encryption	
Data	Session — Interhost communication	
Segments	Transport — End-to-end connections and reliability	Network policies
Packets	Network — Path determination and logical addressing (IP)	
Frames	Data link — Physical addressing (MAC and LLC)	
Bits	Physical — Media, signal, and binary transmission	

Host Layers (Application, Presentation, Session, Transport) — Service Mesh

Media Layers (Network, Data link, Physical) — Container Native Interface (CNI)

Figure 4-4. OSI model showing that a service mesh operates between layers 3 and 7

As an example, when deploying applications into a Kubernetes cluster, a Service can locate and address another Service within the same cluster via a prescribed name that maps to an IP address. Fundamental traffic control security policies can be implemented with NetworkPolicies, which control traffic at the IP address and port level (OSI layer 3 or 4), and additional policy controls are often provided by a cluster's Container Networking Interface (CNI) plug-in.[2]

Service meshes can override the default CNI service-to-IP address resolution and routing and also provide additional functionality. This includes transparent routing across clusters, enforcement of layer 3/4 and 7 security (such as user identity and authorization), layer 7 load balancing (which is useful if you are using multiplexed keepalive protocol like gRPC or HTTP/2), and observability at the service-to-service level and throughout the networking stack.

---

2 You can learn more about Kubernetes networking concepts via the official docs: Service (*https://oreil.ly/ LBZS3*), NetworkPolicies (*https://oreil.ly/KVVUi*), and Container Networking Interface (CNI) (*https://oreil.ly/ wNkuw*).

Why Use a Service Mesh?

In a similar fashion to deciding why you should deploy an API gateway into your existing architecture, determining why to adopt a service mesh is a multifaceted topic. You need to balance both short-term implementation gains and costs against the long-term maintainability requirements. There are many API-related cross-cutting concerns that you might have for each or all of your internal services, including product lifecycle management (incrementally releasing new versions of a service), reliability, multilanguage communication support, observability, security, maintainability, and extensibility. A service mesh can help with all of these.

This section of the chapter will provide you with an overview of the key problems that a service mesh can address, such as:

- Enable fine-grained control of service routing, reliability, and traffic management
- Improve observability of interservice calls
- Enforce security, including transport encryption, authentication, and authorization
- Support cross-functional communication requirements across a variety of languages
- Separate ingress and service-to-service traffic management

Fine-grained Control of Routing, Reliability, and Traffic Management

Routing traffic with a distributed microservices-based system can be more challenging than it may first appear. Typically there will be multiple instances of a service deployed into an environment with the goals of improving both performance (load balancing across services) and reliability (providing redundancy). In addition, many modern infrastructure platforms are built on "commodity hardware" that manifests as ephemeral computing resources that can shut down, restart, or disappear at a moment's notice; and this means the location of a service can change from day-to-day (or minute-to-minute!).

You can, of course, employ the routing technologies and associated techniques that you learned about in Chapter 3. The challenge here is that there are typically many more internal services and APIs in comparison with the number of external APIs that are exposed by your applications, and the pace of change with internal systems and their corresponding APIs and functionality is often much higher. Accordingly, the operational cost would increase dramatically if you were to deploy an API gateway in front of every internal service, both in regards to computing resources required and human maintenance costs.

Transparent routing and service name normalization

Fundamentally, routing is the process of selecting a path for traffic in a network or between or across multiple networks. Within web applications, network-level routing has typically been handled within the TCP/IP stack and associated networking infrastructure (at layer 3/4 of the OSI model). This means that only the IP address and port of both the connection's target and originator are required. Pre-cloud, and often with on-premises data centers, the IP addresses of internal services are often fixed and well-known. Even though DNS is widely used to map domain names to IP addresses, it is still the case that heritage applications and services use hardcoded IP addresses. This means that any changes to a service's location require a redeployment of all services that call this service.

With the adoption of the cloud and the ephemeral nature of our infrastructure that comes with this, IP addresses of computing instances and their corresponding services regularly change. This in turn means that if you hardcode IP and port addresses, these will have to be frequently changed. As microservices-based architectures became more popular, the pain of redeploying increased in relation to the number of services within an application. Early microservice adopters created solutions to overcome this by implementing external "service discovery" directories or registries containing a dynamic mapping of service names to IP address(es) and ports.[3]

Service meshes can handle this dynamic lookup of service name to location, externally to the service and also transparently without the need for code modification, redeployments, or restarts. Another benefit of a service mesh is that it can normalize naming across environments using "environment awareness" in combination with configuration stored external to the application. For example, a service mesh deployed to "production" will recognize that it is running in this environment. The service mesh will then transparently map the code-level service name `sessions-service` to the environment-specific location `AWS-us-east-1a/prod/sessions/v2` by looking up the location from a service registry (that may be integrated with the mesh or run externally). The same code deployed to the staging environment with an appropriately configured service mesh will route `sessions-service` to `internal-staging-server-a/stage/sessions/v3`.

Reliability

The ephemeral nature of modern computing and cluster environments brings challenges related to reliability in addition to location changes. For example, every service must correctly handle communication issues with another service it is interacting with. You will learn more about "The 8 Fallacies of Distributed Computing" shortly,

---

3 Airbnb's SmartStack (*https://oreil.ly/mJDVW*) was one of the first implementations of external microservice service discovery.

but issues to be aware of in this context include a service's connection being interrupted, a service becoming temporarily unavailable, or a service responding slowly. These challenges can be handled in code using well-known reliability patterns such as retries, timeouts, circuit breakers, bulkheads, and fallbacks. Michael Nygard's book *Release It! Design and Deploy Production-Ready Software*, now in its second edition, provides a comprehensive exploration and implementation guide. However, as you will explore in more depth in "Supporting Cross-Functional Communication Across Languages" on page 100, attempting to implement this functionality in code typically leads to inconsistent behavior, especially across different languages and platforms.

As a service mesh is involved with initiating and managing every service-to-service communication, it provides the perfect place to consistently implement these reliability patterns to provide fault-tolerance and graceful degradation. Depending on the implementation, a service mesh can also detect issues and share this information across the mesh, allowing each service within the mesh to make appropriate decisions on how to route traffic—e.g., if a service's response latency is increasing, all services that call the target service can be instructed to instead initiate their fallback actions.

For the case study, a service mesh will enable you to define how to handle any failures when communicating with the new Session service. Imagine several thousand attendees at an event having just watched the morning conference keynote and wanting to view their schedule for the day. This sudden spike of traffic for the Session service may result in degraded behavior. For the majority of use cases you would define appropriate timeouts and retries, but you may also define a circuit-breaking action that triggers an application behavior. For example, if an API call from the Attendee service to the Session service to get an attendee's daily session schedule repeatedly fails, you may trigger a circuit breaker in the service mesh that rapidly fails all calls to this service (to allow the service to recover). Most likely within the mobile application you would handle this failure by "falling back" to rendering the entire conference session schedule rather than a personal schedule.

Advanced traffic routing: Shaping, policing, splitting, and mirroring

Since the dot-com boom of the late '90s, consumer web applications have increasingly handled more users and more traffic. Users have also become more demanding, both in regards to performance and features offered. Accordingly, the need to manage traffic to meet the needs of security, performance, and feature release has become more important. As you learned in "How Does an API Gateway Integrate with Other Technologies at the Edge?" on page 60, the edge of the network saw the emergence of dedicated appliances to meet these requirements, but this infrastructure was not appropriate to deploy in front of every internal service. In this section of the chapter you will learn more about the requirements that have become typical for a microservices-based application in regards to internal traffic shaping and policing.

Traffic shaping.   Traffic shaping is a bandwidth management technique that delays some or all of the network traffic in order to match a desired traffic profile. Traffic shaping is used to optimize or guarantee performance, improve latency, or increase usable bandwidth for some kinds of traffic by delaying other kinds. The most common type of traffic shaping is application-based traffic shaping, where fingerprinting tools are first used to identify applications of interest, which are then subject to shaping policies. With east–west traffic, a service mesh can generate or monitor the fingerprints, such as service identity or some other proxy for this, or a request header containing relevant metadata—for example, whether a request originated from a conference application free-tier user or a paying customer.

Traffic policing.   Traffic policing is the process of monitoring network traffic for compliance with a traffic policy or contract and taking steps to enforce that contract. Traffic violating a policy may be discarded immediately, marked as noncompliant, or left as is, depending on administrative policy. This technique is useful to prevent a malfunctioning internal service from committing a denial of service (DoS) attack, or to prevent a critical or fragile internal resource from becoming overly saturated with traffic (e.g., a data store). Before the advent of cloud technologies and service meshes, traffic policing within internal networks was generally only implemented within an enterprise context using specialized hardware or software appliances such as an enterprise service bus (ESB). Cloud computing and software-defined networks (SDNs) made traffic-policing techniques easier to adopt through the use of security groups (SGs) and network access control lists (NACLs).

When managing east–west communications, services within the network or cluster boundary may be aware of a traffic contract and may apply traffic shaping internally in order to ensure their output stays within the contract. For example, your Attendee service may implement an internal rate limiter that prevents excessive calls to the Session service API within a specific time period.

Service mesh allows granular control of traffic shaping, splitting, and mirroring that makes it possible to gradually shift or migrate traffic from one version of a target service to another. In "Release Strategies" on page 131, we will look at how this approach can be used to facilitate the separation of build and release for traffic-based release strategies.

Provide Transparent Observability

When operating any distributed system like a microservices-based application, the ability to observe both the end-user experience and arbitrary internal components is vitally important for fault identification and debugging corresponding issues. Historically, adopting system-wide monitoring required the integration of highly coupled runtime agents or libraries within applications, requiring a deployment of all applications during the initial rollout and all future upgrades.

A service mesh can provide some of the observability required, particularly application (L7) and network (L4) metrics, and do so transparently. A corresponding update of any telemetry collection components or the service mesh itself should not require a redeployment of all applications. There are, of course, limitations to the observability a service mesh can provide, and you should also instrument your services using language-specific metrics and log-emitting libraries. For example, in our case study the service mesh would provide metrics on the number, latency, and error rate of Session service API calls, and you would also typically decide to log business-specific metrics and KPIs of the API calls.

Enforce Security: Transport Security, Authentication, and Authorization

In much the same way as observability, service-to-service communication security has historically been implemented using language-specific libraries. These highly coupled approaches provide the same drawbacks and nuances. For example, implementing transport-level encryption within an internal network is a relatively common requirement, but different language libraries handle certificate management differently, which increased the operational burden of deploying and rotating certificates. Managing both service (machine) and user (human) identity for authentication and authorization was also difficult across differing languages. It was also often easy to accidentally (or deliberately) circumvent any security implementation by not including the required libraries.

As a service mesh's data plane is included within the path of any traffic within the system, it is relatively trivial to enforce the required security profile. For example, the service mesh data plane can manage service identities (for example, using SPIFFE (*https://spiffe.io*)) and cryptographic certificates, enabling mTLS, and service-level authentication and authorization. This enables us to easily implement mTLS within our case study without the need for code modifications.

Supporting Cross-Functional Communication Across Languages

As you create or extract services within a microservice-based application and move from in-process to out-of-process communication, you need to think about changes in routing, reliability, observability, and security. The functionality required to handle this can be implemented within application code, for example, as a library. However, if your application or system uses multiple programming languages—and a polyglot approach is quite common with microservice-based systems—this means that you will have to implement each library for each language used. As a service mesh is typically implemented using the sidecar pattern, where all service communication is routed through a network proxy external to the service but running within the same network namespace, the functionality required can be implemented once within the proxy and reused across all the services. You can think of this as "infrastructure dependency injection." Within our case study this would enable us to rewrite our Attendee service using a different language (perhaps to meet new performance requirements) and still rely on the cross-functional aspects of service-to-service communication being handled consistently.

Separating Ingress and Service-to-Service Traffic Management

Recall in "Case Study: An Evolutionary Step" on page xxviii that we briefly introduced the key concepts of north–south and east–west traffic. Generally speaking, north–south traffic is traffic that is ingressing from an external location into your system. East–west traffic is transiting internally from system-to-system or service-to-service. The definitions can become tricky when you look further into the definition of "your systems"; for example, does this definition extend to systems designed and operated by only your team, your department, your organization, or your trusted third-parties, etc.

Several contributors to the API space, including Marco Palladino from Kong (*https://oreil.ly/WvLyi*), have argued that the use of north–south and east–west is largely irrelevant and is more of a hangup from the previous generation of computer networking when boundaries between systems were clearer. We'll explore this argument in more detail in Chapter 9, as this touches the idea of API as a product (including API lifecycle management) and layer 7 and layer 4 service connectivity (from the OSI model of networking.) The differences between the core properties and features of ingress and service-to-service traffic are shown in Table 4-3.

Table 4-3. Differences between ingress and service-to-service properties

	Ingress (n/s)	Service-to-service (e/w)
Traffic source	External (user, third-party, internet)	Internal (within trust boundary)
Traffic destination	Public or business-facing API, or website	Service or domain API
Authentication	"user" (real world entity) focused	"service" (machine entity) and "user" (real-world entity) focused
Authorization	"user" roles or capability level	"service" identity or network segment focused, and "user" roles or capability level
TLS	One-way, often enforced (e.g., protocol upgrade)	Mutual, can be made mandatory (strict mTLS)
Primary implementations	API gateway, reverse proxy	Service mesh, application libraries
Primary owner	Gateway/networking/ops team	Platform/cluster/ops team
Organizational users	Architects, API managers, developers	Developers

As illustrated, the properties and associated requirements for managing the two traffic types are often quite different. For example, handling external end-user traffic destined for a product API has fundamentally different requirements in comparison with handling internal service-to-service traffic destined for an internal business, domain, or component API. In practice this means that the control planes for both an API gateway and service mesh must offer different capabilities in order to support the configuration of the respective data planes. As an example in our case study, the Session service development team may want to specify that the service can only be called by the legacy conference application and Attendee service, whereas the Attendee service team would not typically specify which external systems can or cannot call the public API—this would be the responsibility of the associated gateway or networking team.

This difference between managing ingress and service-to-service API calls can be better understood if you compare the evolution and usage of API gateway technology, as explored in "A Modern History of API Gateways" on page 68, with the evolution of service mesh technology, as described in the following section.

Evolution of Service Mesh

Although the term "service mesh" was coined in 2016, several of the early "unicorn" organizations like Twitter, Netflix, Google, and Amazon were creating and using related technologies within their internal platforms from the late 2000s and early 2010s. For example, Twitter created its Scala-based Finagle RPC framework, which was open sourced in 2011. Netflix created and released its "OSS" Java-based microservice shared libraries in 2012, including Ribbon, Eureka, and Hystrix.[4] Later the Netflix team released the Prana sidecar to enable non-JVM-based services to take advantage of these libraries. The creation of the Finagle libraries and adoption of sidecars ultimately spawned Linkerd, arguably the first sidecar-based service mesh and also an initial project in the CNCF when this foundation was formed. Google quickly followed suit by releasing the Istio service mesh that built upon the Envoy Proxy project that had emerged from the Lyft Engineering team.

In a turn that looks like the industry coming full circle, service mesh capabilities are getting pushed back into shared libraries, as we're seeing with gRPC, or added to the OS kernel. This evolution can be seen in Figure 4-5. Although the development and usage of many of these earlier components and platforms are now deprecated, it is useful to take a quick tour of their evolution as this highlights several challenges and limitations of using the service mesh pattern, some of which still remain.

---

4 You should note that the Finagle RPC framework (*https://oreil.ly/wHUOQ*) and Netflix OSS libraries (*https://oreil.ly/BPvAv*) are now both deprecated and not recommended for use in modern production systems.

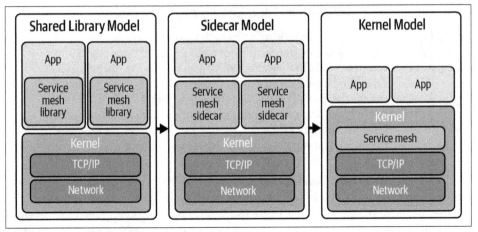

Figure 4-5. Evolution of service mesh technology

Early History and Motivations

In the '90s, Peter Deutsch and others at Sun Microsystems compiled "The 8 Fallacies of Distributed Computing" (*https://oreil.ly/hdvuC*), in which they list assumptions that engineers tend to make when working with distributed systems. They made the point that although these assumptions might have been true in more primitive networking architectures or the theoretical models, they don't hold true in the modern networks:

- The network is reliable
- Latency is zero
- Bandwidth is infinite
- The network is secure
- Topology doesn't change
- There is one administrator
- Transport cost is zero
- The network is homogeneous

Peter and team state that these fallacies "all prove to be false in the long run and all cause big trouble and painful learning experiences." Engineers cannot just ignore these issues; they have to explicitly deal with them.

Ignore the Fallacies of Distributed Computing at Your Peril!

Because the "8 Fallacies of Distributing Computing" were coined in the '90s, it is tempting to think of them as a computing relic. However, this would be a mistake! Much like many of the other timeless computing laws and patterns derived in the '70s and '80s, the issues remain the same, even as the technology changes. When working in the architect role, you must constantly remind your teams that many networking challenges captured within these fallacies hold true today, and you must design systems accordingly!

As distributed systems and microservice architectures became popular in the 2010s, many innovators in the space, such as James Lewis, Sam Newman, and Phil Calçado, realized the importance of building systems that acknowledged and offset these fallacies over and above functionality provided in standard networking stacks. Building on Martin Fowler's initial set of "Microservice Prerequisites," Phil created "Calçado's Microservices Prerequisites" and included "standardized RPC" as a key prerequisite that encapsulated many of the practical lessons he had learned from the fallacies of distributed computing. In his later 2017 blog post, Phil stated that "while the TCP/IP stack and general networking model developed many decades ago is still a powerful tool in making computers talk to each other, the more sophisticated [microservice-based] architectures introduced another layer of requirements that, once more, have to be fulfilled by engineers working in such architectures."[5]

Implementation Patterns

Although the most widely deployed implementation of service meshes today utilize the proxy-based "sidecar" model of deployment, this was not always the case. And it may not be the case in the future. In this section of the chapter you will learn how service mesh implementation patterns have so far evolved and explore what the future may hold.

Libraries

Although many technical leaders realized the need for a new layer of networking functionality within microservice-based systems, they understood that implementing these technologies would be nontrivial. They also recognized that a lot of effort would be repeated, both within and across organizations. This led to the emergence of microservice-focused networking frameworks and shared libraries that could be

---

5 You can learn more via these websites for Fowler's "Microservice Prerequisites" (*https://oreil.ly/GlYvp*), "Calçado's Microservices Prerequisites" (*https://oreil.ly/d4lEh*), and Phil's blog "Pattern: Service Mesh" (*https://oreil.ly/h45Te*).

built once and reused, first across an organization, and later open sourced for wider consumption.

In his aforementioned blog post, Phil Calçado commented that even core networking functionality such as service discovery and circuit breaking was challenging to implement correctly. This led to the creation of large, sophisticated libraries like Twitter's Finagle and the Netflix OSS stack. These became very popular as a means to avoid rewriting the same logic in every service and also as projects to focus shared efforts on ensuring correctness. Some smaller organizations took on the burden themselves of writing the required networking libraries and tools, but the cost was typically high, especially in the long term. Sometimes this cost was explicit and clearly visible—for example, the cost of engineers assigned to teams dedicated to building tooling. But more often the true expense was difficult to fully quantify as it manifests itself as time taken for new developers to learn proprietary solutions, resources required for operational maintenance, or other forms of taking time and energy away from working on your customer-facing products.

Phil also observed that the use of libraries that expose functionality via language bindings or an SDK limited the tools, runtimes, and languages you can use for your microservices. Libraries for microservices are often written for a specific platform, be it a programming language or a runtime like the JVM. If you use platforms other than the one supported by the library, you will most likely need to port the code to the new platform itself, with your costs increasing in relation to the number of languages.

Service Mesh Libraries and the Price of Polyglot

Many organizations embrace a polyglot approach to coding applications and use a variety of languages, choosing the most appropriate one for a service in order to accomplish the requirements. For example, using Java for long-running business services, Go for infrastructure services, and Python for data science work. If you embrace the library-based approach to implementing a service mesh, you will need to be aware that you will have to build, maintain, and upgrade all of your libraries in lock-step in order to avoid compatibility issues or provide a suboptimal developer experience for some languages. You may also find subtle differences between implementations across language platforms, or bugs that only affect a specific runtime.

Sidecars

In the early 2010s, many engineers were embracing the approach to polyglot programming, and it was not uncommon for a single organization to have services written in multiple languages that were deployed to production. The desire to write or maintain one library that handled all of the required networking abstractions led to the creation of libraries that ran externally to a service as standalone processes. The microservice "sidecar" was born. In 2013, Airbnb wrote about "Synapse and Nerve," its open source implementation of a service discovery sidecar. One year later, Netflix introduced Prana, a sidecar that exposed an HTTP interface for non-JVM applications to integrate with the rest of the Netflix OSS ecosystem for service discovery, circuit breaking, and more. The core concept here was that a service did not connect directly to its downstream dependencies, but instead all of the traffic went through the Prana sidecar that transparently added the desired networking abstraction and features.

As the use of the microservices architecture style increased, we saw the rise of a new wave of proxies that were flexible enough to adapt to different infrastructure components and communication requirements. The first widely known system on this space was Linkerd, created by Buoyant and based on its engineering experience of having worked on Twitter's microservices platform. Soon after, the engineering team at Lyft announced Envoy Proxy, which followed a similar principle and was quickly adopted by Google in its Istio service mesh. When using the sidecar pattern, each of your services will have a companion proxy process that runs standalone next to your application. This sidecar typically shares the same process, file, and networking namespace, and specific security guarantees are provided (e.g., that any communication with the "local" network is isolated from the external network). Given that services communicate with each other only through the sidecar proxy, we end up with a deployment similar to the diagram in Figure 4-6.

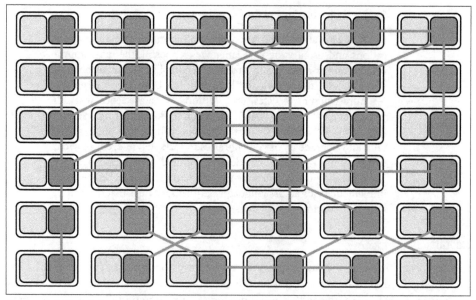

Figure 4-6. Service mesh proxies forming a higher-level networking abstraction

As noted by the likes of Phil Calçado and Buoyant's William Morgan, the most powerful aspect of this integration of sidecar proxies is that it moves you away from thinking of proxies as isolated components and toward acknowledging the network they form as something valuable in itself.

In the mid-2010s, organizations began to move their microservices deployments to more sophisticated runtimes such as Apache Mesos (with Marathon), Docker Swarm, and Kubernetes, and organizations started using the tools made available by these platforms to implement a service mesh. This led to a move away from using a set of independent proxies working in isolation as we saw with the likes of Synapse and Nerve, toward the use of a centralized control plane. If you look at this deployment pattern using a top-down view, you can see that the service traffic still flows from proxy to proxy directly, but the control plane knows about and can influence each proxy instance. The control plane enables the proxies to implement features such as access control and metrics collection that require cooperation and coordination across services, as shown in Figure 4-7.

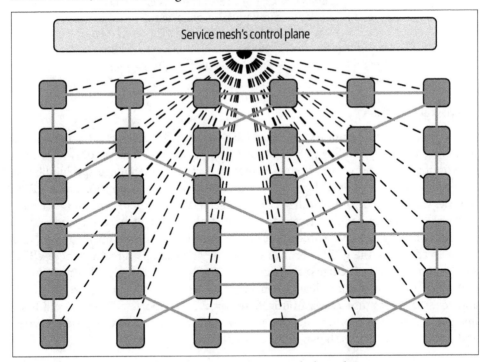

Figure 4-7. Controlling and coordinating a service mesh data plane

The sidecar-based approach is the most common pattern in use today and likely a good choice for our conference system. The primary costs of deploying a sidecar-based service mesh is in relation to the initial installation and ongoing operational maintenance and also the resources required to run all of the sidecars—as our scalability needs are currently modest, we shouldn't require large amounts of computing power to run the sidecar proxies.

The Cost of Running Sidecars at Scale

Many of today's popular service mesh solutions require you to add and run a proxy sidecar container, such as Envoy, Linkerd-proxy, or NGINX, to every service or application running within your cluster. Even in a relatively small environment with, say, 20 services, each running five pods spread across three nodes, you will have 100 proxy containers running. However small and efficient the proxy implementation is, the sheer duplication of the proxies will impact resources.

Depending on the service mesh configuration, the amount of memory used by each proxy may increase in relation to the number of services that it needs to be able to communicate with. Pranay Singhal (*https://oreil.ly/khfYY*) wrote about his experiences configuring Istio to reduce consumption from around 1 GB per proxy to a much more reasonable 60–70 MB each. However, even in the small, imaginary environment with 100 proxies on three nodes, this optimized configuration still requires approximately 2 GB per node.

Proxyless gRPC libraries

In an evolution that appears we may have come full circle, the Google Cloud began promoting "proxyless gPRC" (*https://oreil.ly/ZzbYw*) in early 2021, where the networking abstractions are once again moved back into a language-specific library (albeit a library maintained by Google and a large OSS community). These gRPC libraries are included within each service and act as the data plane within the service mesh. The libraries require access to an external control plane for coordination, such as the Google Traffic Director service. Traffic Director uses open source "xDS APIs" to configure the gRPC libraries within the applications directly.[6] These gRPC applications act as xDS clients, connecting to Traffic Director's global control plane that enables global routing, load balancing, and regional failover for service mesh and load-balancing use cases. Traffic Director even supports a "hybrid" mode of operation, including deployments that incorporate both sidecar proxy-based services and proxyless services, as shown in Figure 4-8.

---

6 You can learn more about Traffic Director (*https://oreil.ly/vao6J*) and the Envoy Proxy–inspired xDS protocol (*https://oreil.ly/rOo5t*) via their respective documentation websites.

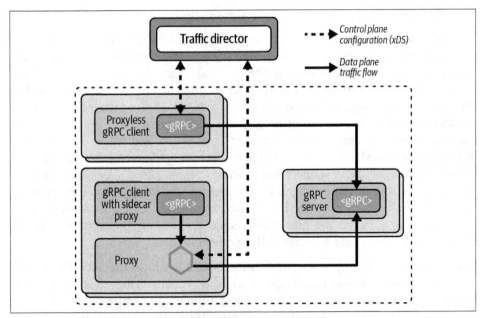

Figure 4-8. Example network diagram of services using both sidecars and proxyless communication

As our conference system uses REST APIs in addition to gRPC APIs, this would currently exclude this choice of a service mesh implementation. If our use of REST APIs internally was deprecated, or the gRPC libraries are enhanced to provide support for non-gRPC-based communication, using this approach could be reevaluated.

Is the Future of Service Mesh Proxyless?

As the popular cliché goes, although history doesn't repeat itself, it often rhymes. Many of the benefits and limitations of the proxyless approach are similar to those when using language-specific libraries. The Google Cloud team has called out the following use cases as examples on when proxyless deployment of service could be beneficial:

- Resource efficiency in a large-scale service mesh: saving resources from not running additional sidecar processes
- High-performance gRPC applications: reducing networking hops and latency
- Service mesh for environments where you can't deploy sidecar proxies: for example, a second process can't be executed, or a sidecar can't manipulate the required networking stack
- Migrate from a service mesh with proxies to a mesh without proxies

Sidecarless: Operating system kernel (eBPF) implementations

Another emerging alternative service mesh implementation is based on pushing the required networking abstractions back into the operation system (OS) kernel itself. This has become possible thanks to the rise and wide adoption of eBPF (*https:// ebpf.io*), a kernel technology that allows custom programs to run sandboxed within the kernel. eBPF programs are run in response to OS-level events, of which there are thousands that can be attached to. These events include the entry to or exit from any function in kernel or user space, or "trace points" and "probe points," and— importantly for service mesh—the arrival of network packets. As there is only one kernel per node, all the containers and processes running on a node share the same kernel. If you add an eBPF program to an event in the kernel, it will be triggered regardless of which process caused that event, whether it's running in an application container or directly on the host. This should remove any potential attempts to circumvent the service mesh, accidentally or otherwise.

The eBPF-based Cilium project provides the capabilities to secure and observe network connectivity between container workloads. Cilium brings this "sidecarless" model to the world of service mesh. Use of Cilium can reduce latency between service calls, as some functionality can be provided by the kernel without the need to perform a network hop to a sidecar proxy.[7] As well as the conventional sidecar model, Cilium supports running a service mesh data plane using a single Envoy Proxy instance per node, reducing resource usage. Figure 4-9 shows how two services can communicate using Cilium and a single Envoy Proxy per node.

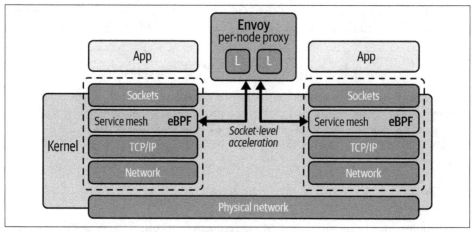

Figure 4-9. Using Cilium, eBPF, and a single Envoy Proxy per node to implement service mesh functionality

---

7 Learn more about this in "How eBPF will solve Service Mesh—Goodbye Sidecars" (*https://oreil.ly/2uxSR*).

Service Mesh Taxonomy

Table 4-4 highlights the difference between the three service mesh implementation styles as discussed in the previous section.

Table 4-4. Comparison of library-, proxy-, and OS/kernel-based service meshes

Use case	Library-based (and "proxyless")	Sidecars, Proxy-based	OS/kernel-based
Language/platform support	Single-language libraries, platform agnostic	Language agnostic, wide platform support	Language agnostic, OS-level support
Runtime mechanism	Packaged and run within the application	Run alongside application in a separate process	Run as part of the OS kernel, with full access to user and kernel space
Upgrading service mesh components	Requires rebuild and redeployment of entire application	Requires redeployment of sidecar components (can often be zero-downtime)	Requires kernel program update/patching
Observability	Complete insight into application and traffic, with ability to propagate context easily	Insight into traffic only, propagating context requires language support or shim	Insight into traffic only, propagating context requires language support or shim
Security threat model	Library code runs as part of application	Sidecars typically share process and network namespace with application	Application interacts directly with OS via syscalls

Case Study: Using a Service Mesh for Routing, Observability, and Security

In this section of the chapter you will explore several concrete examples of how to use a service mesh to implement the common requirements of routing, observing, and securely segmenting (via authorization) your service-to-service traffic. All of these examples will use Kubernetes, as this is the most common platform on which service meshes are deployed, but the concepts demonstrated apply to all platforms and infrastructure for which each service mesh supports. Although we recommend choosing and adopting only one service mesh implementation within your application's technology stack, we'll demonstrate the configuration of the conference system using three different service meshes, purely for educational purposes.

Routing with Istio

Istio can be installed into your Kubernetes cluster with the istioctl tool (*https://oreil.ly/8NyoV*). The main prerequisite for using Istio is enabling the automatic injection of the proxy sidecars to all services that are running within your cluster. This can be done as follows:

```
$ kubectl label namespace default istio-injection=enabled
```

With the auto-injection configured, the two primary Custom Resources you will be working with are VirtualServices and DestinationRules.[8] A VirtualService defines a set of traffic routing rules to apply when a host is addressed—e.g., *http://sessions*. A DestinationRule defines policies that apply to traffic intended for a service after routing has occurred. These rules specify configuration for load balancing, connection pool size from the sidecar, and outlier detection settings to detect and evict unhealthy hosts from the load balancing pool.

For example, to enable routing to your Session and Attendee services within the case study, you can create the following VirtualServices:

```
---
apiVersion: networking.istio.io/v1alpha3
kind: VirtualService
metadata:
  name: sessions
spec:
  hosts:
  - sessions
  http:
  - route:
    - destination:
        host: sessions
        subset: v1
---
apiVersion: networking.istio.io/v1alpha3
kind: VirtualService
metadata:
  name: attendees
spec:
  hosts:
  - attendees
  http:
  - route:
    - destination:
        host: attendees
        subset: v1
```

---

8 You can learn more about VirtualServices (*https://oreil.ly/L01fC*) and DestinationRules (*https://oreil.ly/0069e*) via the Istio docs.

The following DestinationRules can also be created. Note how the attendees DestinationRule specifies two versions of the service; this is the foundation for enabling canary routing for the new v2 version of the service:

```
---
apiVersion: networking.istio.io/v1alpha3
kind: DestinationRule
metadata:
  name: sessions
spec:
  host: sessions
  subsets:
  - name: v1
    labels:
      version: v1
---
apiVersion: networking.istio.io/v1alpha3
kind: DestinationRule
metadata:
  name: attendees
spec:
  host: attendees
  subsets:
  - name: v1
    labels:
      version: v1
  - name: v2
    labels:
      version: v2
```

With Istio installed and the preceding VirtualServices and DestinationRules configured, you can begin routing traffic and API calls between the Attendee and Session services. It really is this easy to get started, although configuring and maintaining Istio in a production environment can be more involved. Istio will handle the routing and also generate telemetry related to each connection. Let's learn more about observability using the Linkerd service mesh.

Observing Traffic with Linkerd

You can install Linkerd into a Kubernetes cluster by following the "Getting Started" instructions (*https://oreil.ly/dfnZ8*). Linkerd's telemetry and monitoring features are enabled automatically, without requiring you to make any configuration changes to the default installation. These observability features include:

- Recording of top-line ("golden") metrics (request volume, success rate, and latency distributions) for HTTP, HTTP/2, and gRPC traffic
- Recording of TCP-level metrics (bytes in/out, etc.) for other TCP traffic

- Reporting metrics per service, per caller/callee pair, or per route/path (with Service Profiles)
- Generating topology graphs that display the runtime relationship between services
- Live, on-demand request sampling

You can consume this data in several ways:

- Through the Linkerd CLI, e.g., with linkerd viz stat and linkerd viz routes
- Through the Linkerd dashboard and prebuilt Grafana dashboards
- Directly from Linkerd's built-in Prometheus instance

To gain access to Linkerd's observability features, you only need to install the viz extension and open the dashboard using your local browser:

```
linkerd viz install | kubectl apply -f -
linkerd viz dashboard
```

This provides access to service graphs showing traffic flow. In Figure 4-10, you can see traffic flowing across the mesh from the webapp to the book and authors services.

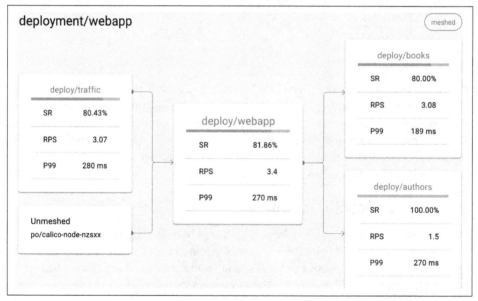

Figure 4-10. Using Linkerd viz to observe traffic flow between services

You can also view the top-line traffic metrics using the prebuilt Grafana dashboards, as shown in Figure 4-11.

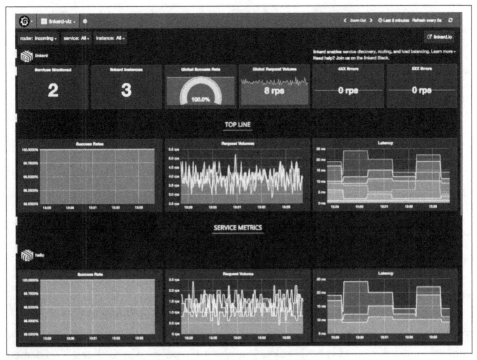

Figure 4-11. Viewing the Linkerd viz Grafana dashboards

Using a service mesh to provide observability into your applications is useful during both development and production. Although you should always automate detection of invalid service-to-service traffic in production, you can also use this service mesh observability tooling to identify when internal APIs or services are being called incorrectly. Let's now explore using policy to specify exactly which services can communicate with each other in the service mesh using HashiCorp's Consul.

Network Segmentation with Consul

You can install and configure Consul as a service mesh within a Kubernetes cluster by following the "Getting Started with Consul Service Mesh for Kubernetes" guide (*https://oreil.ly/RbMcy*). Before microservices, authorization of interservice communication was primarily enforced using firewall rules and routing tables. Consul simplifies the management of interservice authorization with intentions that allow you to define service-to-service communication permissions by service name.

Intentions control which services can communicate with each other and are enforced by the sidecar proxy on inbound connections. The identity of the inbound service is verified by its TLS client certificate, and Consul provides each service with an identity encoded as a TLS certificate. This certificate is used to establish and accept connections to and from other services.[9] The sidecar proxy then checks if an intention exists that authorizes the inbound service to communicate with the destination service. If the inbound service is not authorized, the connection will be terminated.

An intention has four parts:

Source service
Specifies the service that initiates the communication. It can be the full name of a service or be "*" to refer to all services.

Destination service
Specifies the service that receives the communication. This will be the "upstream" (service) you configured in your service definition. It can be the full name of a service or also be "*" to refer to all services.

Permission
Defines whether the communication between source and destination is permitted. This can be set to either allow or deny.

Description
Optional metadata field to associate a description with an intention.

The first intention you will create changes the "allow all" policy, where all traffic is allowed unless denied in specific rules, to a "deny all" policy where all traffic is denied and only specific connections are enabled:

```
apiVersion: consul.hashicorp.com/v1alpha1
kind: ServiceIntentions
metadata:
  name: deny-all
spec:
  destination:
    name: '*'
  sources:
    - name: '*'
      action: deny
```

By specifying the wildcard character (*) in the destination field, this intention will prevent all service-to-service communication. Once you have defined the default policy as deny all, you can authorize traffic between the conference system legacy service, the Attendee service, and the Session service by defining a ServiceIntentions CRD for each required service interaction. For example:

```
---
apiVersion: consul.hashicorp.com/v1alpha1
kind: ServiceIntentions
```

---

9 The identity is encoded in the TLS certificate in compliance with the SPIFFE X.509 Identity Document, which enables Connect services to establish and accept connections with other SPIFFE-compliant systems.

```
metadata:
  name: legacy-app-to-attendee
spec:
  destination:
    name: attendee
  sources:
    - name: legacy-conf-app
      action: allow
---
apiVersion: consul.hashicorp.com/v1alpha1
kind: ServiceIntentions
metadata:
  name: legacy-app-to-sessions
spec:
  destination:
    name: sessions
  sources:
    - name: legacy-conf-app
      action: allow
---
apiVersion: consul.hashicorp.com/v1alpha1
kind: ServiceIntentions
metadata:
  name: attendee-to-sessions
spec:
  destination:
    name: sessions
  sources:
    - name: attendee
      action: allow
---
apiVersion: consul.hashicorp.com/v1alpha1
kind: ServiceIntentions
metadata:
  name: sessions-to-attendee
spec:
  destination:
    name: attendee
  sources:
    - name: sessions
      action: allow
```

Applying this configuration to the Kubernetes cluster will enable these interactions—and only these service-to-service interactions—to process as required. Any other interactions will be prevented, and the API call or request will be dropped.

In addition to Consul's intentions, the Open Policy Agent (OPA) project is a popular choice for implementing similar functionality within a service mesh. You can find an example of using OPA to configure service-to-service policy within Istio in the "OPA Tutorial documentation" (*https://oreil.ly/I4HsD*).

Now that you have explored example configuration that will be applied as we evolve the conference system, let's turn our attention to running and managing the service mesh implementation itself.

Deploying a Service Mesh: Understanding and Managing Failure

Regardless of the deployment pattern and number of instances running within a system or network, a service mesh is typically on the critical path of many, if not all, user requests moving through your system. An outage of a service mesh instance within a cluster or network typically results in the unavailability of the entire system within that network's blast radius. For this reason the topics of understanding and managing failure are vitally important to learn.

Service Mesh as a Single Point of Failure

A service mesh is often on the hot path of all traffic, which can be a challenge in relation to reliability and failover. Obviously, the more functionality you are relying on within the service mesh, the bigger the risk involved and the bigger the impact of an outage. As a service mesh is often used to orchestrate the release of application services, the configuration is also continually being updated. It is critical to be able to detect and resolve issues and mitigate any risks. Many of the points discussed in "API Gateway as a Single Point of Failure" on page 79 can be applied to understanding and managing service mesh failure.

Common Service Mesh Implementation Challenges

As service mesh technologies are newer in comparison with API gateway technologies, some of the common implementation challenges are yet to be discovered and shared widely. However, there are a core set of antipatterns to avoid.

Service Mesh as ESB

With the emergence of service mesh plug-ins or traffic filters, and supporting technologies like Web Assembly (Wasm), it is increasingly tempting to think of service meshes as offering ESB-like functionality, such as payload transformation and translation. For all the reasons already discussed throughout this book, we strongly discourage adding business functionality or coupling too many "smarts" with the platform or infrastructure.

Service Mesh as Gateway

As many service mesh implementations provide some form of ingress gateway, we have seen organizations wanting to adopt an API gateway but instead choosing to deploy a service mesh and only using the gateway functionality. The motivation makes sense, as engineers in the organization realize that they will soon want to adopt service mesh–like functionality, but their biggest pain point is managing ingress traffic. However, the functionality provided by most service mesh gateways is not as rich in comparison with a fully fledged API gateway. You will also most likely encounter the installation and operational costs of running a service mesh without getting any of the benefits.

Too Many Networking Layers

We have seen some organizations provide a rich set of networking abstractions and features that will meet the current service-to-service communication requirements, but the development teams either don't know about this or refuse to adopt this for some reason. As development teams attempt to implement a service mesh on top of the existing networking technologies, additional issues appear, such as incompatibilities (e.g., existing networking technologies stripping headers), increased latency (owing to multiple proxy hops), or functionality being implemented multiple times within the networking stack (e.g., circuit breaking occurring in both the service mesh and the lower-level networking stack). For this reason, we always recommend that all involved teams coordinate and collaborate with service mesh solutions.

Selecting a Service Mesh

Now that you learned about the functionality provided by a service mesh, the evolution of the pattern and technologies, and how a service mesh fits into to the overall system architecture, next is a key question: how do you select a service mesh to be included in your application's technology stack?

Identifying Requirements

As discussed in relation to selecting an API gateway, one of the most important steps with any new infrastructure project is identifying the related requirements. This may appear obvious, but I'm sure you can recall a time that you were distracted by shiny technology, magical marketing, or good sales documentation!

You can look back to the earlier section "Why Use a Service Mesh?" on page 96 of this chapter to explore in more detail the high-level requirements you should be considering during a service mesh selection process. It is important to ask questions that are both focused on current pain points and also your future roadmap.

Build Versus Buy

In comparison with the API gateway build versus buy decision, the related discussions with service mesh are less likely to be had upfront, especially with organizations that have heritage or legacy systems. This can partially be attributed to service mesh being a relatively new category of technology. In our experience, in most vintage systems that are somewhat distributed (e.g., more than a LAMP stack), partial implementations of a service mesh will be scattered throughout an organization—for example, with some departments using language-specific libraries, others using an ESB, and some using simple API gateways or simple proxies to manage internal traffic.

In general, if you have decided to adopt the service mesh pattern, we believe that it is typically best to adopt and standardize on an open source implementation or commercial solution rather than build your own. Presenting the case for build versus buy with software delivery technology could take an entire book, and so in this section we only want to highlight some common challenges:

Underestimating the total cost of ownership (TCO)
Many engineers discount the cost of engineering a solution, the continued maintenance costs, and the ongoing operational costs.

Not thinking about opportunity cost
Unless you are a cloud or platform vendor, it is highly unlikely that a custom service mesh will provide you with a competitive advantage. You can instead deliver more value to your customers by building functionality aligned to your core value proposition.

Operational costs
Not understanding the onboarding and operational cost of maintaining multiple different implementations that solve the same problems.

Awareness of technical solutions
Both the open source and commercial platform component space move fast, and it can be challenging to keep up-to-date. Staying aware and informed, however, is a core part of the role of being a technical leader.

Checklist: Selecting a Service Mesh

The checklist in Table 4-5 highlights the key decisions that you and your team should be considering when deciding whether to implement the service mesh pattern and when choosing the related technologies.

Table 4-5. ADR Guideline: Selecting a service mesh checklist

Decision	How should we approach selecting a service mesh for our organization?
Discussion Points	Have we identified and prioritized all of our requirements associated with selecting a service mesh?
	Have we identified current technology solutions that have been deployed in this space within the organization?
	Do we know all of our team and organizational constraints?
	Have we explored our future roadmap in relation to this decision?
	Have we honestly calculated the "build versus buy" costs?
	Have we explored the current technology landscape and are we aware of all of the available solutions?
	Have we consulted and informed all involved stakeholders in our analysis and decision making?
Recommendations	Focus particularly on your requirement to reduce internal API/system coupling, simplify consumption, protect APIs from overuse and abuse, understand how APIs are being consumed, and manage APIs as products.
	Key questions to ask include: is there an existing service mesh in use? Has a collection of technologies been assembled to provide similar functionality; e.g., have developers created service-to-service communication libraries or have platform/SREs team deployed sidecar proxies?
	Focus on technology skill levels within your team, availability of people to work on a service mesh project, and available resources and budget, etc.
	It is important to identify all planned changes, new features, and current goals that could impact internal traffic management and the other functionality that a service mesh provides.
	Calculate the total cost of ownership (TCO) of all of the current service meshlike implementations and potential future solutions.
	Consult with well-known analysts, trend reports, and product reviews in order to understand all of the current solutions available.
	Selecting and deploying a service mesh will impact many teams and individuals. Be sure to consult with development teams, QA, the architecture review board, the platform team, InfoSec, etc.

Summary

In this chapter you have learned what a service mesh is and explored what functionality, benefits, and challenges adopting this pattern and associated technologies provides:

- Fundamentally, "service mesh" is a pattern for managing all service-to-service communication within a distributed software system.

- At a network level, a service mesh proxy acts as a full proxy, accepting all inbound traffic from other services and also initiating all outbound requests to other services.

- A service mesh is deployed within an internal network or cluster. Large systems or networks are typically managed by deploying several instances of a service mesh, often with each single mesh spanning a network segment or business domain.

- A service mesh may expose endpoints within a network demilitarized zone (DMZ), or to external systems, or additional networks or clusters, but this is frequently implemented by using an "ingress," "terminating," or "transit" gateway.

- There are many API-related cross-cutting concerns that you might have for each or all of your internal services, including: product lifecycle management (incrementally releasing new versions of a service), reliability, multilanguage communication support, observability, security, maintainability, and extensibility. A service mesh can help with all of these.

- A service mesh can be implemented using language-specific libraries, sidecar proxies, proxyless communication frameworks (gRPC), or kernel-based technologies like eBPF.

- The most vulnerable component of a service mesh is typically the control plane. This must be secured, monitored, and run as a highly available service.

- Service mesh usage antipatterns include: service mesh as ESB, service mesh as gateway, and using too many networking layers.

- Choosing to implement a service mesh, and selecting the technology to do so, are Type 1 decisions. Research, requirements analysis, and appropriate design must be conducted.

- If you have decided to adopt the service mesh pattern we believe that it is typically best to adopt and standardize on an open source implementation or commercial solution rather than build your own.

Regardless of your decision to adopt a service mesh, it is important to consider both external and internal operations and security for your APIs. This is the focus of the next section of this book.

PART III

API Operations and Security

In this section you will explore the challenges in operating and securing an API-driven system.

Chapter 5 covers deploying and releasing APIs using an API lifecycle. We will also explore observability topics and how opinionated platforms can help reduce problems with distributed architectures.

Chapter 6 explores threat modeling for APIs and how to think like someone attempting to act maliciously against your APIs.

Chapter 7 examines the use of authentication and authorization for securing APIs.

CHAPTER 5

Deploying and Releasing APIs

In this chapter we will start to tie together how to move from design, build, and test to running in the target environment.

Consider the conference system case study we introduced in the Introduction: we had a single-user interface and server-side application. Deploying an upgrade to the server or user interface would likely mean having some element of downtime. It is likely that the deployment and the release actions are tightly coupled and possibly inseparable. It may also have taken time to roll back the changes if an issue occurred with the deployment. We will explore some options for the legacy conference system, in addition to looking at how a looser coupling between the UI and server components provides more options for deployment and release.

The introduction of traffic management provides you options to separate the deployment and release. In this chapter we will explore this in more detail and look at the conference system options available for rolling out changes. You will need to consider how API versioning impacts the options for modeling releases in the conference system.

One key consideration for a rollout is to understand whether a change has been successful or not. API architectures are by nature decoupled, and it is important to ensure the right metrics, logs, and traces are available to perform a successful release. We will look at the types of considerations for metrics and how they help in releases and incident management/troubleshooting.

Finally, we will touch on how eventual consistency impacts change and where gotchas can creep in at the application level. The introduction of additional layers of infrastructure, such as proxies, requires decisions around caching and header propagation. We will explore these considerations and why you might choose an opinionated platform.

Separating Deployment and Release

It's important for you to understand the difference between deployment and release to get the most out of this chapter. Deployment involves taking a feature all the way into production, because you now have a running process in your system. Although deployed, the new feature is not active or executed by interactions with the production system. There are different ways to achieve this separation and you will explore these shortly. The release involves activating the new feature in a controlled manner, allowing you to control the risk of introducing the new feature. Thoughtworks Technology Radar has a great explanation of the difference between deployment and release:

> Implementing Continuous Delivery continues to be a challenge for many organizations, and it remains important to highlight useful techniques such as decoupling deployment from release. We recommend strictly using the term Deployment when referring to the act of deploying a change to application components or infrastructure. The term Release should be used when a feature change is released to end users, with a business impact. Using techniques such as feature toggles and dark launches, we can deploy changes to production systems more frequently without releasing features. More-frequent deployments reduce the risk associated with change, while business stakeholders retain control over when features are released to end users.
>
> —Thoughtworks Technology Radar 2016

One advantage of moving toward an API-based architecture is that the decoupled nature enables teams to rapidly release change. To realize this benefit, it is important to consider that the mechanisms for ensuring the coupling between systems remains low and the risk of releases resulting in a failure is minimized.

 We have seen teams that move to an API-based architecture without separating deployment and release. This can work for highly coupled services, but quickly puts pressure and downtime on multiple services if releases have to be choreographed across many teams. We will explore further in this chapter how you can use API versioning and lifecycles to help prevent this.

Case Study: Feature Flagging

To effectively consider how to separate deployment and release, we will start with the legacy conference system case study. This is a useful place to start as it will allow us to model an evolutionary architecture nicely, where we can control the rate of change to the new infrastructure we have presented so far in the book. Figure 5-1 shows how the the legacy system for attendees and the database will live side-by-side with the modernized API-based service. Using feature flags, the controller can now

---

make a code-level decision about whether to execute the query against the internal or external API service.

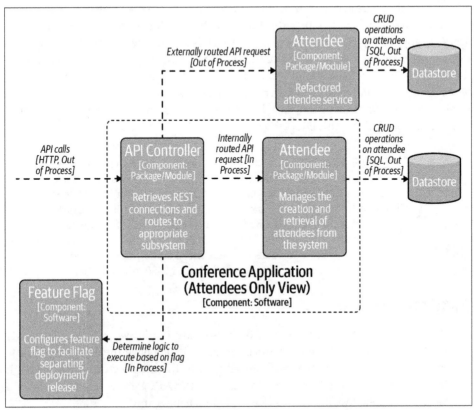

Figure 5-1. Conference application container diagram for attendees and feature flags

Feature flags are typically hosted in a configuration store outside of the running application and allow code to be deployed with the feature off. Once the team (or product owner) is ready to enable the feature, they can toggle the feature on, which causes the application to execute a different branch of code. The granularity could be on a per-user level, or more coarse, as simply enabling a specific option globally. The following is example pseudocode from the popular Java feature-flagging tool LaunchDarkly, where the user's details are in the modern store:

```
LDUser user = new LDUser("jim@masteringapi.com");
boolean newAttendeesService =
    launchDarklyClient.boolVariation("user.enabled.modern", user, false);
if (newAttendeesService) {
  // Retrieves the attendee from the modern store
}
else {
```

```
    // Retrieves the attendee from the legacy store
}
```

Following this approach would allow you to migrate a small batch of users over to the new system and test that the functionality continues to work for the set of users. If anything goes wrong as part of the migration, the switch can simply be toggled back, or else the rollout continues until reaching 100% migration. Like other services that cross-cut the application, a failure in the feature-flagging service would be catastrophic if not managed correctly and be a potential single point of failure. Degrading gracefully using the last known value in a cache or providing default values can help mitigate this effect.

 Feature flags help facilitate the separation between code deploy-ment and release. You must clean up feature flags and always create feature flags with unique names. Once the migration is complete, the feature flag code should be removed completely. For an exam-ple of feature flags going wrong because of this issue, you only have to look at Knight Capital (*https://oreil.ly/WBnE1*), where reusing a feature flag and a failed deployment ended up costing thousands of dollars per second, up to an eventual loss of $460 million.

Traffic Management

One benefit of moving to an API-based architecture is that we can iterate quickly and deploy new changes to our Attendee service. We also have the concept of traffic and routing established for the modernized part of the architecture. This makes it possible to manipulate the traffic in two places: at the API gateway ingress or within the constructs defined within the service mesh for shaping traffic.

For Kubernetes and service mesh–based systems, deployment looks roughly like the following steps:

1. Create a pull request of the changes required to the application, and once the pull request is approved and merged, automatically kick off the deployment build.

2. The build pipeline creates a new image using Docker or the Open Container Initiative.

3. Push the new image to the container registry.

4. Trigger a new deployment of the image into the target environment.

By default, Kubernetes will replace the running deployment with a new deployment. Later in this chapter we will look at techniques to phase in the release of a new pod to actively separate deployment and release. Once the deployment is in place, the job of deploying code is now complete, and a different set of instructions follow for the release configuration of the running system. The configuration may also have multiple stages, and this is a mechanism we can use to set up different release strategies. Before we dive into exploring how to structure the release for traffic management, it is worth exploring the types of releases that you can have within an API system.

Case Study: Modeling Releases in the Conference System

In "Semantic Versioning" on page 16 (semver), we discussed the idea of different version strategies associated with APIs. When considering releases, it can be helpful to couple the ideas in semver with an API Lifecycle.

API Lifecycle

The API space is moving quickly, but one of the clearest representations of version lifecycle comes from the now archived PayPal API standards (*https://oreil.ly/QMCKz*). An approach to modeling lifecycle is presented in Table 5-1.

Table 5-1. API Lifecycle (adapted from PayPal API standards)

Planned	Exposing an API from a technology perspective is quite straightforward, however once it is exposed and live in production you have multiple API consumers that need to be managed. The planning stage is about advertising that you are building an API and gathering initial feedback on the design and shape of the API from consumers. This allows a discussion about the API and the scope, allowing any early design decisions to be included.
Beta	Involves releasing a version of our API for users to start to integrate with; however, this is generally for the purpose of feedback and improving the API. At this stage the producer reserves the right to break compatibility, because it is not a versioned API. This helps to get rapid feedback from consumers about the design of the API before settling on a structure. A round of feedback and changes enables the producer to avoid having many major versions at the start of the API's lifetime.
Live	The API is now versioned and live in production. Any changes from this point onward would be versioned changes. There should only ever be one live API, which marks the most recent major/minor version combination. Whenever a new version is released, the current live API moves to deprecated.
Deprecated	When an API is deprecated, it is still available for use, but significant new development should not be carried out against it. When a minor version of a new API is released, an API will only be deprecated for a short time, until validation of the new API in production is complete. After the new version is successfully validated, a minor version moves to retired, as the new version is backward compatible and can handle the same features as the previous API. When a major version of the API is released, the older version becomes deprecated. It is likely that will be for weeks or months, as an opportunity must be given to consumers to migrate to the new version. There is likely going to be communication with the consumers, a migration guide, and tracking of metrics and usage of the deprecated API.
Retired	The API is retired from production and is no longer accessible.

The lifecycle helps the consumer fully understand what to expect from an API change. With semantic versioning combined with the API Lifecycle, the consumer only needs to be aware of the major version of the API. Minor and patch versions will be received without updates required on the consumer's side and won't break compatibility. By considering the API Lifecycle and what you can control through traffic management, you can start to look at the types of changes and consider the most appropriate way to release new versions of APIs.

Mapping Release Strategies to Lifecycle

Major changes are the most impactful for API consumers. In order to use the new version of software, consumers must actively upgrade their software that interacts with the API. As defined in the lifecycle, this means that we need to simultaneously run a live and deprecated version of the API for a significant amount of time to allow consumers to upgrade and migrate. This allows the consumer to make an explicit choice as to when they upgrade. One way to do this is to add the version in the URL:

```
GET /v1/attendees
```

Adding in the version is practical and easily visible to the consumer. However, it is not part of the resource and in some groups is considered not RESTful. An alternative approach is to have a header describing the major version that will impact the routing at the ingress to the cluster:

```
GET /attendees
Version: v1
```

Minor changes are free from the constraints imposed by major changes. For these types of changes, it is possible to deploy a new minor version of the API without accepting production traffic and then use a release strategy to introduce the new version. This type of change would not require any code changes from the consumer. Patch changes follow a similar pattern, as they do not change the shape of the API specification at all. For this type of transparent release to be possible, it is worth considering adding extra controls into the build process to assure that breaking changes are not accidentally introduced.

In "OpenAPI Specification and Versioning" on page 16, we took a look at using openapi-diff to highlight changes between specifications. In the event that the specification is not backward compatible, the build should fail and prevent a breaking change from entering the architecture without a conscious override in place. The majority of releases against an API will be minor changes or patch changes where loose coupling is a primary concern for the producer and consumer.

If the consumer and producer are tightly coupled, owned by the same team, and always move together, API versioning and lifecycle will not be critical. In this situation it is important to consider a release strategy that allows the release of both components together and traffic is controlled at ingress. Typically blue-green models work well for this scenario, and we will review this further in "Release Strategies" on page 131.

ADR Guideline: Separating Release from Deployment with Traffic Management and Feature Flags

The ADR Guideline in Table 5-2 is helpful when considering how to create an ADR to separate release from deployment.

Table 5-2. ADR Guideline: Separating release from deployment with traffic management and feature flags guideline

Decision	How do you go about separating release from deployment?
Discussion Points	Is it possible to separate deployment and release in the existing systems that are live today?
	What is the degree of coupling between the consumer and producer in the system?
	Do you have a build pipeline where it is possible to enforce the loose coupling requirements of traffic managed APIs, ensuring that compatibility is tested?
Recommendations	Start by working on separating the deploy and release of existing software. This will help to enable an evolutionary architecture and a simplification of the existing system.
	Feature flags are a good way of creating this separation. If the company hasn't used feature flagging before, be sure that you review recommended practices and avoid pitfalls associated with flags.
	Without careful consideration, feature flags have the potential to become a single point of failure.
	Review the type of coupling between APIs in the architecture and decide the correct release strategy for the situation.

In the next section we will explore the different types of release strategies available.

Release Strategies

Once you have adequately separated deployment and release, you can now consider mechanisms for controlling the progressive release of features. It is important to choose a release strategy that allows you to reduce risk in production. Reduction in risk is achieved by performing a test or experiment with a small fraction of traffic and verifying the result. When the result is successful, the release to all traffic triggers. Certain strategies suit scenarios better than others and require varying degrees of additional services and infrastructure. Let's explore a couple of options that are popular with API-based infrastructure.

Canary Releases

A canary release[1] introduces a new version of the software and flows a small percentage of the traffic to the canary. In Figure 5-2, the before stage shows the gateway, the legacy conference at version 1.0, and the Attendee service at v1.0. The concept of a traffic split between the legacy conference service and Attendee service is in place, which will be different depending on the target platform. At the deployment stage a

---

1 Named after canaries that went into the coal mines first to fatally identify the presence of any dangerous gases.

new v1.1 of the Attendee service is deployed, and at release time we can start to flow some of the traffic toward the v1.1 service.

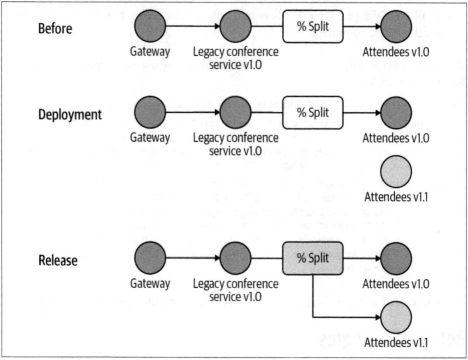

Figure 5-2. Deploying the Attendee service using a canary approach

In Kubernetes, traffic splitting can be achieved by introducing a new pod against a service; you will explore this idea further in "Case Study: Performing Rollouts with Argo Rollouts" on page 135. It's quite difficult to control a small percentage—that is, if you would like 1%, you need to run 99 v1 pods and 1 v2 pod. For most situations this would be impractical.

In service mesh and API gateways, traffic shifting makes it possible to gradually shift or migrate traffic from one version of a target service to another. For example, a new version, v1.1, of a service can be deployed alongside the original, v1.0. Traffic shifting enables you to canary test or canary release your new service by at first only routing a small percentage of user traffic, say 1%, to v1.1, and then over time shifting all of your traffic to the new service. This allows you to monitor the new service and look for technical problems, such as increased latency or error rates, and also look for a desired business impact, such as an increase in key performance indicators like customer conversion ratio or average shopping checkout value. Traffic splitting enables you to run A/B or multivariate tests by dividing traffic destined to a target service between multiple versions of the service. For example, you can split traffic

50/50 across your v1.0 and v1.1 of the target service and see which performs better over a specific period of time.

As a service mesh is involved with all service-to-service communication, you can implement these release and experimentation techniques on any service within your application. For example, you could canary release a new version of the Session service that implements internal caching of an attendees conference session schedule. You would monitor for both business KPIs, such as how often a user views and interacts with their session schedule, and also operational SLIs, such as a decrease in CPU usages within the service.

Separating Deploy and Release: Canary All-the-Things

With the rise in Progressive Delivery (*https://oreil.ly/9qVQe*), and also advanced requirements within Continuous Delivery before this, having the ability to separate the deployment and release of a service (and corresponding API) is a powerful technique. The ability to canary release services or run A/B tests can provide a competitive advantage to your business in both mitigating risks of a bad release and also understanding your customer's requirements more effectively. You will learn more about this in Chapter 9.

Where appropriate, canary releases are an excellent option, as the percentage of traffic exposed to the canary is highly controlled. The trade-off is that the system must have good monitoring in place to be able to quickly identify an issue and roll back if necessary (which can be automated). Canaries have the added advantage that only a single new instance is spun up; in strategies like blue-green, a complete second stack of services is needed. This can save cost and the operational complexity of running two environments in parallel.

Traffic Mirroring

In addition to using traffic splitting to run experiments, you can also use traffic mirroring to copy or duplicate traffic and send this to an additional location or series of locations. Frequently with traffic mirroring, the results of the duplicated requests are not returned to the calling service or end user. Instead, the responses are evaluated out-of-band for correctness, such as comparing the results generated by a refactored and existing service, or a selection of operational properties are observed as a new service version handles the request, such as response latency or CPU required.

Using traffic mirroring enables you to "dark launch" or "dark release" services, where a user is kept in the dark about the new release but you can observe internally for the required effect. The main difference is the ability to mirror traffic, which during the experiment/release phase duplicates the request to the attendees v1.1 service. In

Figure 5-3 the before and deployment stages are identical to the canary release; often dark deployment is referred to as a specialized canary.

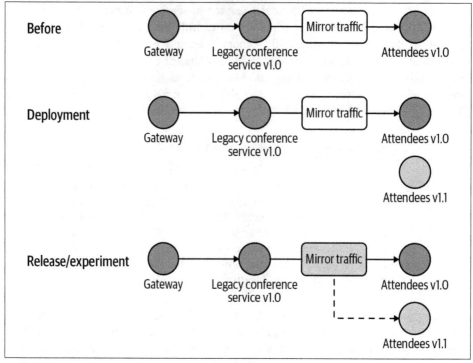

Figure 5-3. Deploying the Attendee service using a traffic mirroring approach

Implementing traffic mirroring at the edge of systems has become increasingly popular over the years, and now a service mesh enables this to be implemented effectively and consistently across internal services. Continuing the example of releasing a new version of the Attendee service that implements internal caching, dark launching this service would allow you to assess the operational performance of the release but not the business impact.

Blue-Green

Blue-green is usually implemented at a point in the architecture that uses a router, gateway, or load balancer, behind which sits a complete blue environment and a green environment. The current blue environment represents the current live environment, and the green environment represents the next version of the stack. The green environment is checked prior to switching to live traffic, and at go live the traffic is flipped over from blue to green. The blue environment is now "off," but if a problem is spotted it is a quick rollback. The next change would go from green to blue, oscillating from first release onward.

In Figure 5-4 the legacy conference service and Attendee service are both at v1.0 and represent our blue model. During deployment we are looking to deploy the legacy conference service v1.1 and attendees v1.1 together, creating a green environment. During the release step, the configuration is updated to target the gateway to point at the green environment.

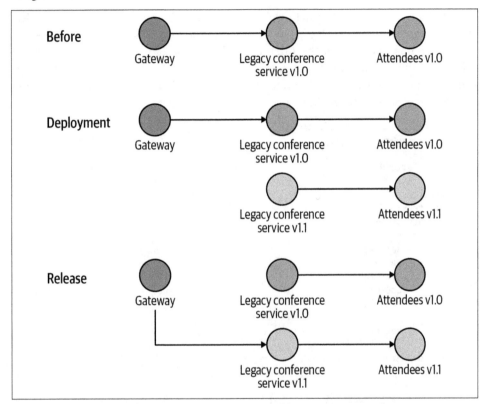

Figure 5-4. Deploying the Attendee service using a blue-green approach

Blue-green works well due to its simplicity and for coupled services is one of the better deployment options. It is also easier to manage persisting services, though you still need to be careful in the event of a rollback. It also requires double the number of resources to be able to run cold in parallel to the current active environment.

Case Study: Performing Rollouts with Argo Rollouts

The strategies discussed add a lot of value, but the rollout itself is a task that you would not want to have to manage manually. This is where a tool such as Argo Rollouts (*https://oreil.ly/Ijj6y*) is valuable for demonstrating practically some of the concerns discussed. Using Argo, it is possible to define a Rollout CRD that represents the strategy you can take for rolling out a new canary of your v1.2 of the Attendee API. A Custom Resource Definition (CRD) allows Argo to extend the Kubernetes API to support rollout behavior. CRDs are a popular pattern with Kubernetes, and they allow the user to interact with one API with the extension to support different features.

The Rollout CRD is a combination of the standard Kubernetes Deployment CRD with a strategy on how to roll out new features. In the following configuration YAML, we are running five pods of the Attendee API, and specifying a canary approach to rolling out the new feature. On triggering the rollout, 20% of the pods will be swapped for the new version. The {} syntax in the pause tells Argo to await confirmation from the user before proceeding:

```
apiVersion: argoproj.io/v1alpha1
kind: Rollout
metadata:
  name: attendees
spec:
  replicas: 5
  strategy:
    canary:
      steps:
        - setWeight: 20
        - pause: {}
        - setWeight: 40
        - pause: {duration: 10}
        - setWeight: 60
        - pause: {duration: 10}
        - setWeight: 80
        - pause: {duration: 10}
  revisionHistoryLimit: 2
  selector:
    matchLabels:
      app: attendees-api
  template:
    metadata:
      labels:
        app: attendees-api
    spec:
      containers:
        - name: attendees
          image: jpgough/attendees:v1
```

After installing Argo to our cluster and applying the preceding configuration, the cluster will have five pods of the version 1 Attendee service running. A really nice feature of Argo is that the dashboard helps to clearly visualize the current status of the rollout. Figure 5-5 shows the starting point of the rollout, running five pods of the attendees v1 service.

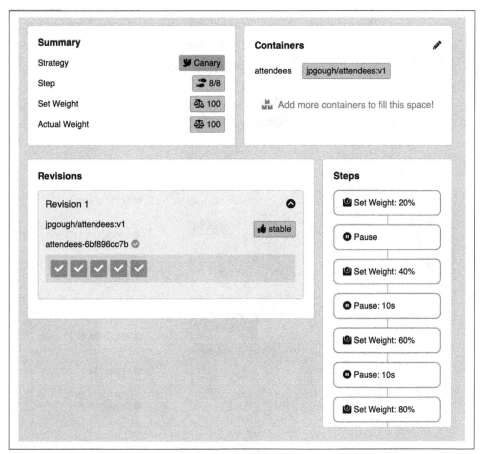

Figure 5-5. Argo Rollouts starting point

Executing the following command introduces the v1.2 canary into the platform:

```
kubectl argo rollouts set image attendees attendees=jpgough/attendees:v1.2
```

Figure 5-6 shows that the release is on the first step of the strategy with a 20% weight now set to the canary for attendees v1.2. As the UI demonstrates, the rollout is now in the Pause step, waiting for the manual promotion to be triggered to continue the rollout, either from the UI or command line. It is also possible to quickly roll back the canary release if an issue is encountered.

Figure 5-6. Argo Rollouts canary

In this simple example, you have explored the Kubernetes level only; however, it is possible to fully integrate with features of service mesh to control rollouts. It is also possible to integrate with ingress gateways such as NGINX and Ambassador to coordinate traffic management with the release. Tools like Argo make rollouts and traffic-based releases quite compelling.

In addition to manual promotion steps explored in this walkthrough, it is also possible to drive promotion based on the analysis of metrics. The following is an example of an `AnalysisTemplate` that uses Prometheus metrics to observe the success rate of deploying a canary. This analysis stage can be represented in the `Rollout` definition, allowing the rollout to progress if the success criteria are met:

```
apiVersion: argoproj.io/v1alpha1
kind: AnalysisTemplate
metadata:
```

```
      name: success-rate
spec:
  args:
  - name: service-name
  - name: prometheus-port
    value: 9090
  metrics:
  - name: success-rate
    successCondition: result[0] >= 0.95
    provider:
      prometheus:
        address: "http://prometheus.example.com:{{args.prometheus-port}}"
```

Success rate is a fairly simple metric; however, there are situations where APIs fail that are not indicative of a fault in infrastructure but rather the client request. Let's explore some of the key principles that are important from an API perspective that you can use to both operate the plant and also inform your rollout strategies.

Monitoring for Success and Identifying Failure

Consider the legacy conference system case study in the Introduction and how you would go about investigating an issue in a single application. A single service has a single logfile to trace requests and processing by the application. There is only one application to look at for the overall health of the process on the server. Separating out multiple services, such as the Attendee service, results in an increase in operational complexity. The more *hops* between services introduces a potential for failure and manually finding what has gone wrong soon becomes difficult.

Three Pillars of Observability

API-driven architectures are decoupled and, without appropriate support, are complex to reason about and troubleshoot. Observability provides transparency into your system, providing a full understanding of what is happening at all times. Observability is best described by the three pillars, an operational minimum required to reason about distributed architecture:

- *Metrics* are a measurement captured at regular intervals that represent an important element to the overall platform health. Metrics can be at different levels across the platform, and the freedom of structure means that a platform can determine what metrics are important to capture. For example, a Java platform may choose to capture CPU utilization, current heap size, and garbage collection pause time (to name a few).

- *Logs* are granular details of processing from a given component, and often the quality of logs is closely tied to the application or infrastructure component emitting them. Log format influences the utility of searching and processing of log data significantly, with structured logging facilitating a better search and retrieval of relevant data. In a distributed system, logs alone are usually not enough, and they are often better explored with the addition of context provided by traces and metrics.

- *Traces* are essential when moving to a distributed architecture, enabling the tracking of each request through all the components interacted with in the architecture. For example, if a request fails, tracing will enable you to quickly locate the exact component in the architecture that is failing. Tracing works by adding a unique header as close to the origination of the request as possible; this header is propagated in all subsequent processing of a given request. If the context of the request moves over to a different type of infrastructure (e.g., a queue), the unique header will be recorded in the message envelope.

You can find a more detailed introduction in *Distributed Systems Observability* (O'Reilly) by Cindy Sridharan.

 Implementing the three pillars across the platform is not enough. In "Reading the Signals" on page 141, we will cover how to make use of the three pillars of observability to operate infrastructure involved with an API platform.

For the three pillars of observability, the OpenTelemetry project (*https://oreil.ly/fJPPd*) is the best place to start. The project provides an open standard in the Cloud Native Computing Foundation (CNCF), preventing vendor lock-in and facilitating the widest possible compatibility. Although metrics and tracing standards have been created and are stable, logging is a slightly more difficult problem to solve (due to the vast array of different possible emitters), but it is also covered in the OpenTelemetry project.

Important Metrics for APIs

Considering which metrics are important for an API platform is a key decision that will help discover outages early, and possibly even prevent them. You could measure and gather a wide range of different metrics, but some metrics will also be dependent upon your platform. Rate, Error, Duration (RED) metrics are often noted as one approach to measuring traffic-based service architectures. Part of the appeal is that these metrics provide a good overview of what is going on at a point in time. Rate shows how many requests per second a service is processing (or throughput), what errors are returned, and the duration (or latency) of each request. In the Site Reliability Engineering (SRE) world, these metrics help us to derive The Four Golden Signals (*https://oreil.ly/iv1bJ*)—latency, traffic, errors, and saturation.

Perhaps one of the biggest drawbacks of RED/golden signals is that it is easy to apply the rules and miss out on the wider context (or understanding) of the system. For example, is every error from an API caused by a service in the request chain? For APIs the context of the error is really important—for example, a 5xx range error is important as it highlights a failure caused by an infrastructure component or service. A 4xx error isn't a service problem and is more the problem of the client, but can you simply ignore this error code? A series of 403 Forbidden errors could indicate that a malicious actor is attempting to access data that they are not entitled to. This is one example of why context is critical, and time spent investigating what metrics are important takes API reasoning beyond RED metrics.

Important metrics should be tied to alerting in order to ensure that you can swiftly deal with problems (or upcoming problems). You have to be careful when setting alerts to avoid false positives. For example, if an alert is generated on low or no activity this could be triggered on bank holidays or weekends. Only having this type of alert scheduled for core business hours could help, or perhaps tying it to the current number of website logins.

In our conference system case study, the following would be considered important example metrics to capture:

- The number of requests per minute for attendees.
- The service-level objective (SLO) for attendees is average latency for responses. If the latency starts to significantly deviate, it could be the early signs of an issue.
- Number of 401s from the CFP system could indicate a vendor compromise or a stolen token.
- Measure of availability and uptime of the Attendee service.
- Memory and CPU usage of the applications.
- The total number of attendees in the system.

Reading the Signals

So far we have discussed observability and why this is important, along with the purpose of each pillar. We have looked at some key metrics for APIs, but also added a caution that implementation alone or metrics without context is not enough. We mentioned the idea of capturing metrics from the running application such as garbage collection time. Increasing time spent garbage collecting might be an early symptom that your application is about to fail. Garbage collections typically spend time pausing applications, which in turn results in requests being delayed and can impact latency. Spotting this early is the equivalent of a car engine making a strange noise; it still works but something isn't quite right.

In order to read the signals, establishing an expectation or baseline is really helpful, and then measuring within this range and alerting when outside the range can help spot a problem. The next step would be observing the actual metric for API latency being impacted—the equivalent of the check engine light now showing. The sooner you can read the signals of a potential issue, the less the likelihood of there being a client-impacting problem. If both measures are ignored, the application eventually falls over, leaving the team scrambling to repair.

Understanding the software and the link into key metrics helps lead to a mature operational platform with early identification and hopefully resolution of problems. In distributed architectures, failure is inevitable, and in an outage scenario, traces would be the first port of call to narrow down the root cause. We have seen it take hours to dig into the cause of a problem without tools like tracing, with developers turned detectives poring over logs trying to find clues as to "whodunnit." Another key consideration is how quickly the team responds to various events. If the first time is when all API traffic is not working, it's going to be stressful (and possibly business impacting).

Application Decisions for Effective Software Releases

Distributed architectures introduce new challenges and considerations for releasing software and require changes at the application level. In this section you will explore some of the gotchas when releasing in a distributed architecture and how to resolve them.

Response Caching

Response caching can be a real issue when it comes to application components in particular gateways and proxies. Consider the following scenario. We try to perform a canary release of the Attendee service, and everything looks to be going nicely, so we proceed with the rollout of all new services. However, the service calling GET /attendees was using a proxy, which now bounces, producing 500s everywhere. It turns out the cached result was masking the fact that our new software was broken.

To avoid caching results it is important to set a header on the client making the GET request, i.e., Cache-Control: no-cache, no-store. Eventually the cache will expire and we achieve a consistent state.

Application-Level Header Propagation

Any API services that terminate an API request and create a request to another service need to copy headers across from the terminated request to the new request. For example, any tracing- or observability-related headers need to be added on to the downstream request to ensure distributed tracing is observed.

For authentication and authorization headers, it is important to have an opinion on what can safely be sent downstream. For example, forwarding an authentication header can end up with a service being able to impersonate another service or user, causing issues. An OAuth2 bearer token, however, is safe to send downstream (as long as the transport is secure).

Logging to Assist Debugging

Things are going to go wrong in a distributed architecture! Often, being able to see that a request made it to a service is really valuable, especially if you don't consider caching. It is useful to think of logs in two different types: journal and diagnostics. A *journal* allows the capturing of important transactions/events within the system and is used sparingly. An example of a journal event is the receipt of a new message to process and the outcome of that event. *Diagnostics* are more concerned with failures in the processing and any unexpected errors outside of a journal-based event. As part of the structured log, you can add a field to represent the log type, allowing quick access to either only journals or full diagnostics.

Considering an Opinionated Platform

Often there is no conscious decision about what approach to take with the decisions we have covered in this section, which can lead to repeated work or inconsistent approaches. One option to solve this problem is to create a platform team and develop an opinionated platform. The opinionated platform would make key decisions on how to solve problems as part of the technical platform, avoiding the need for every developer to implement the same platform features.

For opinionated platforms to be successful, they need to enhance the path to production, taking into account DevOps and other key factors required to operate on the platform. This is often referred to as the *paved path* or *golden path* to production. Creating a platform that development teams want to use and that makes solving business problems easier will have a far greater chance of adoption. It is important to remember that creating opinions creates constraints, so there is a trade-off between developer freedom and applications that work as expected within an organization.

ADR Guideline: Opinionated Platforms

Choosing to create an opinionated platform is most successful when the developers of the platform are involved in the design process. In the guideline in Table 5-3, you will explore what points to consider and the importance of involving developers to create a successful opinionated platform.

Table 5-3. ADR Guideline: Opinionated platforms

Decision	Should you adopt an opinionated platform for your deployments and releases?
Discussion Points	What are our languages for developing software in the organization? Is it possible to center around a few to live within the opinionated platform?
	Is the organization set up in a way where you can empower developers as customers and run the opinionated platform as an internal product?
	What are the constraints or features that are going to add benefit to introducing a platform? For example, should monitoring and observability be features supplied out of the box to developers?
	How do you update the platform recommendations and help provide changes to teams already using the platform?
Recommendations	Consider developers as customers of the platform product and create a mechanism that supports developers providing input.
	The key features should be as transparent as possible to developers (e.g., configures a library to introduce open telemetry).
	New applications always get the latest features in the stack. However, how do you ensure that existing platform users can easily get access to the latest features?

Summary

In this chapter we have provided an introduction to deploying and distributing software in an API architecture:

- A valuable starting point is to understand the importance of separating deployment and release. In existing applications, feature flagging is one approach to configuring and enabling new features at a code level.

- Traffic management provides a new opportunity to use the routing of traffic to model releases.

- Major, minor, and patch releases help to separate the style of release options. Applications that have a tightly coupled API may use a different strategy.

- You have reviewed the release strategies and the situations in which they apply, and you saw how tools like Argo can help to facilitate rollouts effectively.

- Monitoring and metrics are an important measure of success in an API platform. You have reviewed why some metrics can be gotchas and could suggest a problem where there isn't one. You have learned a primer to observability and why applying these technologies is critical to successfully operating an API platform.

- Finally, you explored application decisions to support effective rollouts and what platform owners may wish to consider when aiming for consistency across the plant.

Deploying and releasing APIs effectively is critical to a successful API-driven architecture. However, it is important to think about security threats API systems will face and consider how to effectively mitigate the risk. This is the focus of Chapter 6.

Operational Security: Threat Modeling for APIs

At this stage you have explored the full API Lifecycle—taking into consideration design and testing, options for deployment, and strategies for releasing APIs. The Attendee API may appear like it is ready to be exposed to external systems. APIs are quick to build, tricky to design for future compatibility, and even harder to secure. The truth is that developers and architects focus on delivering functionality, and security is often not considered until toward the end of a project.

In this chapter, you will see why security is important and how not having proper security in place can damage your reputation and be expensive. You will learn how to examine a system's architecture for security weaknesses and determine the threats that could be encountered within a production environment. Of course, you won't be able to identify all the threats—attackers are devious, and the threat landscape continually evolves—but the critical skill for architects is to be able to "shift left" the design and implementation of security concerns, both for themselves and for the wider development teams.[1] The earlier you consider security within your software development lifecycle (i.e., the further left this can be shifted), generally speaking, the easier and more cost effectively you can adapt to the evolving threat landscape. This will help you make informed decisions when engaging in the security design for APIs.

In "Enforce Security: Transport Security, Authentication, and Authorization" on page 100, we reviewed how communication within a control plane or system is possible to secure using mTLS. However, once "external" systems outside of the control plane's reach are introduced, a new approach is required.

---

[1] Ideally security should "start left" to bring security in as a foundation.

Case Study: Applying OWASP to the Attendee API

You will begin your journey toward designing secure systems with an introduction to threat modeling. You will then explore how to conduct a threat model exercise, using the Attendee service and API as an example, as shown in Figure 6-1.

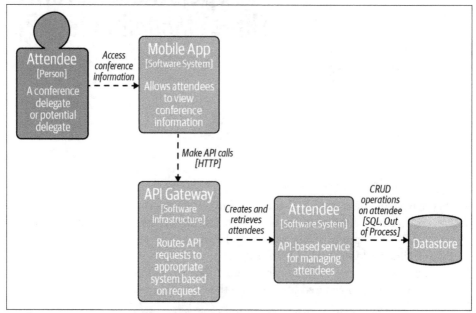

Figure 6-1. The Attendee API that will be used in the threat modeling exercise

A core component of threat modeling is looking for potential security weaknesses, so you will explore the OWASP API Security Top 10 (*https://oreil.ly/k9MSt*), which you can use both as a source of inspiration when hunting for issues and as a source of mitigations when you are attempting to address the threats found. By the end of the chapter you will understand what threat modeling is and how you can apply this to your own projects.[2]

Open Web Application Security Project (OWASP) is a nonprofit foundation that works to improve the security of software. The most well-known project by OWASP is the OWASP Top 10; this project is a list of the most critical security risks faced by web applications. In 2019 OWASP produced a new top 10 list—this was the API Security Top 10. The list is based on the work of security experts who examined security breaches and bug bounty programs, and penetration testers also gave their

---

2 For an exhaustive reference and description of ways to perform threat modeling, please refer to *Threat Modeling* by Izar Tarandach and Matthew J. Coles (O'Reilly).

input on what should be in this top 10. This is not an exhaustive list of all the threats you will face. However, you should keep them in your mind when looking at how your API might be exploited. These lists are updated periodically, so it is important to look for changes and updates to the top 10 as they evolve.

The Risk of Not Securing External APIs

Though security has become more appealing and been brought into the limelight as a topic,[3] it has struggled to gain the same popularity as technologies such as machine learning, big data, and quantum computing. For the majority of software professionals, security is not always at the forefront of their minds. Developers are focused on coding business solutions, SRE teams ensure the plant is running, and product owners focus on the planning of new valuable features. Security is often deferred, and if you are fortunate to have a security team, then it may get delegated to them. The perceived value for the customer is (normally) not in the security controls implemented but rather in the service that your system provides.

Security breaches can have catastrophic impact: there is a usually significant risk to an organization's reputation. Financially, the impacts are huge: "the average cost of a cyber-breach to a publicly traded company was $116 million" (*https://oreil.ly/W70CP*) and the average cost of a data breach for an organization in 2021 was $4.24m (*https://oreil.ly/FpH3D*), up 10% from the previous year.

Following are a few example headlines of security breaches that have had a huge cost, both financially and socially:

- Databases Leak Data Of 419 Million Users (*https://oreil.ly/iCZOb*)
- Data Breach Impacts 143 Million Americans (*https://oreil.ly/sK321*)
- Security Breach Exposes personal information of 47 Million Users (*https://oreil.ly/DREQ0*)
- $17.5 million settlement over data breach (*https://oreil.ly/RfiQh*)
- 106m customer records stolen and issued a $80m fine (*https://oreil.ly/8fR4j*)
- £16.4m fine for failings surrounding a cyber-attack (*https://oreil.ly/LnEuX*)

The last two articles are interesting, as the regulators issued penalties for breaking regulatory rules or not responding appropriately. It is important to look at your operating environment to see what requirements exist for client data governance. A fair assumption from users is that appropriate measures are being taken to protect their privacy and data; if not, your organization is accountable. One such regulatory

---

3 Individuals like Edward Snowden and TV shows like *Mr. Robot* have increased security conversations in the general public.

requirement is the General Data Protection Regulation (GDPR), which gives greater control to individuals over their personal information. These can carry serious financial penalties if not followed. Currently, the biggest fines issued for breaking GDPR include Amazon with a £636m fine (*https://oreil.ly/rcWyY*) and WhatsApp with a €225m fine (*https://oreil.ly/TuYnM*).

 The accountability of an organization goes beyond APIs and systems developed by the organization. Vendor products and open source software present real challenges if not carefully managed. Ensure that vendor products are held to the same standard that you would hold your own software development standards to. Open source software vulnerabilities can be wide reaching. Ensuring that an organization tracks Common Vulnerabilities and Exposures (CVEs) and is able to rebuild impacted software is critical.

Threat Modeling 101

Threat modeling is a "technique you can use to help you identify threats, attacks, vulnerabilities, and countermeasures that could affect your application" (*https://oreil.ly/ahFgn*). To use a real-world analogy, if you were conducting a threat modeling exercise for your house or apartment, you would identify things like points of entry (doors, windows) and whether you have given a front door key to a neighbor. This approach is beneficial as it is only possible to mitigate security risks once the threats have been clearly identified. It also helps to prioritize efforts to improve security and avoid meaningless efforts or security theater (*https://oreil.ly/peFDx*). To continue the house example, it would not be beneficial if you spent a large amount of money on a steel reinforced front door only to leave the key under your doormat or the flower pot right outside.

Threat modeling is a process that should be integrated into your entire software development lifecycle. Ideally it is conducted at the beginning of a project and is continually revisited as the system and architecture evolves. The good news is that there are a number of well-defined methodologies for threat modeling. In this book we will use the STRIDE methodology designed by Praerit Garg and Loren Kohnfelder at Microsoft. You'll learn more about this methodology later in the chapter.

Threat modeling of software systems has historically been performed using data flow diagrams (DFDs).[4] DFDs capture the dynamic (data flow) aspects of a system, while C4 models primarily capture the static (structural) aspects of the system. DFDs are simple to understand and data-centric, which makes it easy to see how data flows through the system. The core components for DFDs are:

---

4 For a full breakdown of DFDs, visit the OWASP DFD introduction page (*https://oreil.ly/0VlaM*).

External entities
> These are applications/services that are not part of your system. In our case this would be the mobile application.

Processes
> An application/task that is in our domain, such as the API gateway.

Datastores
> A location where data is stored. For the case study, this would be the database.

Data flows
> Connection that represents the flow of data, such as the mobile application to the API gateway.

Boundaries
> A privileged or trust boundary to show a change in trust levels. A boundary for the case study would be the internet boundary between the mobile application to the API gateway.

As part of our threat modeling, we have created a DFD as shown in Figure 6-2.

Thinking Like an Attacker

Architects and development teams can at times be reluctant to consider security issues, as they believe this is the job of a specialist team. However, who better than the people designing and building the key structural components of a software system to identify and understand potential weaknesses? Architects and security experts can then collaborate on addressing these problems and work together to explore different angles of attack. The good news is that to conduct a threat modeling exercise, you do not need to be a security expert yourself, but you need to think like an attacker or bad actor.

Thinking like an attacker is often easier than you think, as you do it all the time (just by asking yourself "what would the attacker do?")! For example, when you park your car in the evening, what do you do with your car keys? Do you leave them in the car? Probably not if it is left on the street, though you may if it is in a garage. You could leave the keys by the front door. However, someone could use a coat hanger through the letter box to take your keys, or, if a wireless car, the attacker could use signal amplification. So do you take them upstairs? And with the rise of electronic locking systems and immobilizers, do you put them in a Faraday cage (*https://oreil.ly/AAdsK*)? What you are doing here is looking at a situation and evaluating the threat and weighing up the risk. You now need to apply this approach to designing software systems, with a little help from existing well-defined methodologies.

How to Threat Model

As with many methodologies within software design and development, there are well-defined goals, approaches, and techniques to threat modeling that architects and engineers have refined over the years. The high-level approach to threat modeling is:

1. Identify your objectives—Create a list of the business and security objectives. Keep them simple (e.g., avoid unauthorized access).

2. Gather the right information—Generate a high-level design of the system and ensure you have the right information. To be able to understand how your systems work and work together, this will include having the right people involved in the conversation.

3. Decompose the system—Break down your high-level design so that you can start to model the threats. This may require multiple models and diagrams.

4. Identify threats—Systematically look for threats to your systems.

5. Evaluate the risk of the threats—Prioritize threats to focus on the most likely ones, then identify mitigations to these likely threats.

6. Validate—Ask yourself and your team if the changes in place have been successful. Should you perform another review?

Let's now explore these steps in more detail, using the case study as the system that you want to perform a threat modeling exercise on.

Step 1: Identify Your Objectives

The first step of threat modeling is to identify your objectives; this is the driver for performing the threat modeling. When deciding objectives for your own systems, you should focus on what security goals you are trying to achieve. These goals should be sourced from across your entire organization, and not just your team and the InfoSec teams. Security objectives are often driven from business goals, such as avoiding data leakage to prevent being sued or being compliant with regulations like GDPR. If these are just sourced from your immediate area, then you do not have a complete picture of the most important issues that face your organization. Your objectives for the Attendee service is to prepare the API for external consumption by third parties by ensuring that the OWASP Top 10 are mitigated.

Step 2: Gather the Right Information

Once you have the goals in mind, Step 2 of threat modeling is acquiring the information about how the system works. With threat modeling, you need to bring in experts on each area of the system and associated codebases or products. This is to ensure that you understand how everything works and that no hidden assumptions are made. For the Attendee API, this will require bringing in members of the team who work across all of your components; mobile, gateway, databases, and Attendee service.

Step 3: Decompose the System

The third step of the threat modeling process is to create a diagram of the system that shows the component interactions with the flow of data. The information gathered collaboratively is then used to create the DFDs. Creating diagrams can be time-consuming, so we recommend using dedicated threat modeling tooling. For the case study data flow diagram, shown in Figure 6-2, we used the Microsoft Threat Modeling Tool, although other tools are available.[5]

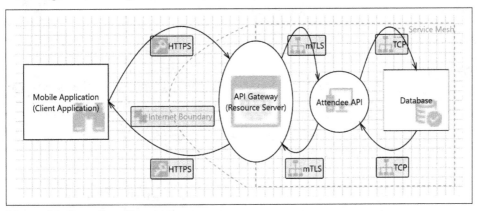

Figure 6-2. Data flow diagram

Step 4: Identify Threats—Taking This in Your STRIDE

The fourth step of threat modeling is all about looking at the threats to the system. When you start looking at the data flow diagram, it is important to keep your threat modeling objectives in mind, otherwise it can be tempting to go off on a tangent.

The benefit of using the dedicated Microsoft Threat Modeling Tool is that it can conduct some automated analysis for you using the STRIDE methodology. The generated list is not complete, but it can be used as a starting point. The list of generated threats for our Attendee API System is seen in Figure 6-3. In this case the tooling has found 27 potential threats.

---

5 You can find the Microsoft Threat Modeling Tool here (*https://oreil.ly/ahFgn*) and explore other options via the OWASP Threat Dragon GitHub repo (*https://oreil.ly/NXF8U*).

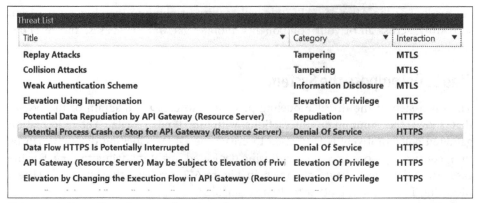

Title	Category	Interaction
Replay Attacks	Tampering	MTLS
Collision Attacks	Tampering	MTLS
Weak Authentication Scheme	Information Disclosure	MTLS
Elevation Using Impersonation	Elevation Of Privilege	MTLS
Potential Data Repudiation by API Gateway (Resource Server)	Repudiation	HTTPS
Potential Process Crash or Stop for API Gateway (Resource Server)	Denial Of Service	HTTPS
Data Flow HTTPS Is Potentially Interrupted	Denial Of Service	HTTPS
API Gateway (Resource Server) May be Subject to Elevation of Privi	Elevation Of Privilege	HTTPS
Elevation by Changing the Execution Flow in API Gateway (Resourc	Elevation Of Privilege	HTTPS

Figure 6-3. Data flow diagram threat analysis

The STRIDE acronym stands for:[6]

Spoofing

> Breaching the user's authentication information. In this case, the hacker has obtained the user's personal information or something that enables him to replay the authentication procedure. Spoofing threats are associated with a wily hacker being able to impersonate a valid system user or resource to get access to the system and thereby compromise system security.

Tampering

> Modifying system or user data with or without detection. An unauthorized change to stored or in-transit information, formatting of a hard disk, a malicious intruder introducing an undetectable network packet in a communication, and making an undetectable change to a sensitive file are all tampering threats.

Repudiation

> An untrusted user performing an illegal operation without the ability to be traced. Repudiability threats are associated with users (malicious or otherwise) who can deny a wrongdoing without any way to prove otherwise.

Information disclosure

> Compromising the user's private or business-critical information. Information disclosure threats expose information to individuals who are not supposed to see it. A user's ability to read a file that she or he was not granted access to, as well as an intruder's ability to read the data while in transit between two computers, are both disclosure threats. Note that this threat differs from a spoofing threat in that

---

6 The definitions used come from the paper "The threats to our Products" (*https://oreil.ly/a7NHe*) (download) written in 1999 by Loren Kohnfelder and Praerit Garg, the creators of STRIDE.

here the perpetrator gets access to the information directly rather than by having to spoof a legitimate user.

Denial of Service

Making the system temporarily unavailable or unusable, such as those attacks that could force a reboot or restart of the user's machine. When an attacker can temporarily make the system resources (processing time, storage, etc.) unavailable or unusable, we have a denial of service threat. We must protect against certain types of DoS threats for improved system availability and reliability. However, some types of DoS threats are very hard to protect against, so at a minimum, we must identify and rationalize such threats.[7]

Elevation of privilege

An unprivileged user gains privileged access and thereby has sufficient access to completely compromise or destroy the entire system. The more dangerous aspect of such threats is compromising the system in undetectable ways whereby the user is able to take advantage of the privileges without the knowledge of system administrators. Elevation of privilege threats include those situations where an attacker is allowed more privilege than should properly be granted, completely compromising the security of the entire system and causing extreme system damage. Here the attacker has effectively penetrated all system defenses and become part of the trusted system itself and can do anything.

You can use this acronym when evaluating your system at each point of your architecture to see what threats exist. There are also other threat modeling methodologies that can be used.[8]

As you look at the data flow diagram in Figure 6-2, you can see the boundary that exists between the client application and the API gateway. An API gateway is often located at the edge of our network and can also be internet-facing, as you learned in "Where Is an API Gateway Deployed?" on page 59. You are going to explore a number of different threats related to the API gateway and learn how this can be used to protect your system against many of the common API vulnerabilities. If you protect your system at the edge, the risks can often be reduced throughout your system, but this is not always the case. You will learn more about the move from zonal architecture, where traffic inside your security perimeter is treated differently than traffic outside, toward zero-trust models, where traffic is constantly re-authenticated, in "From Zonal Architecture to Zero Trust" on page 217.

---

7 Though this definition is about individual machines, the context of what a denial of service attack is, is still the same today. It's about taking resources offline.

8 Two additional methodologies include P.A.S.T.A (*https://oreil.ly/OYYQq*) and Trike (*https://oreil.ly/TQayg*).

Your case study security goals are quite specific: the Attendee API should be prepared for external consumption, and to achieve this we will ensure that each process mitigates the OWASP API Security Top 10 issues. As this is a direct objective, the DFD can be used to map data flows to the issues and vulnerabilities listed on the OWASP site. However, typically a threat modeling objective may be something like "Prevent data leakage of PII to conform with GDPR," or "Provide 99.9% availability for APIs to fulfill contractual obligations." This second objective may not appear to be related to security, however you will want to keep DoS at the forefront of your mind, as not fulfilling this obligation, even when under a DoS attack, could result in a financial penalty.

Let's now review the system and apply STRIDE. To highlight the OWASP API Security Top 10, the threats will be grouped under the applicable STRIDE value. This is to showcase both the application of STRIDE and the OWASP API Security Top 10 along with their mitigations. When you are identifying threats in your own architecture, it is recommended you apply STRIDE to each process and connection—this is known as STRIDE per element.

Spoofing

Spoofing is when a person or program is able to masquerade as another person or program. To mitigate this, you will want to authenticate any requests that are made and ensure that they are legitimate. Within the OWASP API Top 10, one of the security issues is Broken User Authentication (*https://oreil.ly/59Tgo*). This is definitely related to the spoofing category, so you are going to want to ensure that the authentication flow is not broken. To learn more about this, "Authentication" on page 167 provides information and an example using the case study.

Tampering

Next in the STRIDE methodology is "tampering," with the goal that users or clients should not be able to modify the system, application, or data in an unintended manner. For example, it should not be possible that a bad actor can modify the Attendee service by redirecting traffic intended for the Attendee service to an external location, or by updating attendee user data inappropriately. There are two primary ways that tampering occurs: through payload injection and mass assignment.

Payload injection.   Payload injection occurs when a bad actor attempts to inject a malicious payload into the request made to an API or application. Note that in the OWASP Security Top 10, this relates not only to the commonly known SQL injection but also to injection for any user input. In the case study, you can aim to prevent injection attacks early in the request handling chain, by using the API gateway to validate that the request made conforms to a defined contract or schema. Any request that does not fulfill the contract can be denied or the corresponding traffic dropped.

This approach is described in "Practical Application of OpenAPI Specifications" on page 13. Increasingly, OpenAPI Specifications are used for validating HTTP requests.

It is worth mentioning that although input validation is valuable when conducted at the API gateway, it does not mean you can omit further input validation and sanitization within the backend services; trust, but verify!

An example of this for the Attendee service would be receiving the following POST request with this sample payload to create a user:

```
POST /attendees
{
  "name": "Danny B",
  "age": 35,
  "profile": "Hax; DROP ALL TABLES; --"
}
```

The OpenAPI Specification for the Attendee API defines that `name` should only accept letters, `age` accepts positive integers, and `profile` accepts letters, numbers, and special characters in the value (because it is for the user to write a little about themselves). The API gateway, which in this case is performing the input validation, will inspect the payload and only let it pass if the input validation is successful. Even if the input validation passes, the Attendee API should still sanitize the input to prevent an attack. The Attendee service would use prepared statements when communicating with the database. It is important to have multiple lines of defense in case one of them fails.

Mass assignment. Modifiable properties that are bound to database entities are vulnerable to being inappropriately changed. They can be exploited by the vulnerability known as mass assignment (*https://oreil.ly/5Q6aC*). This is an important case to consider, particularly if your underlying application uses the Active Record pattern[9] or some form of automated entity database serialization/deserialization, as often provided by object-relational mapping (ORM) frameworks.

Let's examine a hypothetical case for our Attendee API. Imagine that there is a property called `devices` that is returned when making a request for an attendee. This property is designed to be an externally read-only list of devices that the attendee has used to connect to the API, and this should only be updated by the attendee application code.

A bad actor makes a GET request for an attendee (`/attendees/123456`) and receives the following response:

---

9 The Active Record pattern is the practice of exposing a data object and its functions, which more or less map to the underlying database model.

```
{
  "name": "Danny B",
  "age": 35,
  "devices": [
    "iPhone",
    "Firefox"
  ]
}
```

Now the bad actor issues a PUT request to the Attendee API to update the `age` attribute, and they also maliciously attempt to update the `devices` list:

```
PUT /attendees/123456
{
  "name": "Danny B",
  "age": 36,
  "devices": [
    "vulnerableDevice"
  ]
}
```

Any data in the `devices` list should be ignored when the entity is saved to the database. Mass Assignment is typical where client input data is bound to internal objects without thought of the repercussions, which is often a consequence when exposing a database API as a web-based API. In Chapter 1 the concerns of exposing an underlying data model are discussed from a usability point of view, which provides additional reasons not to do this.

This vulnerability is not something that can typically be solved at the API gateway level; instead, this must be guarded against within the API implementation itself.

Repudiation

According to STRIDE, a repudiation attack happens when an application or system does not adopt controls to properly track and log users' actions, which permits malicious manipulation or forging the identification of new actions. For many requests that are made to an API, it is important to understand the details of the request, the payload, and the response generated (and corresponding internal actions). In certain regulatory or compliance use cases, you may need to arbitrarily inspect what was in an exchange. If a request can be repudiated—i.e., there is no proof of what the attacker has done—then the attacker can reject or disagree that they have tried to perform any such malicious action. This is why repudiation threats (the "R" in STRIDE) are included in STRIDE methodology.

To identify requests that are passing through your system and to understand what is happening, you need to add logging and monitoring. Insufficient logging and monitoring (*https://oreil.ly/Gmzj6*) is a vulnerability in the OWASP API Top 10. With all requests from users flowing through the API gateway, this is an obvious centralized point to monitor the traffic and to log the requests and responses. Many API gateways will provide this functionality out-of-the-box, but you need to understand how to store, search, and extract this information, particularly over the course of time. As with any disaster recovery and business continuity (DR/BC) capabilities, logging and monitoring must be regularly verified in order to ensure that you are capturing what is expected.

Information disclosure

Information disclosure is the "I" in STRIDE, and this is focused on not exposing information that should only be used internally or kept secret. Two common antipatterns in this category of threat include excessive data exposure and improper assets management.

Excessive data exposure. The OWASP API Top 10 Excessive data exposure (*https://oreil.ly/5pHdH*) is focused on making sure data is not exposed inappropriately. As a hypothetical scenario, imagine the Attendee service holds PII such as a passport number. When designing your API, it is important to prevent the inappropriate exposure of this data. It is all too easy to make naive assumptions about how an API will be called, especially as a system evolves over time. APIs that were initially intended only for internal consumption can be exposed publicly (with good intentions), or a previous API that was only accessible to a trusted client application can be opened to public consumption.

If an API is called via a web application, it is easy to examine requests, responses, and corresponding payloads via the developer tools included within modern web browsers. For example, any user information request made to the Attendee API may accidentally return passport information:

```
{
  "values": [
    {
      "id": "0",
      "name": "Danny B",
      "age": 65,
      "email", "danny.b@masteringapis.com",
      "passport": "Abc12408NJUILM"
    },
    {
      "id": "1",
      "name": "Jimmy G",
      "age": 93,
      "email": "jimmy.g@masteringapis.com",
      "passport": "ZYX123ASJJ0072M"
    }
  ]
}
```

It is possible to perform response validation in an API gateway. However, it is the responsibility of those building the API to know what they are exposing and to not expose sensitive data that should be private. Any implementation in an API gateway should be seen as the verification of last resort (or part of a "belt and braces" approach to verification). You will also need to ensure that you don't leak sensitive data back to calling clients, such as the versions of a web server being used or an application stack trace that has been generated as a result of a crash.

Improper assets management.   Improper assets management (*https://oreil.ly/ZViZw*) typically occurs as your systems evolve, and the organization loses track of which APIs (and which versions) are exposed or which APIs were designed for internal consumption only. As a hypothetical example with the Attendee API, it could be possible to have multiple versions of the API deployed into production, with an early version of the API exposing all attendee properties by default. As the data model evolves, several private fields that contain PII are added, and new versions of the Attendee service remove this information when the API is queried. Even if the old version of the Attendee service does not fully function, it can still be used to extract the additional information contained in the data model.

A hypothetical example for the Attendee service is that the `/beta/attendees` endpoint is publicly exposed. This early version was exposed for some testing and then forgotten about. As there is no proper management over exposed assets, it is not noticed, but an attacker could try to call the endpoint. If all API traffic is managed through your gateway, you should have a registration within it to know what exists. You can also examine requests and look for anomalies of requests called to unexpected endpoints.

To counteract this problem, an API management or developer portal platform can be used to catalog and track all APIs deployed to production. Many API Management solutions include this functionality as standard, as it is seen as a vital component to manage the lifecycle of APIs.

Denial of service

Within the STRIDE methodology, the "D" is focused on denial of service (DoS). A DoS attack attempts to overwhelm a system or any of its defenses for malicious purposes. For example, a firewall that becomes overloaded may default to allowing all traffic, which enables an attacker to make malicious calls that previously would have been blocked. Or a bad actor may simply want to deny availability of a critical service, such as a voting website. By overloading the system with traffic, no legitimate requests can be made and no user can vote. The OWASP API Top 10 has a security issue (*https://oreil.ly/ccNCH*) that covers DoS extensively.

The Attendee API needs to meet your scalability demands, but it should also guard against becoming overloaded with traffic. To accomplish this, you can use the techniques of rate limiting and load shedding.

Malicious DoS attacks or Distributed DoS attacks are best handled by specialist service providers, software, or hardware. For example, many content delivery network (CDN) providers include DoS prevention by default, and most public vendors offer a similar service that can be attached to public domain names and IP addresses.

 A denial of service can occur by accident, such as "friendly fire DoS," that is caused by your own systems. As systems evolve, it is not uncommon to accidentally introduce circular dependencies, and given the right conditions, this can involve internal services calling each other's, APIs in an infinite loop. This is why implementing rate limiting and error monitoring on internal API calls can be invaluable!

Rate limiting and load shedding. Rate limiting, as the name suggests, limits the number of requests that can be made to your API over a period of time.[10] The use of rate limiting typically refers to rejecting traffic based on properties of individual requests (too many from a given user, client application, or location). Load shedding refers to rejecting requests based on the overall state of the system (database at capacity, no more worker threads available). By default, many applications, web servers, and API gateways do not implement rate limiting or load shedding and the corresponding failure modes may be undefined. Performing load testing can provide insight into the limits, breaking points, and visible behavior.

 It is important to understand if your API gateway and other edge security tools have "fail open" or "fail closed" polices. Fail open policies will continue to permit access to your services even if there are failure conditions. A hypothetical example is that in medical emergency services, it is more important to serve information about a patient's medical history than to authenticate the request. A fail close policy is when connections will be blocked in failure conditions. There is no single correct implementation, and the default should meet your requirements. For example, the majority of financial APIs would want a fail closed policy by default, whereas a public weather service may implement a fail open policy.

---

10 One of the authors, Daniel, has written a series of articles about rate limiting and its application to API gateways. The first article of the series is available online at: "Part 1: Rate Limiting: A Useful Tool with Distributed Systems" (*https://oreil.ly/2rzHx*).

For the case study, the most appropriate location to implement rate limiting would be the API gateway. To perform rate limiting, you will typically want to identify the originator of each request (or set of requests on aggregate). Example properties include IP address, geo-location, or a client ID that is sent by the client. You may not want to limit on an incoming property and instead treat all requests as being equal.

Once a request property has been selected (none, or otherwise), a strategy needs to be applied to perform the limiting. The most common examples include:

Fixed window
 A fixed limit within a period, e.g., 2,400 requests per day.

Sliding window
 A limit within the last period, e.g., 100 requests within the last hour.

Token bucket
 A set number of total requests are allowed (bucket of tokens) and each request takes a token when a request is made. The bucket is refilled periodically.

Leaky bucket
 Like the Token bucket, however, the rate at which requests are processed is a fixed rate; this is the leak of the bucket.

You can see rate limiting enforcement in Figure 6-4.

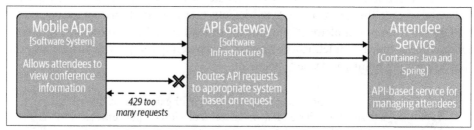

Figure 6-4. Rate limiting example with the API gateway

An example of load shedding is shown in Figure 6-5.

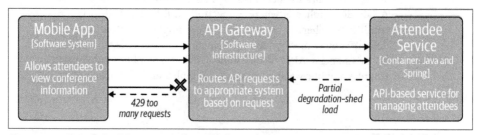

Figure 6-5. Load shedding example with the API gateway

Elevation of Privilege

The final letter "E" in STRIDE is focused on "Elevation of Privilege." This occurs when a user or application finds a way to perform a task that is outside the scope of what should be allowed given the current security context—e.g., a user is able to execute tasks that are only meant to be executed by an administrator. The two OWASP Security Top 10 that relate to this are:

- Broken Object Level Authorization (*https://oreil.ly/26Dpz*)
- Broken Function Level Authorization (*https://oreil.ly/gPaqN*)

These are both focused on enforcing authorization and ensuring that requests to your API are entitled to perform the operation. This was covered in "Authorization Enforcement" on page 185.

Security misconfiguration

Security misconfiguration is not limited to one of these STRIDE categories, as misconfiguration can happen in a range of places, such as information disclosure, where a permission is incorrectly assigned, or within denial of service and a rate-limiting policy is incorrectly set to fail open. Security misconfiguration is focused on ensuring that the security that you have in place is not incorrectly configured, and it is another piece that you must think about when evaluating each element of STRIDE for threats. It is a truism that having misconfigured security can be worse than having no security at all, as users behave very differently when they believe their actions and data are not secure. There are certain features of security that you are most likely always going to want, such as Transport Layer Security (TLS), and others that may be bespoke to an API or a setup, such as IP allowlisting.[11]

Within our case study, the API gateway is a key place where security misconfiguration could have a disastrous effect. Extra attention must be paid to its configuration as the API gateway is acting as the "front door."

TLS termination. TLS will ensure that the traffic that you receive has not been intercepted and modified. Also, TLS certificates provide information about the owner of a domain, so you can be confident in who you are contacting. As the API gateway deals with all incoming traffic, TLS can be enabled here. Having a centralized location to manage the external TLS certificates for incoming requests is also convenient. This, in comparison to not using a gateway, where TLS certificates need to be added to each web server, proxy, and application that is handling request traffic, is more difficult to manage and more likely prone to error. It is important to use a modern protocol and

---

11 IP allowlists are a literal list of IPs that are allowed to connect to your system. If the IP that connects is not in that list, then the request is rejected.

strong encryption, and, at the time of writing, using TLS 1.2 or later is recommended due to known issues with earlier versions of this protocol.[12]

Cross-Origin Request Sharing (CORS). CORS is an HTTP-header-based mechanism that allows a server to indicate any origins (domain, scheme, or port) other than its own from which a browser should permit loading resources. Supporting CORS is a core requirement for any modern web browser, and for security reasons, browsers restrict cross-origin HTTP requests initiated from scripts. CORS works by the web browser performing "preflight" requests to see if it is allowed to make the desired call. You can explore this by checking the "Developer Tools" features of a browser. In the "Network Calls" section, you can typically see the HTTP Options requests; these are commonly CORS requests.[13]

Security directive hardening. A request to an API endpoint can contain an arbitrary payload, including headers and a data payload. Although all genuine requests will correspond with your expected contract, an attacker can add unknown, incorrect, or malformed headers and data in an attempt to gain access or otherwise compromise your system. Actions need to be taken to mitigate this. In our case study, for example, you will want to think about implementing an HTTP header allowlist in the API gateway and removing all invalid HTTP headers. An attacker could send through additional HTTP headers to the Attendee API like `X-Assert-Role=Admin` or `X-Impersonate=Admin`. The attacker would hope that these headers will not be removed and are used internally, which may give some extra privileges.

Step 5: Evaluate Threat Risks

When you perform your own threat modeling and end up with a list of threats, it is important to understand the priority of fixing them. This is what Step 5 of the threat modeling process is about. To evaluate threats, you can employ a qualitative risk calculation known as DREAD. Like STRIDE, DREAD was developed at Microsoft. This methodology provides you with an approach to start adding risk values to threats. Although DREAD is no longer used by Microsoft, it is still used by many companies and promoted as a useful way to establish a metric on the risk of a threat.

DREAD has a simple scoring system based on the underlying acronym:

Damage
    How bad would an attack be?

---

12 Most commercial API gateways will by default only allow current versions of TLS to be used, so you will need to enable weaker versions with known vulnerabilities if this is required.

13 To read a full explanation of CORS, you can take a look at this article by Mozilla (*https://oreil.ly/k70rh*).

Reproducibility
>   Can an attack be easily reproduced?

Exploitability
>   How easy is it to mount a successful attack?

Affected Users
>   How many users are impacted?

Discoverability
>   What is the likelihood of this threat being discovered?

Each threat is scored against these DREAD categories, where each category is scored from 1–10. The risk value assigned to a threat is (Damage + Reproducibility + Exploitability + Affected User + Discoverability) / 5.

In this example for our case study, you will look at the threat shown in Figure 6-6. This threat is a DDoS attack against the API gateway where no rate limiting is in place.

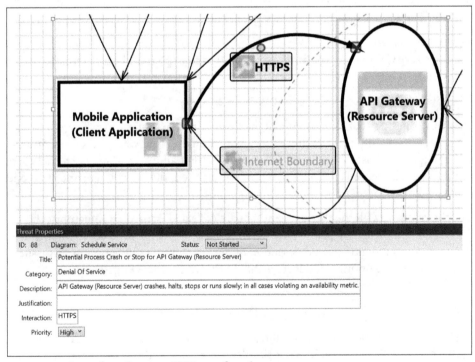

Figure 6-6. Data flow diagram TCP spoofing threat

Here is the ranking of this threat:

Damage: 8
> There is no rate limiting in place. This is a serious cause for concern as it allows anyone to send as many requests to the API gateway as they like, and potentially overload it, making it unusable.

Reproducibility: 8
> Calling the API gateway repeatedly with many requests every second will start to degrade and eventually stop the gateway from working.

Exploitability: 5
> The attacker can be outside our network to start attempting to run a DoS attack. The API gateway first checks the authentication and authorization to enforce the request. This means that the request must come from one of our legitimate and known client applications that integrate with our system.

Affected Users: 10
> This can have devastating effects because if the gateway is unavailable, it will affect all our users.

Discoverability: 10
> This is trivial to discover for anyone wanting to exploit and cause damage to our system.

The total score is (8 + 8 + 5 + 10 + 10) / 5 = 8.2.

It is worth noting that the values assigned to the risk are subjective. To get a somewhat consistent rating, for each category you should define what the values mean—for example, if all users are affected, the score is 10; if all internal or all external users are affected, the score is 7; if half of a group is affected, the score is a 3; and if no one is affected, the score is 0.

For the case study, all the threats identified are collected, scored, and then prioritized. In this case the highest-priority item is the lack of DDoS protection for the API gateway. As you identified in this section of the chapter, the mitigation to this issue is to implement rate limiting and load shedding for within the API gateway.

Other Risk Evaluation Tools

There are other ways to evaluate threats—one of them is DREAD-D (pronounced Dread minus D). In the DREAD risk calculation, one of the D's is Discoverability, which in some cases could be security through obscurity (*https://oreil.ly/rGpCD*), which is a terrible way to protect any data. So the Discoverability element is dropped; this why it is called DREAD-D. Another tool that can be used is the Common Vulnerability Scoring System (CVSS) (*https://oreil.ly/YJmOE*), which can be used to

---

measure the severity (i.e., the damage) of an exploited vulnerability. CVSS is used by NIST to evaluate CVEs, so if you ever look at a CVE, a CVSS can be found. For example, you can see this looking at the Log4J CVE (*https://oreil.ly/d4EMu*) and the NIST CVSS (*https://oreil.ly/XIcbd*).

Step 6: Validation

The sixth and final step of the threat modeling process is to validate that your security objectives are complete and ask if another review is needed. As part of threat modeling, you should have evaluated all the threats that are discovered and identified and taken action to mitigate the risks. You also want to ensure that you have completed the security objectives that you set out at the beginning of the threat modeling exercise. Threat modeling should be a recursive process with each run through the process identifying previously unknown issues. You should also periodically and continually run the threat modeling process, especially when adding new functionality to the system, but also as the external threat environment continually evolves.

Threat modeling is a skill and it takes time to learn the process itself, and it is also time-consuming. However, as with any skill, the more it is used and integrated into your regular workflow, the easier it gets.

Summary

In this chapter you have learned how to conduct a threat modeling exercise, both against the case study and also how to apply it to your own systems and APIs:

- There are strong financial penalties and reputational damage for failing to secure APIs.
- Threat modeling of an API-based system typically begins by creating a data flow diagram (DFD). Automated tooling can be used in order to rapidly analyze and identify potential threats.
- You don't need to be a security expert to conduct threat modeling, and a key skill is "thinking like an attacker."
- The process of threat modeling includes: identifying your objectives, gathering the right information, decomposing the system, identifying threats, evaluating the risk of those threats, and validating the results and actions.
- The OWASP API Security Top 10 is an excellent resource to understand the threats you can expect.

- The STRIDE methodology focuses your action on the threats of spoofing, tampering, repudiation, information disclosure, denial of service, and elevation of privilege.

- The DREAD methodology can be used to calculate a qualitative risk metric that can help you prioritize which threats to mitigate first.

- Within an API-based system, an API gateway can often provide high-level mitigation to risks that have been identified. However, as systems become more distributed, you should always consider individual service implementations and interservice communication.

You have seen a variety of threats that exist and ways to mitigate them. However, when you are returning data to the API consumer, you want to ensure that they are who they say they are, and the API consumer can only perform actions that they have permissions for. To see how you identify who the callee is and what they can do, you will take a deeper dive into authentication and authorization in the next chapter.

CHAPTER 7

API Authentication and Authorization

In the previous chapter you learned how to threat model API-based systems and about the OWASP API Security Top 10. The Attendee API is ready to receive traffic from the outside world; however, how exactly is the consumer of the API identified? In this chapter we are going to explore authentication and authorization for APIs. Authentication tells us who the callee is and authorization tells us what they are allowed to do.

We will begin by highlighting what authentication and authorization is for APIs. This leads to the importance of securing APIs and the potential limitations with using API keys and tokens. OAuth2 is a token-based authorization framework introduced in 2012 and has rapidly become the industry standard for securing APIs and determining what actions an application can perform against an API. A large part of this chapter will focus on OAuth2 and the range of security approaches offered for both end users and system-based interactions. Consumers of APIs will sometimes need to know details of the user they are acting on behalf of—to show how this can be achieved we will introduce OIDC.

The chapter will illustrate the different approaches to security by looking to prepare the Attendee API for external usage by the CFP system.

Authentication

Authentication is the act of verifying an identity. For the case of a user, the most traditional method is that the user presents their credentials in the form of a username and the password. It is now becoming more common for Multi-Factor Authentication (MFA) (*https://oreil.ly/4WQkd*) to be part of a standard login flow. MFA is useful to give higher levels of assurance that the user is who they say they are. For machine-to-machine authentication, credentials can be in the form of keys or certificates. By verifying the identity of the presented credentials, we know who is trying to communicate with our systems.

Let's look at this in the context of our Attendee service. The Attendee API contains personally identifiable information (PII) such as name and email address, which a user expects to be protected. In order to protect this information, the first step is to challenge and identify the caller of the API. Asserting this identity is called authentication. Once the caller is authenticated, the Attendee API establishes what the caller is allowed to access and retrieve: this type of entitlement checking is authorization.

Figure 7-1 demonstrates the interaction with the Attendee API. The mobile application connects via the API gateway and queries the Attendee API. Another interaction follows a similar path from the CFP system, however the CFP system is owned by a third party. Let's consider the options that we have for authenticating an end user (the mobile application user and the CFP system speakers) and a system-to-system interaction (the CFP system).

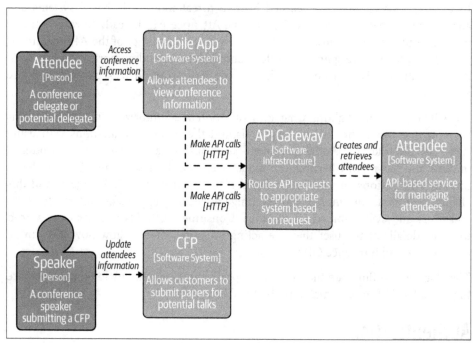

Figure 7-1. Securing our case study

End-User Authentication with Tokens

The mobile application is acting on behalf of the attendee and retrieves and displays information about the attendees. In token-based authentication, the user would enter their username and password, which is exchanged for a token. The token issued depends on the implementation, but in the simplest case it could be an opaque string. The token is sent in the REST request as part of the Authentication Bearer header (*https://oreil.ly/cU6Al*). Tokens are sensitive and it is important that the REST request is sent over HTTPS to secure the information in transit. Once a token is received as part of a request, it is inspected and checked to confirm the token's validity. Figure 7-2 demonstrates a historically typical token lookup process where the token is stored in a database.

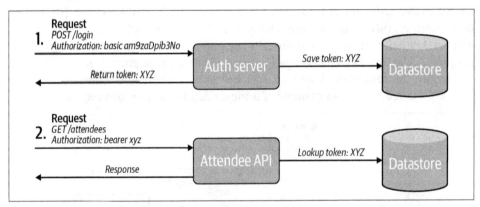

Figure 7-2. Server-side token lookup verification process

The token should have a limited lifetime—for example, an hour—and after the token expires, the user would need to obtain a new token. Tokens have the advantage that long-lived credentials, such as passwords, are not going across the network for every request to access resources.

Things might seem ideal on the surface with tokens; however, a major disadvantage is the user having to enter the username and password into the application that is making calls to an API to retrieve their data. Also, when a token is placed into storage, looking up the token to check validity each time can be a performance concern and would need to be mitigated. What would be preferable is to use a token that has integrity and can be validated in-process.

It is possible to access APIs using HTTP Basic, however, if a third-party application asks to access an API on your behalf, it means handing over your username and password.[1] We recommend that you do not allow HTTP Basic to be used to access your APIs.

System-to-System Authentication

In some situations an end user is not involved in the interaction and system-to-system communication is required. One option would be to use an API key, which does not conform to any particular standard. Whenever you do use an API key, it should be secure, meaning that it should be generated using a cryptographically secure random number generator and of an unguessable length. Typically API keys are 32-character-length strings (256 bits). If the API key is guessable (short and deterministic), this creates a vulnerability of a client being hacked. To access an API with an API key, you simply add the API key into a request header and send it to the endpoint.[2] The API key is associated with an application or project, so it is possible to identify the requester.[3] Using an API key is very similar to using a password. Figure 7-3 demonstrates an example of using an API key as part of a request.

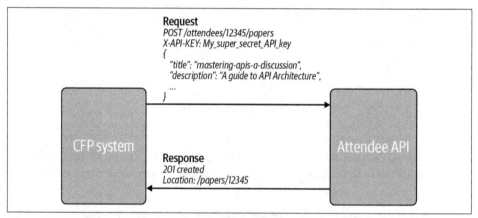

Figure 7-3. External CFP system calling Attendee API with an API key

---

1 If you do not know what HTTP Basic is, refer to the spec rfc7617 (*https://oreil.ly/NAKYY*).

2 The request header is either a custom header (e.g., X-API-KEY: My_super_secret_API_Key) or the authorization header.

3 Google has a good piece on this here (*https://oreil.ly/fraOb*).

Why You Shouldn't Mix Keys and Users

Consider the scenario where a speaker is using the CFP system, owned by a third party, and the CFP is requesting an update to the email address associated with that user's data. Just because the CFP system is using an API key and can be identified does not mean that this third-party system should be able to assert who the end user is or who they are acting on behalf of. This puts trust of the entire system in the hands of the third party. A solution to this would be that the CFP system also passes the user's username and password (using HTTP Basic) along with the API key to allow the Attendee service to authenticate the user. However, as we have already warned, this means that the user must hand their username and password for the Attendee service to the CFP system, which is undesirable. The ideal scenario would be a situation where the CFP system can call the Attendee service, but any request performed on behalf of a user by the CFP system does not require sharing credentials and is done with the user's specific approval. The solution to this problem is in essence the use of OAuth2.

OAuth2

OAuth2 is a token-based authorization framework and has been around since 2012. It is the replacement for OAuth (*https://oreil.ly/hQl1g*), which is still around—however, it is used in very few places. OAuth2 allows a user to consent that a third-party application can access their data on their behalf. The consent that the user gives is the authorization—they are allowing or denying the access. OAuth2 removes the need for a user to hand over their credentials to the third party, which gives the user control over their data. This makes OAuth2 appealing as it supports the challenges faced in the previous section.

In order to explore OAuth2 further, it is important to first understand the different roles within the OAuth2 specification. The definitions have been taken directly from the OAuth2 specification (*https://oreil.ly/I9I6b*):

Resource Owner
> An entity capable of granting access to a protected resource. When the resource owner is a person, it is referred to as an end-user.

Authorization Server
> The server issuing access tokens to the client after successfully authenticating the resource owner and obtaining authorization. Most identity providers, such as Google or Auth0, will be OAuth2 authorization servers.

Client

An application making protected resource requests on behalf of the resource owner and with its authorization.

Resource Server

The server hosting the protected resources, capable of accepting and responding to protected resource requests using access tokens.

Authorization Server Role with API Interactions

The authorization server has two endpoints:

- The authorization endpoint is used when a *resource owner* needs to authorize access to protected resources.

- The token endpoint is used by the *client* to get an access token.

If the Attendee service was called directly by the client, then the Attendee service would be the *resource server* as it is hosting protected resources. However, a resource server does not need to be an individual application; it could represent a complete system. One popular pattern is to use the API gateway as a resource server, as shown in Figure 7-4. The two clients, the mobile application and the CFP system, are calling the Attendee service via an API gateway. There could be multiple services behind the API gateway but for the client the API gateway would still be the resource server as it is hosting the protected resources. The two resource owners in this case are the attendees using the mobile app and the speakers using the CFP system.

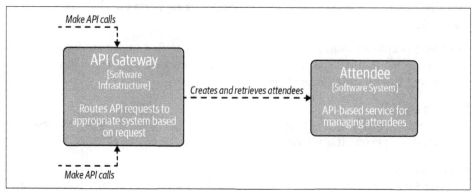

Figure 7-4. API gateway as the resource server

JSON Web Tokens (JWT)

JavaScript Object Notation (JSON) Web Tokens are an RFC standardized (*https://oreil.ly/9AAYt*) token format that is the de facto standard token for OAuth2. A JSON Web Token, also known as a JWT (pronounced "jot"), consists of claims and these claims have associated values. JWTs are structured and encoded using standards to ensure the token is unmodifiable and additionally can be encrypted. They are especially useful in the transfer of information in "space constrained environments such as HTTP Authorization headers" (*https://oreil.ly/hArh0*).

Here is an example JWT:

```
{
    "iss": "http://mastering-api/",
    "sub": "18f913b1-7a9d-47e6-a062-5381d1e21ffa",
    "aud": "Attendee-Service",
    "exp": 1618146900,
    "nbf": 1618144200,
    "iat": 1618144200,
    "jti": "4d13ba71-54e4-4583-9458-562cbf0ba4e4"
}
```

In this example the claims are iss, sub, aud, exp, nbf, iat and jti—these are all reserved claims in the JWT RFC. Reserved claims have a special meaning. They are not mandatory in a token, however they offer a starting point for a minimum amount of information. Looking at our example token, let's list what the claim abbreviations are and how they are typically used:

iss *(Issuer)*
: The authority that issued the token. This is normally an identity provider (e.g., Google or Auth0).

sub *(Subject)*
: A unique identifier to identify the principal of the JWT. In the case of the mobile application that is acting on behalf of the user, this would be attendee (e.g., Matthew Auburn); if this was a server-to-server connection, this may be the application (e.g., the CFP System).[4] The subject value does not follow any format, and if you are defining what the subject should be, you must decide if it should be unique within your system or universally unique (e.g., using a UUID (*https://oreil.ly/NmTRn*)).

aud *(Audience)*
: Who this token is intended for.

---

4 An email or username is normally not a good choice as users modify these over time. Having a consistent identifier is simpler to manage.

exp *(Expiration time)*
> When the token expires (45 minutes after being issued in this case).

nbf *(Not before)*
> Token should not be used before this time (same time as the issued time in this case).

iat *(Issued at)*
> The time the token was issued.

jti *(JWT ID)*
> A unique identifier for the JWT.

> Tokens can contain more information such as preferred name, email of the user, claims about the issuing party, and which application requested the token. For high-security APIs it is common that the authentication method to the authorization server is a claim, which can be used to check if MFA was used by the resource owner to authenticate themselves.

Encoding and verifying JSON Web Tokens

There are two popular encoding mechanisms for JWT, which have their own format:

- JSON Web Signatures (JWS) (*https://oreil.ly/SOfsT*) provides integrity to a JWT. The contents of the token are visible to anyone who receives the token; however, the claims are digitally signed, which ensures that if the contents of the token are changed, the token is immediately invalid.
- JSON Web Encryption (JWE) (*https://oreil.ly/ZHlfR*) provides integrity but is also encrypted. This means that the contents of the token cannot be examined.

> Generally, when JWT is used, that implies JWT using JWS, and Encrypted JWT means JWT using JWE.

The most common mechanism used is JWS, where the digital signing is performed using a private key. The public key is used by the receiver of the token to validate that the token was signed by the specific issuing party. The public key is freely shared with any party that needs to verify the integrity of the token.

If you're using JWT with JWS, you should not insert confidential data into the claim values. JWS provides integrity to the claims; however, anyone who has the JWT can read the claims. To ensure the JWT can't be read, use JWE.

JWTs are a great option for a token format. API services consume the JWT, validate it by verifying the signature, and do not need to look up a token in a database. As the access token will be from an authorization server that is (most likely) under your control, you can add all the information you expect/require to your JWT.

When the JWT is received, there are multiple parts to verify. First, the signature is checked to confirm that it was issued from the expected party and has not been modified or tampered with. Then other claims in the token should be validated, such as checking that the token has not expired (exp claim) or that the token is not used before it is allowed (nbf claim). All tokens that are issued should be short-lived; long-lived tokens are a risk if they are lost or stolen. On the topic of long-lived assertions, the NIST (National Institute of Standards and Technology) (*https://www.nist.gov*) Digital Guidelines state:

> Long-lived assertions have a greater risk of being stolen or replayed; a short assertion lifetime mitigates this risk.

There is no official standard for how long a short-lived or long-lived token should be valid for. The typical suggested lifetime of a short-lived token is between 1 and 60 minutes, and a long-lived token is from one year to ten years. It is suggested that you keep the lifetime of tokens as short as possible.

There are many positives to using JWTs for an access token. Now let's look at their usage within OAuth2.

Terminology and Mechanisms of OAuth2 Grants

OAuth2 is designed to be extensible. The official OAuth2 spec was released in 2012 with four grants, and since then additional grants and modifications have been approved to extend its usage. This is made possible as OAuth2 presents an abstract protocol (*https://oreil.ly/BSldZ*), shown in Figure 7-5:

A. The client requests authorization from the resource owner.

B. The resource owner will grant or deny the client access to their resources.

C. The client will ask for an access token from the authorization server for the authorization it has been granted.

D. The authorization server will issue an access token if the client has been authorized by the resource owner.

E. The client makes a request for the resource to the resource server, which in our case is the API. The request will send the access token as part of the request.

F. The resource server will return the resource if the access token is valid.

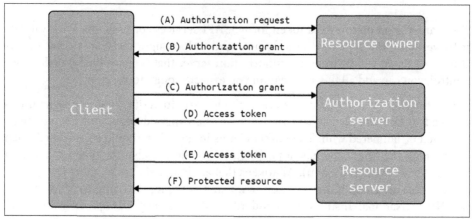

Figure 7-5. Abstract protocol flow

This abstract protocol about how OAuth2 grants should work highlights that the resource owner has control over their own resources. The client is requesting authorization from the resource owner—i.e., "can I (the application) access your resources on your behalf?" The way in which authorization is given is not important. What is essential is that the resource owner has the opportunity to grant or deny access. When requesting a resource from the resource server (i.e., calling the API), how the client obtained the access token does not matter. As long as the request contains a valid access token, the resource server will issue the resource. Each step is isolated and does not require information about the previous step. This is why there are different grants for different scenarios, as they have their own implementation to ensure that these steps are secure for that environment.

ADR Guideline: Should I Consider Using OAuth2?

It is important that you understand the reasons to adopt using OAuth2 and whether it is even the right choice for you. To help with this decision, use this ADR Guideline (see Table 7-1) to help you determine what is right for you and the conversations you may want to have.

Table 7-1. ADR Guideline: Do I need to use OAuth2?

Decision	Should OAuth2 be used or is there another standard for authentication and authorization that is preferred for the operating environment?
Discussion Points	When you start working with APIs, you have the opportunity to decide or influence the security mechanisms for them: • Examine the current security requirements and how things might potentially change. For example, are APIs just used within a control plane or are they also used outside of a control plane/potentially with third parties? • What security model are you expected to support? Have external integrators requested that you use a certain security model? • Do you need to support multiple authentication and authorization models? This is important if you are looking to migrate from an existing authentication model to another.
Recommendations	Using OAuth2 will provide the maximum compatibility with other API users. It is an industry standard with documentation and client libraries that ease integration. OAuth2 supports both the end user and system-to-system cases.

Authorization Code Grant

The Authorization Code Grant (Auth Code Grant) (*https://oreil.ly/CqMhB*) is an implementation of an OAuth2 grant; it is an implementation of the abstract protocol that you saw previously in Figure 7-5. This is a most well-known grant, and you will likely have used it without realizing you did.[5] The typical use case for the Authorization Code Grant is a website backed by a server, which is not publicly available to the internet (i.e., it can protect a secret). A client application that can protect a secret is called a confidential client. Figure 7-6 describes in more detail how the grant works:

A. The client application directs the web browser (the User Agent in the diagram is a web browser) to an authorization server. The redirect to the authorization server will include the identification of the client (a client ID), and as part of the redirect it also has what grant is being used (in this case the Authorization Code Grant is known as code).

B. The authorization server asks the resource owner (end user) to identify themselves. The authorization server needs to know who the resource owner is, so the resource owner will need to authenticate to the authorization server. The authorization server is then able to get consent from the resource owner if they grant authorization to the client application. (Steps A and B of the Authorization Code Grant are all about the authorization request; this is shown as a single step (A) in the abstract protocol from Figure 7-5.)

---

5 A typical scenario is when you are using LinkedIn and LinkedIn asks to access your GMail contacts. LinkedIn redirects you to Google and you log in to your Google account. You are then presented with a message saying "LinkedIn would like to access your email contacts." After you accept, LinkedIn can access your emails.

C. Assuming authorization is granted, an authorization code is passed to the client application, via the User Agent. (This step matches to Step B of the abstract protocol where it shows the authorization grant returned.)

D. The client then requests an access token from the authorization server presenting the authorization code. The authorization server cannot just accept the authorization code from anyone. The client application must authenticate itself to the authorization server by using a secret that is known to the authorization server and the client application. (In the abstract protocol this is Step C where the authorization grant is sent to the authorization server to be exchanged.)

E. If the client application successfully authenticates and presents a valid authorization code, it is granted an access token. (This step lines up with Step D in the abstract protocol where the access token is issued.)

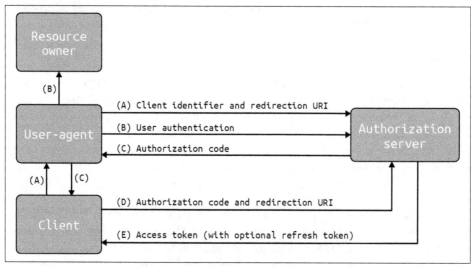

Figure 7-6. Authorization Code Grant

This solution works really well and was the default model for web applications. However, the world of websites has evolved, and Single Page Application (SPAs) now exist. SPA websites are JavaScript-based and run in the user's browser, which means that the source code is fully available for the user to look at. It means also that an OAuth2 client SPA cannot protect a secret and is known as a public client, so using Auth Code Grant as it stands is not possible.

Authorization Code Grant (+ PKCE)

This is when you would use Authorization Code Grant + PKCE (*https://oreil.ly/Kb0r2*), which allows you to use OAuth2 for SPA applications. PKCE stands for Proof Key for Code Exchange and is used to mitigate interception attacks. Within the Auth Code Grant + PKCE grant, two additional parameters are needed: one for the authorization request, which is the code_challenge, and one for the access token request, which is the code_verifier. The code_verifier is a cryptographically random string generated by the client, and the code_challenge is the hashed value of the code_verifier. When the client application initiates the request to the authorization server, it sends the code_challenge, and when an access token is requested, the authorization code is presented along with the code_verifier. The authorization server can hash the code_verifier to check that it matches the code_challenge used to initiate the token request. This extension makes the grant more secure as only the original client should have the code_verifier; this prevents attacks where an authorization code could be intercepted and swapped for an access token. We can see this grant in action in Figure 7-7.

A. The authorization request is made and the code_verifier is sent to the authorization server. In the diagram t(code_verifier) is the transformation of the code_verifier to the code_challenge and t_m is the transformation method (as described previously, this is a hash).

B. Like in the Authorization Code Grant, an authorization code is returned.

C. The client requests the access token by sending the authorization request, which is the authorization code and the code_verifier. No client secret is sent as this is a public client.

D. The access token is then issued to the client application.

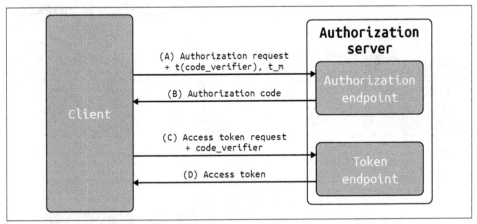

Figure 7-7. Authorization Code Grant + PKCE

You may be looking at these steps and wondering how this maps back to the Authorization Code Grant without PKCE. The diagram looks different from Figure 7-6, but the only real difference is the first step, Step A. In Step A of Figure 7-7, it is all about the authorization request (like in the abstract protocol Step A), and the process will be the same as in the Authorization Code Grant in Steps A and B.

PKCE must be used for public clients. However, you can use PKCE for confidential clients as well as for additional protection.

The Authorization Code Grant and its PKCE extension will work in the most common scenarios for your public and confidential clients when you have an end user in your case.

Case Study: Accessing Attendee API with the Authorization Code Grant

There are two client applications for accessing the Attendee API. Both of these applications will use the Authorization Code Grant to access the Attendee API on behalf of users (the resource owners). The External CFP system is a confidential client. The client can maintain a secret, which means that Authorization Code Grant can be used. The mobile application is a public client, and it is not able to maintain a secret, therefore Authorization Code Grant + PKCE must be used. The steps for the External CFP system and the mobile application requesting an access token and using them to access the Attendee service are shown in Figure 7-8. This also highlights that using PKCE does not change the high-level steps taken or the user's journey.

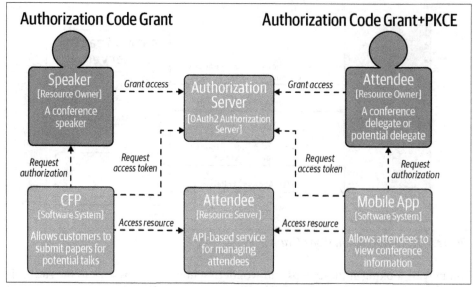

Figure 7-8. Authorization Code Grant applied to our case study

Refresh Tokens

It is good practice to issue tokens that are short-lived; however, asking a user to reenter their username and password would soon become a jarring experience. A refresh token is a long-lived token used by the client to request additional access tokens when the previous token expires. Refresh tokens are requested as part of the authorization request, meaning the end user is not involved in requesting further access tokens. As part of the latest security best practices (*https://oreil.ly/veXgR*), the detection of a refresh token used twice immediately revokes the active refresh token. Refresh tokens are an additional credential and long-lived, so it is important that these are kept secure and not leaked. If at any point a client needs to be denied access, including if the resource owner does not want the client to have further access to their resources, the refresh token can be revoked. The next time the client application requests a new access token (which are short-lived) they will be stopped. This does mean that there can be a window when a client has a valid access token but should not have access. This is why it is important to have short-lived tokens.

Client Credentials Grant

The client for the Client Credentials Grant (*https://oreil.ly/6GA8r*) is a confidential client as it needs to maintain a secret. As this is for machine-to-machine communication, the connection is set up in advance and the access (what the client is authorized to do) should be pre-arranged.

The process of the client obtaining an access token is very straightforward as shown in Figure 7-9:[6]

A. The client application authenticates to the authorization server and requests an access token. The client also identifies the grant being used, which is `client_credentials`.

B. The authorization server returns an access token if the client application successfully authenticates.

Figure 7-9. Client Credentials Grant

---

6 If you want to look further at adding even more security to the client application getting access tokens, see RFC8705 (*https://oreil.ly/kQGTQ*). This specification uses Mutual TLS instead of secret strings to obtain access tokens.

There are no additional steps as there is no resource owner to give permission. The client is acting on its own behalf so only is required to identify itself.

Case Study: Accessing Attendee API from the CFP system with Client Credentials Grant

The External CFP system produces a report every three months to show how many attendees go on to submit talks and become speakers. This report generation is not on behalf of an attendee but instead happens for the External CFP system. The client (External CFP system) is registered into the authorization server.[7] In the Attendee service the client is added into a list of clients that can access the service and is configured to be able to read information about attendees and query which users have submitted talks—this is the pre-arranged access. When the client wants to access the Attendee API, it will request an access token from the authorization server and then use the access token when it calls the Attendee API.

You have now seen how to use OAuth2 for machine-to-machine communication, but what if your case has not been covered so far?

Refresh tokens are not used with the Client Credentials Grant; instead, the client requests a new access token.

Additional OAuth2 Grants

There are more OAuth2 grants available than just the previous two discussed. The other standardized grants available are listed here, but we will not explore them in further detail:

- The Device Authorization Grant is used for devices that have limited input or lack a browser. This makes it useful for IoT devices, such as your smart fridge or a Raspberry Pi project.
- Implicit Grant was used commonly for SPAs, but it has been replaced by the Authorization Code Grant + PKCE.
- Resource Owner Password Credentials Grant was historically used as a stepping stone from HTTP Basic to get client applications off the ground using OAuth2. It is recommended not to use this grant.

---

7 It is fine to have a client registered for multiple grant types; the subject of the callee will be different depending on the grant used. As we see here in the client credentials, the subject is the client making the request and not on behalf of a resource owner.

ADR Guideline: Choosing Which OAuth2 Grants to Support

As we have seen, there are many OAuth2 grants. It is important to pick the grant that is right for your case or the grants you want to support. The ADR Guideline in Table 7-2 provides discussion points and considerations you should think about before picking your grant.

Table 7-2. ADR Guideline: Which OAuth2 Grants

Decision	Which OAuth2 Grants should be supported?
Discussion Points	Determine what types of clients will be interacting with your APIs:

- Do you need to support IoT devices and the Device Authorization Grant?
- Do you have older clients that are SPAs that only support the Implicit Grant?
- Should you outright forbid the use of the Resource Owner Password Credential Grant?

If you already have a security model for authentication and authorization, should you move to OAuth2?

- Which grant best represents your interaction model?
- Will the clients be able to migrate to the grant? If they are under your control or you have a small number of third parties, this will be significantly easier to start getting third parties to migrate.
- Should all new onboarded clients use the new OAuth2 Grant?

Recommendations	We recommend that you use OAuth2 and use only the grants you need and add more if required. If you have a security model in place that works and many paying customers, it may not be feasible to force them to migrate over to use OAuth2. However, you may have to evolve your security architecture to use OAuth2 to be more standard, as this can also be a request from third parties so they do not need to build a custom interaction for your security model. Starting with the Client Credentials Grant is often the easiest way to introduce OAuth2 into an API system.

OAuth2 Scopes

Scopes are an important mechanism in OAuth2 and are effectively used to limit the access of a client acting on behalf of a user. When a user first authenticates, the end user receives a consent screen, which will state what the client is requesting access to do. For example, "Application would like to read appointments in your calendar" and "Application would like to book meetings in your calendar." The end user is in control and can restrict what actions the client can perform on their behalf.

Case Study: Applying OAuth2 scopes to the Attendee API

Let's explore a practical example to show scopes for modeling attendees using some endpoints. To help with this example, let's imagine that the legacy conference system has two endpoints exposed as well:

Attendee API

- GET – /attendees—Get a list of attendees
- GET – /attendees/{attendee_id}—Get details of an attendee
- POST – /attendees—Register a new attendee
- PUT – /attendees/{attendee_id}—Update attendee information

Legacy Conference API

- GET – /conferences—Get a list of conferences
- POST – /conferences—Create a new conference

The External CFP application needs to only access the Attendee API, so as a resource owner you do not want the External CFP to access conference information. There should be a separation where you can authorize the External CFP system to just the Attendee API.

Two scopes are created: the Attendee scope and a Conference scope. This is shown as the HTTP Method – endpoint – scope.

Attendee API

- GET – /attendees – Attendee
- GET – /attendees/{attendee_id} – Attendee
- POST – /attendees – Attendee
- PUT – /attendees/{attendee_id – Attendee

Legacy Conference API

- GET – /conferences – Conference
- POST – /conferences – Conference

This achieves the separation of conferences and attendees, however it is possible to take this a step further and differentiate between read and write operations:

Attendee API

- GET – /attendees – AttendeeRead
- GET – /attendees/{attendee_id} – AttendeeRead
- POST – /attendees – AttendeeAccount
- PUT – /attendees{attendee_id} – AttendeeAccount

Scopes don't have a defined standard, however they are typically used as a coarse-grained separation within an API. Scopes must make sense to the end user, as they are going to need to consent to their usage. Once the resource owner grants authorization to a resource, this information needs to be used by the resource server to enforce this. When using access tokens in a JWT format, a claim is normally added to the JWT; e.g., `"scope"`: `"AttendeeRead AttendeeAccount`.[8] This will have the list of all the scopes that have been authorized. Scopes are not mandatory for OAuth2, though it is very useful and something that you should consider for coarse-grained authorization.

Authorization Enforcement

Authorization needs to be enforced as this is fundamental in API security. Two of the most common security authorization issues listed in the OWASP API Security Top 10 are Broken Object Level Authorization (BOLA) (*https://oreil.ly/3HH5T*) and Broken Function Level Authorization (*https://oreil.ly/V08ul*). BOLA is when a user is able to request information for an object that they should not have access to, often discovered by tampering with a resource ID. Broken Function Level Authorization is when the user can perform tasks they are not authorized to do, for example executing an administration-only endpoint as a standard user.

Authorization is typically based on some sort of entitlements. This is popularly enforced using Role Based Access Control (RBAC) (*https://oreil.ly/U3ahp*). Though the exact entitlement choice is a detail, some sort of access control should exist and it is important that every endpoint has an authorization check before fulfilling the request.

When you look at authorization with OAuth2, you must keep in mind that scopes are used to specify what a resource owner has stated regarding the range of actions a client can perform. This does not mean that the client should have access to all end-user data. For the Attendee service there could be different actions that are possible, such as admin rights to manage attendees and view-only rights on attendees. An attendee may only have permission to read the attendees' profile description; however, a client may ask for permission to read attendees' information and to manage attendees. A user may grant access to the client to perform these tasks on their behalf; however, the user themself may not have access. This overlap of authorization is highlighted in Figure 7-10.

---

8 This may be an array—comma-separated, or like this case, space separated.

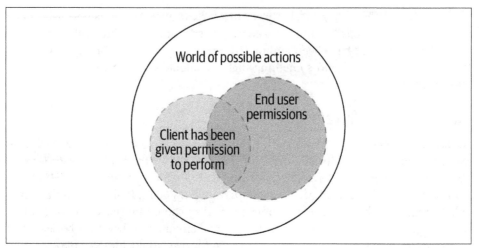

Figure 7-10. Venn of authorization

Scopes are useful for an API gateway to enforce scope authorization and to reject requests when a client does not have the correct scope to access an API.

Introducing OIDC

OAuth2 provides a mechanism for the client to access APIs using authentication and authorization. A common requirement is for the client to know the identity of the resource owner. Consider the External CFP system. It will need to store data about the speaker, but OAuth2 grants do not provide a way to obtain the identity of the end user.

This is the purpose of OpenID Connect (OIDC) (*https://oreil.ly/umHmK*); it provides an identity layer. This layer builds on top of OAuth2, by having the OAuth2 authorization server implement additional functionality. The functionality required turns the OAuth2 authorization server into an OpenID provider as well. It is now possible for a client to request information about the user by using a special scope called *openid*. This scope is requested along with any the scopes required for any access tokens. Using the openid scope provides the client with an ID token, which is a JWT that contains claims about the user.

The ID token returned when using just the openid scope contains a very limited amount of information about the user. The only claim that identifies the user is the subject claim, which is a unique ID of the user and must never change (usually this is a UUID). Having just a unique ID about the user is not usually enough for the client. That is why OIDC specifies additional scopes that can be added to the request to get information in the ID token:

profile
> name, family_name, given_name, middle_name, nickname, preferred_username, profile, picture, website, gender, birthdate, zoneinfo, locale, and updated_at

email
> email and email_verified

address
> address

phone
> phone_number and phone_number_verified

You can end up with a very rich ID token that contains a lot of information about the user. These scopes are used in the context of ID tokens—you would not see these scopes in your access token as you saw in "OAuth2 Scopes" on page 183.

Three flows are declared by OIDC: Authorization Code Flow, Implicit Flow, and Hybrid Flow. The OIDC specification calls steps to acquire an ID token "flows." The recommendation is to use the Authorization Code Flow for the same reasons as the Authorization Code Grant (+ PKCE)—it is more secure.

Many people think that OAuth2 and OIDC are the same thing and will refer to OIDC being used to access APIs. The reality is that they are not the same; they are two distinct things. OIDC has its role, providing user identity to clients; however, it does not provide access to APIs. If OIDC is something that you need, then you should be sure that your identity provider has support for it. Do not try to build your own identity layer.

 Never substitute ID tokens for access tokens. This is very dangerous practice as ID tokens are not intended for this purpose. They are long-lived tokens with the purpose of providing information about the user to a client. They are not for accessing resources.

SAML 2.0

In enterprise environments it is common to use SAML 2.0, often referred to as just SAML. SAML (Security Assertion Markup Language) is an open standard that transfers assertions. It is often used for single sign on, and the assertions that are transferred are user identities. SAML is popular within the enterprise world as it is used to allow employees to sign on to external applications. SAML is not aligned to be used by APIs in its raw form. However, there does exist an OAuth2 extension: Security Assertion Markup Language (SAML) 2.0 Profile for OAuth 2.0 Client Authentication and Authorization Grants (*https://oreil.ly/AVVHY*). This extension allows a client to request an access token using SAML, assuming that the authorization server has implemented the functionality. You should be aware of this if SAML is something that you need to use as part of a migration to OAuth2.

Summary

In this chapter we have explored the importance of securing APIs and robust industry standards to achieve this:

- Authentication establishes the identity of the resource owner, which in APIs is either an end user or an application performing system-to-system communication.

- OAuth2 is the de facto standard for securing APIs and often leverages JWT as part of the bearer header. JWT tokens are often encoded and signed to ensure they are tamper free.

- Different OAuth2 grants support different scenarios. The most common are the Authorization Code Grant + PKCE and the Client Credentials Grant.

- Refresh tokens help to smooth out the end-user experience of needing to keep asking the user to enter a username and password.

- OAuth2 scopes help to provide coarse-grained authorization and allow the end user to configure the access of a client.

- OIDC is used when the client requires information about the end user. OIDC provides basic information about the authenticated user and can optionally provide additional details.

Fundamentally, you should now understand how you can identify an API callee and how you can secure your own APIs. However, this is not the end of the journey, as the majority of software architectures don't stay still. You will learn about evolutionary architecture with APIs in the next chapter.

PART IV

Evolutionary Architecture with APIs

This section explores how to evolve the architecture of a system or series of systems using APIs. This includes evolving existing legacy applications toward API-based, service-oriented architectures, and also using API infrastructure for evolving or replatforming a system for effective deployment into a cloud environment.

Chapter 8 explores redesigning monolithic applications toward an API-driven architecture.

In Chapter 9, you will learn how to use API infrastructure to evolve your current systems toward cloud platforms.

Chapter 10 provides a summary of key lessons you have learned throughout the book. This chapter also presents ways in which you can continue to evolve the case study and advance your learning about API architecture.

CHAPTER 8

Redesigning Applications to API-Driven Architectures

Now that you have a solid grasp of API operations and security, you will explore how APIs can be used to evolve and augment existing applications. In *Building Evolutionary Architectures* (*https://oreil.ly/ojdwr*) (O'Reilly), the authors discuss how an evolutionary architecture supports guided, incremental changes, across multiple dimensions. Whether you want to adopt an evolutionary architecture as defined in that book or not, the reality is that almost every successful system will have to evolve over time to meet new user requirements or to react to a changing environment. It is rare for a business or organization not to change its products based on customer feedback or changing market conditions. Equally, it is uncommon for a long-running system not to be impacted by changes in infrastructure (e.g., hardware failing and becoming obsolete), the underlying application frameworks, or a third-party service.

APIs are the natural interfaces, abstractions, and (encapsulated) entry points to and within a system, and as such can be instrumental in supporting an evolutionary architecture. In this chapter you will learn about why change is needed, how to design for this, and where to implement useful patterns.

Although you may not have realized it, you have been applying many of the skills discussed in this chapter throughout the conference system case study. We recommend that you think about the evolution of the case study as you read this chapter, and you will review the final end state of the conference system architecture in "Case Study: A Look Back on Your Journey" on page 225.

Why Use APIs to Evolve a System?

Changing software in a safe manner can be difficult. This challenge is further compounded if the software has any of these three characteristics: a large number of users, inherent complexity in the design, or tight integration with a number of other systems. And here's the kicker: these characteristics are almost inevitable within a software system that is well adopted, meets user needs, and is a key part of an organization's workflow. The majority of "legacy" systems have also evolved in a somewhat ad hoc manner, with many temporary workarounds, quick fixes, or shortcuts becoming an embedded part of the system design.

As an architect, APIs can help you evolve a system. An API can be a boundary to a module or component, and this makes an API a natural point of leverage when trying to ensure a system is highly cohesive and loosely coupled.

Creating Useful Abstractions: Increasing Cohesion

Cohesion refers to the degree to which the elements inside a system belong together. Implementing APIs and systems with high cohesion enables the easier evolution of both the API provider and consumer. As a provider, you can alter the internals of your service, such as changing algorithms, refactoring code to improve performance, or changing datastores, and you only have to avoid modifying the external interface in a way that breaks backward compatibility. As a consumer, you can be more confident in modifying and scaling your service, with clear and understandable integration points into the existing API.

Closely related to designing cohesive APIs is thinking critically about the abstractions you are creating. We can all understand and appreciate the differences in abstractions for controlling different vehicles. With a car, you typically interact with the dashboard, pedals, and steering wheel. When operating a space shuttle, the control panel contains many more fine-grained dashboards, control sticks, and buttons. The space shuttle controls are cohesive to the task at hand, but the level of control and complexity offered here would not be appropriate when designing a car. Hopefully, you can see the analogy with API design. It can be tempting to design the equivalent of a space shuttle control panel—particularly in relation to the goal of "future-proofing" APIs—when in reality, your underlying business service is analogous to driving a car.

Aim for APIs with High Cohesion

APIs that are highly cohesive are easier for an architect to understand, build mental models of, and reason about. Cohesive APIs also don't violate the principle of least surprise. Highly cohesive APIs can also become focused points of change within a system. For example, a series of related changes may only require the modification of a single API, versus the modification of a series of APIs required when modifying a system with low cohesion. Always strive for and evolve toward highly cohesive systems.

As a counterexample of high cohesion within the case study, imagine if you created a "utils" API that exposed a collection of convenience functions that could be used across all of the conference entities. This could easily lead to a situation where a change in the code behind one API, such as the Attendee API, requires that another utility API also be updated. Unless you are the original author of the APIs, or you have very good documentation and tests, it could be easy to miss this and leave the system with inconsistent or incompatible behavior.

There Are Many Types of Cohesion to Consider!

Although cohesion often gets talked about as if this could be measured in one dimension, there are several types of cohesion that architects should be aware of. For example, systems can be coupled in a number of ways:

- Functional cohesion
- Sequential cohesion
- Communicational cohesion
- Procedural cohesion
- Temporal cohesion
- Logical cohesion
- Coincidental cohesion

Joseph Ingeno's *Software Architect's Handbook* (*https://oreil.ly/hkS1F*) (Packt Publishing) provides a more comprehensive overview for readers who want to know more.

Of course, cohesion is only one property to strive for when designing and evolving systems. Let's now look at cohesion's close relation in software: coupling.

Clarifying Domain Boundaries: Promoting Loose Coupling

A loosely coupled system has two properties. First, components are weakly associated (have breakable relationships) with each other, which means that changes in one component do not affect the functionality or performance of another component. And second, each of the system's components has little or no knowledge of the definitions of other separate components. Components in a loosely coupled system can be replaced with alternative implementations that provide the same services and are less constrained to the same platform, language, operating system, or build environment.

Designing or refactoring toward a loosely coupled API will enable providers and consumers to evolve their systems more effectively. As a provider, a loosely coupled API will enable the maximum adoption of your service across the organization, both from the perspectives of ease of integration and supporting ease of change. And for consumers, an API that is loosely coupled will support easier swapping of components (potentially even at runtime), allow easier testing, and reduce the cost of managing dependencies.

Loose Coupling Enables Easier Mocking and Virtualizing When Testing!

An API designed with loose coupling in mind will typically be much easier to mock or virtualize when performing integration and end-to-end testing. A loosely coupled API enables the provider implementation to be easily swapped. When testing a consumer, the provider API implementation can be swapped for a simple stub or virtual service that returns the required response.

In comparison, it is often not possible to mock or stub an API that is highly coupled. Instead you will find yourself running the API provider as part of your test set or attempting to use a lightweight (less functional) or embedded version of the service.

Case Study: Establishing Attendee Domain Boundaries

As an example with the conference system use case, imagine if our Attendee service was highly coupled with the underlying datastore and exposed data in the format of the underlying data schema. If, as the service provider, you wanted to swap out the datastore to something different, you have two choices. You can implement a new system to adapt any data created or retrieved between the old and new format, which will likely require complicated and error-prone translation code. Or, you can modify your external API and get all of your consumers to adopt this—and don't underestimate the difficulty in doing this with a widely adopted service!

The Power of Information Hiding

When you design an API to be both highly cohesive and loosely coupled, you benefit from the principle of information hiding. This is the principle of segregation of implementation decisions that are most likely to change. If you get this right, you can protect other parts of the system from extensive modification if the design decision is changed.

The protection involves providing a stable interface that protects the remainder of the system from the underlying (changeable) implementation. In regards to APIs, information hiding is the ability to prevent certain aspects of a provider being accessible to its consumers This can be achieved by using only business- or domain-focused API endpoints and by not leaking any of the internal abstractions or the implementation-specific data model or schema.

End State Architecture Options

As you evolve and redesign your monolithic applications and APIs, you should have a clear vision of what you want your system to be able to do as a result of the changes being made. Otherwise, this now infamous scene in *Alice in Wonderland* will become all too true:

> "Would you tell me, please, which way I ought to go from here?" "That depends a good deal on where you want to get to," said the Cat. "I don't much care where—" said Alice. "Then it doesn't matter which way you go," said the Cat. "—so long as I get SOMEWHERE," Alice added as an explanation.

You will learn more about the approach to determining your overall goals for evolving systems in the next section of this chapter, but for the moment let's take a tour of the potential options for your architecture and how they impact API design.

Monolith

Over the last several years, the monolithic architectural style has gotten a bad rap. However, this is mostly because the word "monolith" has become synonymous with "big ball of mud."[1] In reality, a monolith is just a software system that is composed all in one piece and runs as a single-process, self-contained application. There is nothing fundamentally wrong with a monolithic architecture. For many systems, particularly proof of concept applications, or systems that are being created as the underlying business product market fit is being found, this architectural style will

---

[1] For more insight and the history of the big ball of mud, check out these articles from Wikipedia (*https://oreil.ly/Toz8J*) and InfoQ (*https://oreil.ly/lPDpX*).

allow you to move the fastest at the beginning of the project. This is because it is easy to understand and modify as there is only one thing to look at, reason about, and work on.

The challenge when implementing APIs within a monolithic application is that it is easier to accidentally create a highly coupled design, which will only become apparent when you are making modifications in the future. Following best practices, such as using domain-driven design (DDD) and potentially using a hexagonal architecture, will pay dividends later.

Service-Oriented Architecture (SOA)

Service-oriented architecture (SOA) is a style of software design where services are provided to the other components by applications or services that communicate over a network. The first use of SOA, often referred to as "classic SOA," also has somewhat of a bad rap. This is mostly due to the use of heavyweight technologies with early SOA, such as SOAP, WSDL, and XML, and vendor-driven middleware such as ESBs and message queues. There was a focus on the network using "smart pipes" for communication, and business logic was incorporated into middleware.

Evolving your applications toward SOA can be beneficial, but care should be taken to avoid the use of frameworks or vendor middleware that promotes high coupling or low cohesions. For example, always avoid adding business logic to an API gateway or enterprise service bus (ESB). One of the biggest challenges with designing SOA-based systems is getting the size and ownership of services "correct"—i.e., striking a good balance with the cohesiveness of the API, having clear ownership of the code across the organization, and the design and runtime cost of having many services.

Microservices

Microservices are the latest implementation of SOA, where software is composed of small independent services that communicate over well-defined APIs. There are several differences with classic SOA—i.e., the use of "smart endpoints and dumb pipes" (*https://oreil.ly/cTt3j*) and avoiding the use of heavyweight middleware that can become highly coupled to your services. Many books have been written about microservices,[2] and so we will refer you to these if you are looking to dive deep into the topic. However, the core principles with evolving microservices include creating loosely coupled and highly cohesive API-driven services.

As with classic SOA, one of the biggest challenges when designing APIs using a microservices architecture is getting the boundaries (and cohesiveness) of an API and the underlying services correct. Using techniques like context mapping and event

---

2 Sam Newman's *Building Microservices*, 2nd Edition (O'Reilly) is our personal favorite.

storming from the world of DDD, before building or evolving towards microservices, will often greatly reward your future efforts. Microservice APIs should ideally use lightweight technologies that encourage loose coupling. This includes technologies that you have already explored within this book, such as REST, gRPC, and lightweight event-driven or message-based technologies like AMQP, STOMP, or WebSockets.

Functions

Although an initial promise of functions being the next evolution of microservices hasn't quite come to fruition, there is good adoption of this architecture across a range of organizations. This architectural style can be a useful target to aim for if you have a highly event-driven system—for example, a market-based trading system that is highly reactive to news and market events, or an image-processing system with a pipeline of standardized transformations to apply and reports to be generated.

The biggest challenge with designing a function-based system and the corresponding APIs is typically related to getting coupling correct. It's all too easy to design functions or services that are so simplistic that many of them have to be orchestrated together to provide any business value. These services and their APIs tend then to become highly coupled. The balance here between reusability and maintainability can be difficult, and therefore this architecture style should not be chosen without recognizing that you and your team may take some time to adjust to it.

Managing the Evolutionary Process

Evolving a system must be a consciously managed activity. Let's look at the things you need to keep an eye on when making changes to your API.

Determine Your Goals

Before attempting to evolve a system, you should be clear about the motivation behind the changes. The goals should be catalogued and clearly communicated with your team and organization. Identifying incorrect assumptions and targets early in the change process is less costly than at the point where coding begins. The goals largely fall into two categories: functional and cross-functional.

Functional evolutionary goals are feature or functionality change requests. They are typically driven by end users or business stakeholders. There may be refactoring required, but these types of goals focus on writing more code or integrating more systems.

Cross-functional goals, also referred to as nonfunctional goals, focus on the "ilities," such as maintainability, scalability, and reliability. For example, maintainability changes are often driven by the technical leadership team wanting to reduce the time taken by engineers on understanding, fixing, or changing a system. Scalability changes are often driven by business stakeholders that are forecasting increased usage or more demand for the system. Reliability work often focuses on attempting to reduce the number and impact of failures within a system. These types of goals typically focus on refactoring existing systems or introducing new platform or infrastructure components.

Creating cross-functional requirements makes total sense, but how do we set clear goals around the changes we are looking to make to our system, and how will we know if we've succeeded? This is where fitness functions can help.

Using Fitness Functions

Aiming for an architecture that avoids rapidly becoming legacy requires active decisions that prevent degradation over time. Defining fitness functions is a mechanism that provides a constant interrogation of the system architecture and code artifacts that make up the system. Think of a function as a sort of unit/integration test for architecture, assessing the "ilities" of the architecture in a quantifiable metric. A fitness function is included into the build pipeline to help provide a constant assurance of the goals for the system. In the Thoughtworks blog on fitness functions (*https://oreil.ly/hl9eB*), several categories of focus are suggested, as outlined in Table 8-1.

Table 8-1. Categories of fitness functions

Code Quality	This is a fitness function category that many teams likely already have in place to a certain extent. Executing tests allow you to measure the quality of code ahead of releasing into production. Additional metrics are also worth considering—for example, ensuring that cyclic complexity is minimized.
Resiliency	An initial test for resiliency is to deploy a system into a preproduction environment, run sample (or synthetic) traffic into this, and observe that the error rate is below a certain threshold. An API gateway or service mesh can often be used to inject faults into the system and facilitate the testing of resiliency and availability to certain scenarios.
Observability	Ensuring that services conform (and do not regress) and publishing the types of metrics that are required by the observability platform is critical. In "Important Metrics for APIs" on page 140, you reviewed what would be a good set of API metrics to publish; this could be measured and enforced by an ongoing fitness function.
Performance	Performance tests are often an afterthought; however, if you can set out latency and throughput targets, these can be measured in the build pipeline. Perhaps one of the hardest parts to this objective is getting production-like data to make the type of performance tests you'd need to run be meaningful. We will consider this further in "Performance Issues" on page 206.
Compliance	This section is very business/organization-specific in terms of assessing what is critical to monitor. It could include audit or data requirements that are key to continuing to provide evidence that a business is running as expected.
Security	Security has many different aspects to it and you explored some of the considerations in Chapters 6 and 7. One possible fitness function might be to analyze the library dependencies in the project and check for any known vulnerabilities. Another could be to run an automated scan over the codebase to ensure that there are no OWASP-style vulnerabilities present.
Operability	Many applications are built, put into production, and then start to evolve; users onboard and then problems start. Deciding on a minimum set of requirements for operating the platform is key to ensuring the plant remains operational. Assessing whether monitoring and alerting are in place is a good place to start.

Creating ADRs around the fitness functions that you would like to introduce is a good place to start. It might be tricky to immediately implement everything presented in the preceding table.

Some decisions are difficult to reverse and it is important that, where possible, these types of decisions are identified.

 An irreversible decision is not a bad thing! However, an irreversible decision without careful thought and consideration is. An ADR helps with the common *"What were they thinking...?"* style question and shares historical context. Decisions made collectively through the use of ADRs and open discussion will lead to an architecture that has longevity.

Decomposing a System into Modules

Have you ever worked on a codebase that is bashed for being a monolith (perhaps by yourself or others)? One of the authors has worked on a four-million-line codebase that had 24 years of technical debt (according to SonarQube). The code structure connected ad hoc from many different classes, creating a high degree of uncontrolled coupling across the application. Refactoring any part of the application was difficult—often fixing one bug created other unexpected bugs. None of the problems were due to the monolithic nature of the system but instead were due to a lack of code organization and design.

One approach to prevent the spaghetti code/ball of mud is breaking up software applications using modules. Designing modular components within a codebase helps to define clear boundaries and logical grouping based on cohesion of functionality. Modules aim to form well-defined boundaries that hide implementation details. Where you set the definition of the module can be a complicated issue; in languages such as Java, there are options such as method, class, package, and module. Each of those constructs allows a different degree of information hiding that overlaps with object-oriented encapsulation constructs. For the purpose of our discussion, we will consider a module to define an architectural partitioning on a larger scale than methods and individual classes.

Sam Newman has some excellent advice on limiting what you expose to start with when designing modules. Sam's book *Monolith to Microservices* (O'Reilly) is a fantastic deep-dive into the subject of modularity and migrations from monolith to microservices:

> Personally, I adopt the approach of exposing as little as possible from a module (or microservice) boundary. Once something becomes part of a module interface, it's hard to walk that back. But if you hide it now, you can always decide to share it later.

Let's consider what modules we could potentially have introduced in the conference system case study that we started with in the Introduction. Figure 8-1 introduces a module to represent the controllers, services, and data access object (DAO) patterns. Each controller exposes the RESTful endpoints and will be exposed by the web server hosting the application. The service module is where the business logic lives behind the controller, exposing a clear interface to the controllers. The DAO module is where the data access object lives behind the services, exposing clear interfaces to the services. Module layers are quite common, and getting to the point where there is a clear single directional dependency between modules is a good application of modularity.

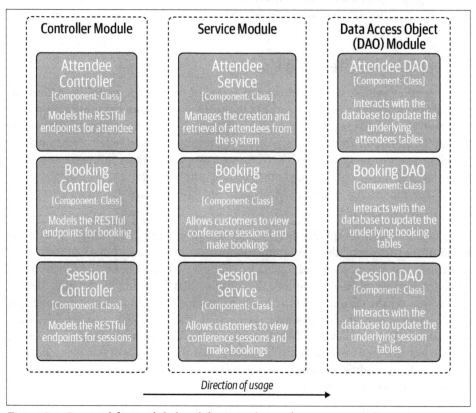

Figure 8-1. Proposal for module breakdown in the conference case study

Now that we have clear separation, each module can apply a strategy for testing the subject in isolation. Another advantage of a modular approach is the ability for developers to reason about and test within a module.

In a recent project, one of the authors created a DAO pattern for interacting with the database as a module of the application. An interface exposed the functionality to the other modules of the application, making interactions with the module clear. A decision was taken later to split the business logic into three modules that utilized the DAOs into independent services—a monolith first evolution. The three new modules nicely separated into their own services, using the DAO module as a library. Designing well-defined modules enabled independent evolution and evolutionary decisions to be made about the system.

Using C4 diagrams to express software is a lightweight approach at the component level for defining relationships between components in the system. The component diagram, first discussed in the Introduction, helps provide a mechanism for reviewing relationships and helps in defining modular structures.

Defining modules within your applications is a good design step, though there are many options for how modularity is achieved. Look to use language-level support to help enforce modules and agree as a team on the approach that will work best for your technical stack.

Creating APIs as "Seams" for Extension

The concept of "seams" was first introduced in Michael Feather's 2004 book *Working Effectively with Legacy Code* (*https://oreil.ly/EtYnR*) (Pearson). A seam is a point where functionality is stitched together—it can be considered as the point where one subject under consideration[3] interacts with another. This is usually achieved by techniques like dependency injection, injecting the collaborator and executing against an interface allowing for substitutability. The substitutability consideration is important; this allows for effective testing without the requirement to run the whole system (e.g., using mocks or test doubles).

If the application was built without a good design, the definition of a seam may be complex and make it hard to understand the full range of behavior. When working with legacy code, it can make it difficult to break apart and refactor code to work in a more modular way. Nicolas Carlo (*https://oreil.ly/Xqzpm*) presents a useful recipe for breaking apart seams of legacy code, assuming that tests do not already exist:

- Identify change points (seams)
- Break dependencies
- Write the tests
- Make your changes
- Refactor

---

3 In this context "subject under consideration" is a class or set of classes.

When designing changes, consider creating an API design for how two (or potentially more) collaborators connect together. If there is potential that the definition of the seam could be used outside of the subject under consideration, an interservice API could be a great choice. For example, if the seam is a similar execution across many different parts of the codebase, and the goal is to break up a service into smaller service-based architectures, this is an opportunity to define cross-service reuse.

Identifying Change Leverage Points within a System

Sometimes it is easy for architects or developers to identify "change leverage points," or code and services that are obvious candidates to refactor and change in order to make a system "better" in some way—for example, more performant, extensible, secure. If you've worked in the industry for more than a few years, I'm sure you've worked on a system with a particularly challenging area of the codebase, or a module that is constantly changing and churning (and often the two issues are correlated!), and you've thought to yourself that you would like to spend time properly addressing the issue. However, these leverage points are not always obvious, particularly if you have inherited a codebase or system. For this situation, books such as Adam Tornhill's *Your Code as a Crime Scene* (Pragmatic Bookshelf) will prove useful for understanding your code and applications. Related tooling can be very useful, such as version control system churn detection utilities that locate constantly changing parts of a codebase, or software complexity measuring tooling that analyzes a codebase or service with each build pipeline run.

Continuous Delivery and Verification

In Chapter 5 you reviewed the importance of automating the deployment and releases of loosely coupled systems. The need to continually verify systems as we deploy more is critical to enabling an evolutionary architecture.

Architectural Patterns for Evolving Systems with APIs

APIs provide a powerful abstraction for evolving systems toward a modern architecture and also to introduce new features and change. As you discovered in Chapters 3 and 4, gateways and service mesh–based constructs allow an operational migration using gateways. When creating an evolutionary change, a primary consideration during the evolutionary period is to mitigate the risks of evolution and maximize the benefits as soon as possible. Let's review some architectural patterns that can assist with migrating to APIs.

Strangler Fig

A strangler fig is any of the numerous species of tropical figs that grows around an existing tree. Although a strangler fig often smothers and outcompetes its host, there is some evidence that trees encased in strangler figs are more likely to survive tropical storms, suggesting that the relationship can be somewhat mutualistic. Ultimately this is the goal of an evolutionary architecture—to support a changing system, which may result in completely removing what was there before. This is achieved by introducing new components of the application while the old mechanism is still in place. The goal is to gradually migrate over to the new API-based approach.

In "Case Study: Feature Flagging" on page 126, you reviewed how a feature flag could be used to query the legacy service or invoke a new API-based service. Figure 8-2 shows a C4 diagram of the use of feature flags. This works well for seams that previously existed as in-process interactions for the introduction of new APIs into a service. However, if there are many consumers already interacting with the service out of process it would be unrealistic to expect all to implement and control a feature flag.

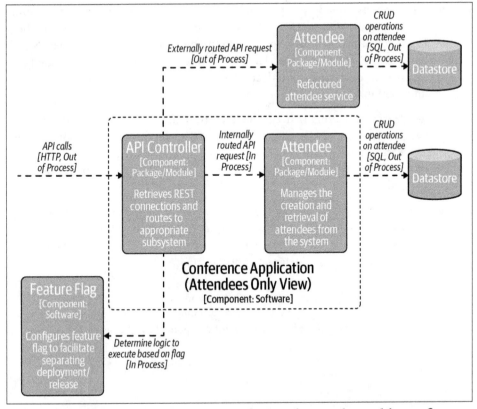

Figure 8-2. Conference application container diagram for attendees and feature flags

Another model is to use a proxy or gateway to front the API interaction, routing to the legacy implementation or to the new implementation. This is a type of facade using a proxy, meaning that the API consumer uses the same API and is unaware of the migration from one service to another that is happening behind the scenes.

Managing the strangler fig pattern behind the scenes can be tricky, and the introduction of a new component can be a single point of failure or bottleneck unless this is mitigated. The proxy should not take on business logic or this will make it difficult to remove at the end of the migration. Managing the legacy and modern process side-by-side is a challenge to ensure data coherency between the two services. You can find more guidance for overcoming these challenges in *Monolith to Microservices*.

Facade and Adapter

Facade and adapter patterns are well-known patterns that can assist with migrating to modern services. The strangler fig pattern is a type of facade, intercepting API calls and hiding the complexity behind the scenes.

A common situation we have encountered is present in existing large-scale distributed applications already using a form of API. Perhaps interservice communication is driven over SOAP-RCP or another vintage protocol. Adapters can help evolve the architecture by introducing a component that converts a given SOAP request into a new RESTful API call. However, protocol rewriting can be challenging to implement correctly. Care should be taken here to avoid reducing cohesion or introducing coupling.

It's not just legacy situations that can benefit from the use of the adapter pattern. In Chapter 1 we explored the use of gRPC as a technology that is popular and effective for east–west communication. Using the grpc-gateway project, it is possible to present a RESTful JSON endpoint that is converted to the gRPC representation in the background.

Facade and Adapter patterns are very similar, in the sense that they *get in the way*. A facade is usually less complex than an adapter; a traditional API gateway simply routes API requests, whereas an adapter will be responsible for converting into a representation understood by the target application.

 If an API gateway steps over the line from acting as a facade pattern to the adapter pattern, the coupling immediately increases. Be sure to ask if you are still using the right component for the task!

API Layer Cake

An API migration pattern that is talked about a lot within enterprise contexts is the "Layered APIs" or "API Layer Cake," which builds upon the "separation of concerns" layering pattern seen within traditional enterprise monolithic applications. During the 2000s, it was considered a best practice in Java or .NET enterprise applications to implement application functionality in a series of layered tiers—for example, presentation, application, domain, and datastore tiers. The core idea was that each user request entering an application flowed sequentially down and then up of each tier/layer. This pattern allowed for the abstraction and reuse of functionality specific to each tier, with the trade-off being that an end-to-end slice of functionality often required modifying many layers—i.e., cohesion within each tier's layer came at the expense of high coupling of tiers to provide a unit of business functionality.

The modern API-based approach to this pattern is seen in Gartner's *Pace-Layered Application Strategy*.[4] New names are used for each API or microservice layer, with presentation being translated approximately to systems of engagement (SoE), application to systems of differentiation (SoD), and datastore to systems of record (SoR).

Over time, this pattern has earned a bad reputation, particularly as the legacy systems that implemented it became more and more challenging to evolve. This pattern encourages architects and developers to take shortcuts, like duplicating functionality between many layers to avoid calling an additional layer, or circumventing layers when dealing with requests, such as the presentation tier directly communicating with the datastore tier. We generally recommend avoiding the use of this pattern.

Identifying Pain Points and Opportunities

It is often tempting to avoid working on parts of a system or codebase that have a bad reputation, whether this is for poor code quality, high complexity, or just frequent failure. Some pain points are not always obvious until you have severe outages to resolve. However, never let a good crisis go to waste—identification and cataloguing problematic components within the system can help to track and improve known issues. Let's explore some of the common issues that occur within a distributed API-based system and how to approach this as an opportunity for change.

Upgrade and Maintenance Issues

Identification of where upgrades and reported bugs occur in the overall system can help create a "hit list." Watch for the following issues that occur within the system:

---

4 For more information on Pace, see "Accelerating Innovation by Adopting a Pace-Layered Application Strategy" by Gartner (*https://oreil.ly/EB1du*) and "A Pace-Layered Integration Architecture" by Dan Toomey (*https://oreil.ly/dHaBE*).

- High change fail percentage for a specific subsystem
- High volume of support issues raised for a system
- Large amounts churn of a specific part of the system or codebase
- High complexity (identified via static analysis and cyclomatic complexity)
- Low level of confidence provided from development teams when asked about the ease of a required change

Consider adding code quality metrics as this can provide a rough guide to potential underlying issues. A maintenance issue or subsystem issue could be a good opportunity to introduce an API abstraction to pull functionality out and use strangler fig to drive improvement. It might also be a code smell that good coding principles are not followed. In Chapter 9 we will also consider how we approach applications as we migrate toward API-based architectures on new infrastructure.

Performance Issues

Service-level agreements (SLAs) are an excellent upper bound to track and monitor performance against. In Chapter 5 you reviewed monitoring and metrics that help to signal an issue with an API service. The reality is that many applications do not build in proactive protections against the introduction of problems. If the first time the team hears about a performance problem is from direct customer feedback or from production monitoring—e.g., an edge system that has exhausted a user request-response latency budget—the team is immediately at a disadvantage when reacting to the problem.

Performance issues can be architectural; for example, do you have a service calling a service located in a different region or across the internet? When it comes to performance issues, measuring and creating an objective plan is critical. Take a measurement of the existing system, create a hypothesis on where performance could be improved, and then test and verify. It is important to consider the system as a whole, rather than attempting to optimize a specific component in isolation. Automating the measurement process allows you to introduce the performance measurement as part of the build process.

Breaking Dependencies: Highly Coupled APIs

Moving toward a distributed architecture is only going to pay dividends if parts of the architecture can evolve independently. A particular antipattern to watch out for is the synchronized coordination of releases across different parts of the system. This is a sign that APIs are potentially highly coupled, and breaking this could be an opportunity to further reuse and reduce release friction.

One skill that is often overlooked in training courses and in teams is working effectively with legacy code. Often developers are unsure about how to introduce the types of changes that help to break up dependencies. There are two techniques that are useful to consider when looking to break dependencies.

The sprout technique is covered in Michael Feather's 2004 *Working Effectively with Legacy Code*. It is often very difficult to unit test code that wasn't built with testing in mind. Sprout involves creating the new functionality elsewhere, testing it and adding it to a legacy method known as the insertion point. Another technique is to wrap the existing functionality by creating a new method with the same name and signature as the old method. The old method is renamed and called from the new method, with any additional logic before the legacy method is called.

If a service is predominantly legacy, working with legacy code is a critical skill to develop. Working on coding katas or pair programming on complex areas of the codebase will help promote understanding across the team. Sandro Mancuso created an excellent video on YouTube (*https://oreil.ly/p2jWO*) that several of us have used to understand practical approaches to working with legacy code.

Summary

In this chapter you have learned how to use an API-driven approach to evolve vintage monolithic applications toward a service-based architecture:

- APIs often provide a natural abstraction or "seam" within systems, supporting decomposition of services and facades to support gradual change. As such, they are a powerful force in any architect's toolbox when evolving a system.

- Key concepts to understand when evolving a system using APIs include coupling and cohesion. Designing and building systems with these universal architectural concepts in mind will make evolution, testing, and deploying of systems easier and safer.

- When evolving a system, you should always be clear about your current goals and constraints. Without clearly establishing and sharing these, migrations can become open-ended, which drains resources while providing little value and can affect morale.

- Well-established patterns, such as the strangler fig, can increase the speed and safety of evolving a system and prevent the need to reinvent the wheel.

The next chapter builds on the focus of this chapter and extends the scope of evolutionary architecture to also include migrating to cloud infrastructure.

CHAPTER 9

Using API Infrastructure to Evolve Toward Cloud Platforms

In the previous chapter we provided an overview of architectural approaches that you can use when evolving APIs and the services that power them. An equally important topic to consider within the evolution of systems is the underlying infrastructure, platforms, and hardware. Often this changes and evolves on its own rhythm: as hardware breaks, companies and technology become merged or acquired, or organization-wide IT policies dictate that infrastructure be upgraded. However, at times an API program will drive infrastructure changes, particularly in relation to modernization and moving to more cloud-like (software-defined) infrastructure. Now, you will learn how to implement and manage evolving a system and the corresponding API infrastructure.

This chapter builds on the architecture foundations presented in the previous chapters and explores how you can use API infrastructure, such as API gateways, service meshes, and developer portals, to evolve a system when moving to a cloud-based environment. You will learn the differences between a "lift and shift" of applications, a "replatform," and a "refactor or re-architecture," and develop the skills to know which is the most appropriate given a specific context. The accompanying case study will show how the existing API gateway and the Attendee service can be migrated to the cloud. The use of an API gateway can provide location transparency for services and APIs being served, which allows the deployment of a service into the cloud and traffic to be gradually shifted from the existing service to the new with limited (or no) impact on consumers. You will also explore nascent migration options for migrating services to the cloud using the multilocation/cluster functionality of a service mesh.

Case Study: Moving the Attendee Service to the Cloud

For the next evolution of the conference system case study, you will focus on moving the Attendee service to a cloud vendor's infrastructure. The primary motivation for doing this is that conference system owners want to eventually remove the burden of running their own data center. This will ultimately involve moving all of the new services, the monolithic application, middleware (such as API gateways), and datastores, to the cloud. We've chosen to migrate the Attendee service first, as it is the newest component and also one of the services that receives the most traffic. Figure 9-1 shows how the extracted Attendee service is currently running outside of the main conference system application's context.

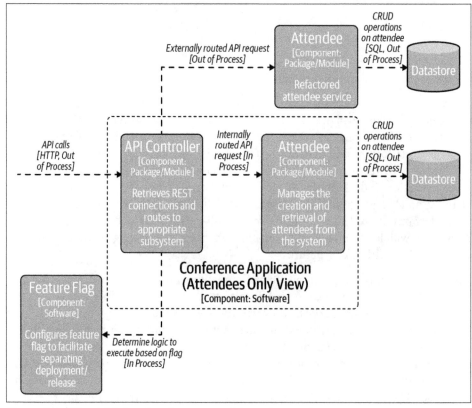

Figure 9-1. C4 model showing the extracted Attendee service

As you will explore in this chapter, there are multiple approaches to moving this service and supporting infrastructure to the cloud. Before you dive into the mechanics of the preceding approach, let's first explore the options that we should consider before deciding on the migration strategy.

Choosing a Cloud Migration Strategy

Building on Gartner's 2010 article, "Migrating Applications to the Cloud: Rehost, Refactor, Revise, Rebuild, or Replace?" (*https://oreil.ly/vHnc9*) Amazon Web Services published a blog in 2016 that presented the "six Rs" of cloud migration.[1] These articles are a great jumping-off point if you have been tasked with evaluating or leading a migration of your existing architecture and systems to the cloud. As APIs are often the closest business-driven component to the user—and a key point of ingress for the majority of requests—you should pay special attention to them when deciding on your approach to migration. The six Rs present a spectrum of options from "do nothing" all the way through to a complete rebuild or retiring of a system. They are:

- Retain or Revisit
- Rehost
- Replatform
- Repurchase
- Refactor/Re-architect
- Retire

Let's examine AWS's six Rs in more detail and explore how you can use this framework to evolve API infrastructure.

Retain or Revisit

This is the do nothing (for now) strategy. Although it can be tempting to discount this approach, many architects (us included) will suggest you "pick your battles," and sometimes the battle of migrating an API is not worth the return on your effort. This decision should, of course, be based on a sound business and technical evaluation, and you should communicate the decision to not take action internally and externally as appropriate. This is where ADRs shine—in terms of providing the paper trail and rationale of these decisions for future reference.

---

1 See "6 Strategies for Migrating Applications to the Cloud" (*https://oreil.ly/ilyJe*).

Communicating Change and Deprecations

A business and technical evaluation of a current API or system may lead you to decide against evolving the system at the current time. In this situation, it's still important to communicate any known dates by which action must be taken. For example, if a business unit is shutting down on a known date, or a system will reach end-of-life (EOL), or a key software or datastore license will expire at a known time, this should be communicated to consumers as a deprecation warning. You will most likely have a required deprecation notice baked into contracts and SLAs, and so be sure to consult these.

One key factor when considering moving applications to the cloud is the introduction of latency between two services during evolutionary steps. If you have a high-traffic service, a slowdown will be incurred for each request when crossing network boundaries. Ensuring that there is an understanding of what the degradation looks like is an important consideration, and if this violates an SLA, moving the service may not be an option. In "Modeling Exchanges and Choosing an API Format" on page 20, you learned how to choose a protocol and design an API within constraints, which is an important consideration when crossing boundaries.

Retaining would not be a viable strategy for our conference use case, as this would simply be "kicking the can down the road" and deferring the goal of migrating to the cloud.

Rehost

"Rehost" is otherwise known as "lift-and-shift." It involves moving systems and workloads to a cloud platform without any re-architecting. If you are looking to consolidate workloads or simply have to migrate away from your current infrastructure, this can often be an effective strategy. However, be aware that cloud infrastructure does not always behave in the same way as on-premise hardware, and so identify and confirm any assumptions that you have made.

Be Cautious with Specialist Systems and Bespoke Hardware

Although many "lift-and-shift" projects work as expected, some don't. This is especially true in relation to specialist bespoke systems and custom hardware. For example, older specialist systems may assume that all communication within the system occurs over a local bus or dedicated network connections (which isn't the case in the cloud), and certain datastore technologies assume specific hardware characteristics (or guarantees) of the underlying block storage system. When in doubt, do your research.

Rehosting could be a viable approach for our case study, although we have chosen the option of replatforming to allow us to take advantage of some cloud features.

Replatform

This approach is sometimes referred to as "lift-tinker-and-shift." It is very similar to rehosting but also takes advantage of some cloud services that require minimal re-work. For example, an existing datastore that is run as a system component may be swapped out for a protocol-compatible cloud service. You could swap a native MySQL datastore with a MySQL-compatible AWS RDS, an Azure Database, or GCP Cloud SQL. Another common replatforming is to update or change a language-specific application server or container.

This is the approach we have chosen for our conference system case study, so we can avoid major rework while still taking advantage of new cloud services as we migrate away from our existing on-premise infrastructure.

Repurchase

Repurchase primarily involves moving to a different product—for example, subscribing to a SaaS-based email-sending service rather than continuing to run an email server in-house.

As our conference system example primarily consists of bespoke applications and standard datastores, there is no option to repurchase (other than perhaps purchasing an off-the-shelf conference management system, which is out of scope for the migration).

Refactor/Re-architect

Refactoring means a re-imagining of how the application is architected and developed, typically using cloud native features. As with any refactor, the core (external) functionality of the application or system should not change, but how the functionality is accomplished internally will definitely change. This is typically driven by a strong business need to add features, scale, or performance that would otherwise be difficult to achieve in the application's existing environment. For example, if an organization has decided to decompose an existing monolithic application into microservices, a move toward adopting cloud native patterns is very often also considered. This pattern tends to be the most expensive to implement, but, if you have a good product-market fit and are being limited by your existing technology choices, it can also be the most beneficial.

We have not explicitly chosen this approach for our case study, as you have already been re-architecting the conference system throughout this book. One important point to consider is that API infrastructure and design lead toward a more cloud native way of thinking. Defining and modeling APIs as discussed in Chapter 1 facilitates a neat mechanism for representing services during refactor/re-architecture. It is also key that many cloud-based services or interactions are based on APIs too. The strategy around APIs when re-architecting is just as important as the service and systems that you plan to use on the cloud.

With the re-architecture now complete, it makes the most sense to replatform onto the cloud before making additional changes to the architecture.

Retire

"Retiring" systems during a migration simply means that you get rid of them. During many large migrations we have taken part in, there is often at least one existing system that is not being used any more and has simply been forgotten. As there is no longer a need for this functionality, the system can simply be decommissioned and the hardware resource freed or recycled.

It goes without saying that, as our conference system is relatively small and cohesive, there are no parts of it that can be retired quite yet! One of the overall goals was to retire the legacy conference system, and once the replatforming and refactoring is complete we can move forward with this.

Case Study: Replatforming the Attendee Service to the Cloud

Given the context provided in the previous section of this chapter, we have decided to "replatform" our Attendee service in addition to migrating the API gateway to the cloud. Retaining or retiring the service were not valid options, given the requirements to migrate toward the cloud. Repurchasing also did not make sense in this context. As we have already re-architected the attendees' functionality, by extracting this to a service early in this book, the refactor/re-architect did not appear appropriate. However, when you are adding new functionality into the conference system in the future, re-architecting the system (potentially extracting a service) and moving this to the cloud would be an option to strongly consider. Rehosting could be a solid strategy, but we are keen to take advantage of a cloud-based database-as-a-service rather than "lift and shift" our own MySQL database instance.

As shown in Figure 9-2, the "replatforming" approach will provide a good foundation on which to continue the migration as we move more services to the cloud. Moving the API gateway to the cloud now will also help to support API traffic being incrementally routed from the existing on-premises location to the cloud.

Figure 9-2 shows the final state of the replatformed architecture.

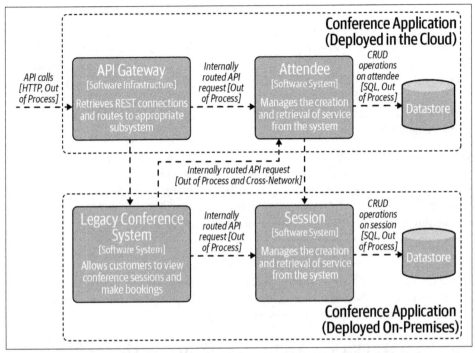

Figure 9-2. Infrastructure diagram showing extracted API gateway and Attendee service

Let's now consider how you could implement other requirements, such as API management, as the conference system evolves.

Role of API Management

Regardless of the strategy taken for your evolutionary journey, API management can play a key role in migration and also in unlocking the value of APIs across and even outside of an organization. API managers are essentially a supercharged gateway at the heart, providing a wide variety of additional features for publishing and controlling APIs. API managers provide policies that enable edge concerns, such as OAuth2 challenges, content validation, rate limiting, throttling, and many other features that are typical in a gateway. Additionally, they can provide developer portals containing a marketplace of all APIs that developers can use when building systems to consume offered APIs. Organizations can also use API management to monetize accessing APIs, both to external customers and for internal "chargebacks," which are common in enterprises and cross-divisional deployments. In "Current API Gateway Taxonomy" on page 73, we shared taxonomies for API gateways, and API management sits within the enterprise gateway category.

Perhaps the most important part of API management is that it can offer a central point to discover APIs, while you continue to make changes behind the scenes. It is possible to front the legacy conference system with an API, for example, while also offering the new broken-out Attendee API. In the case of the conference organizers, they could potentially look at offering an API that provides "conference management as a service" that would allow other conferences to use this, or to interface in a controlled manner with the external CFP system. Assuming that contracts on the API don't change, it is possible to evolve behind an API management layer.

Organizations often talk about the concept of being *API First*, meaning that all interactions between systems are carefully designed and modeled as APIs. This was a concept that we explored in Chapter 1. By following good design principles and striving for "API-First" design, this enables you to unlock value both externally to customers or internally within the wider organization by using tools like API management.

To modernize and migrate applications to be able to take advantage of using a tool like external API management, you need to reconsider traffic patterns. As architecture evolves to become hybrid, spanning different networks and deployments, thoughts about traffic also needs to be challenged.

North–South Versus East–West: Blurring Lines of Traffic Management

With a tour of the various options available for an API infrastructure migration complete, let's now explore how our chosen approach to replatforming will impact the management of API traffic within the evolving conference system. As we have chosen to incrementally migrate our services—rather than risk a big bang—the running of services across multiple cloud environments and on-premise data centers does present additional challenges. As is the case with many incremental cloud migrations, traffic will need to transit multiple networks in order to satisfy an API request made by a user.

Start at the Edge and Work Inward

In our case study, we have chosen to start at the edge by migrating the API gateway to the cloud along with a single service. Doing this can provide a migration team the chance to initially set up a completely new cloud environment without disrupting the existing system. For example, a duplicate of the current API gateway can be deployed into the cloud while the existing gateway is left running as is. This enables you to minimize risk by incrementally configuring the cloud-based API gateway without disrupting the existing production system.

It is often sensible to build an isolated proof of concept purely within the cloud, and only when this has been verified, start experimenting with routing into and out of the cloud environment. Designing for cloud-based architectures is often a paradigm shift from a design perspective. Don't underestimate the time needed to learn and understand new infrastructure.

Crossing Boundaries: Routing Across Networks

Before a migration to the cloud can go live, it is often necessary to ensure that the new and old systems can interact across the different networks. As discussed in Chapters 3 and 4, you have a range of options to implement this routing. If there is a single monolithic application and a small number of simple routes, it can be easiest to temporarily route from the new API gateway to the old, potentially with a simple HTTP redirect. However, if there are a large number of routes that will cross networks, or traffic must not leave the network once it has entered, you will have to consider other options, such as virtual private network peering or endpoints, or multicluster service mesh.

With API traffic transiting multiple networks, you will most likely need to consult your InfoSec teams, as this will disrupt the traditional approach to perimeter defenses and zonal architecture. Let's explore this topic in more depth and learn how the move to zero trust networks can help.

From Zonal Architecture to Zero Trust

Before learning how modern API gateways and service meshes can help you implement zero trust networks, let's first explore the traditional approach to zonal network architecture.

Getting in the Zone

As the commercial internet grew in popularity, more and more regulated industries began providing access to applications. This meant that both new systems and existing internal systems were made to be user facing. The emergence of zonal architectures provided a best practice in designing secure networks. Zoning is used to mitigate the risk of a completely open or flat network by segmenting infrastructure services into logical groupings that have the same networking security policies and security requirements. Consider a vulnerability like Log4Shell (CVE-2021-44228), a zero-day vulnerability posing significant risk to Java applications using affected Log4J libraries. Using the exploit, an attacker could gain access to a host in a network and start to run malicious activities. The range of impact and services under exploit is known as the blast radius of the attack. If all untrusted requests enter a zone that has access to very little high-value information, the blast radius is minimized and security operations have time to act to prevent serious outage. Zones tend to cascade, with each traversal into the next zone applying more defense-in-depth mitigation to challenge the inbound traffic.

The zones are separated by perimeters (Zone Interface Points) implemented through security and network devices. Zoning is a logical design approach used to control and restrict access and data communication flows only to those components and users as per security policy.

There are many approaches to defining zones and the associated security requirements, both standardized (often at the country level) and bespoke. However, as shown in Figure 9-3, four typical zones are found in most zonal architectures:[2]

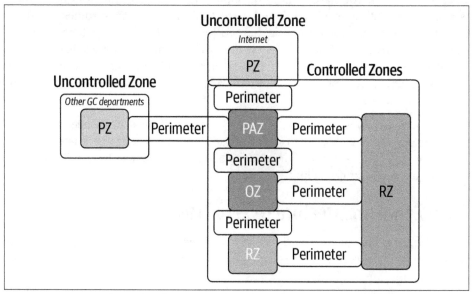

Figure 9-3. A typical zonal architecture, taken from the Canadian government's ITSG-22

Public Zone (PZ)
> This zone is entirely open and includes public networks such as the public internet, the public switched telephone network, and other public carrier backbone networks and services.

Public Access Zone (PAZ)
> This zone mediates access between operational systems and the Public Zone and often includes a demilitarized zone (DMZ).

---

2 Interested readers can learn more about zonal architectures from the Canadian government's Network Security Zoning (*https://oreil.ly/vYrDQ*).

Operations Zone (OZ)

An OZ is the standard environment for routine operations and with appropriate security controls at the end systems. This zone may be suitable for processing sensitive information; however, it is generally unsuitable for large repositories of sensitive data or critical applications without additional strong, trustworthy security controls that are beyond the scope of this guideline.

Restricted Zone (RZ)

This zone provides a controlled network environment generally suitable for business-critical IT services or large repositories of sensitive information and supports access from systems in the Public Zone via a PAZ and an OZ.

This approach to perimeter-based network design is somewhat similar to the old "castle and moat" defense, in that an attacker will struggle the most at the ingress point, but once inside the castle walls, they will generally have an easier time navigating around. This is largely because assumptions are made about any communication originating from within the system perimeter, network, or location. However, cloud infrastructure can challenge these assumptions. In many cloud platforms, the geographical and network location of the underlying infrastructure is abstracted away or not available. Even with protections in place from cluster providers, there is still the risk of a supply chain attack, where software is manipulated with malicious content at build time. Another possibility is a malicious user at the infrastructure provider's site, accessing information from the platform level.

Running different types of security across different types of deployment is possible, however a more homogeneous approach reduces the risk of assumptions being made and the requirement to learn different security techniques. There is inherent trust designed into a zone-based architecture, which prompted the evolution of a new approach: that of zero trust.

Trust No One and Verify

The zero trust security model, also known as zero trust architecture or perimeterless security, describes an approach to the design and implementation of modern network systems. The main concept behind the zero trust security model is "never trust, always verify," which means that devices should not be trusted by default, even if they are connected to a permissioned network such as a corporate LAN and even if they were previously verified. The reasoning for zero trust is that the traditional approach—trusting devices within a notional "corporate perimeter," or devices connected via a VPN—is not relevant in the complex environment of a corporate network. The zero trust approach advocates mutual authentication, including checking the identity and integrity of devices without respect to location, and providing access to applications and services based on the confidence of device identity and device health in combination with user authentication.

The eight principles outlined in our guidance will help you to implement your own zero trust network architecture in an enterprise environment. The principles are:

- Know your architecture, including users, devices, services, and data.
- Know your user, service, and device identities.
- Assess your user behavior, device, and service health.
- Use policies to authorize requests.
- Authenticate and authorize everywhere.
- Focus your monitoring on everything in regard to access: users, devices, and services.
- Don't trust any network, including your own.
- Choose and design services for zero trust.

The eight principles outlined are perfectly reasonable, however they are very tricky to consider in zonal architecture. The concept of a zone's trust assumptions would challenge many of these points. For example, a zonal architecture often only authenticates a user once at the edge of the system, and all networks within the perimeter are trusted by default. Let's explore how we can potentially evolve to a zero trust–based architecture.

Role of Service Mesh in Zero Trust Architectures

Zero Trust Architecture (*https://oreil.ly/8r8aC*), published by NIST in 2020, is a fantastic document in defining zero trust and key architectural considerations. Service mesh and API gateways combined provide a fantastic platform for implementing zero trust–based architectures. Using service mesh helps provide a homogeneous modeling of how your architecture components are represented and how the traffic flows between them. Underlying technologies enable a concrete model around running process identity and management of certificates helps to assert and prove identity. Integration of active tracing and monitoring enables analysis at all points in the platform, both for users but also for underlying services and Kubernetes pod health. All ingress traffic must have a strong challenge, often asserting that request with OAuth2 as discussed in Chapter 7, and traffic within the cluster can use mTLS for a strong assertion of authentication and authorization.

Don't trust any network, including your own is an interesting challenge for service mesh. In most service mesh models, a sidecar is tightly coupled with a service or app, enabling traffic management and security by routing via the sidecar. However, the simplicity of this deployment means that you cannot make concrete assertions on the platform that you are running on. What sits under the application and the sidecar needs to be secured to not make trust-based assumptions.

Augmenting Service Mesh with Network Policies

Platform security underpins any assumptions that you make at the application level. You therefore need to move down a level to get full zero trust. Kubernetes has the concept of NetworkPolicies (*https://oreil.ly/zxYkZ*) allowing the use of a network plug-in, such as Calico (*https://oreil.ly/5ds3n*). The controls allow you to create an isolation of pods from the platform that they operate on.

For example, the following policy will lock down all inbound and outbound traffic from being able to enter a given pod. For a zero trust architecture, this would be the default for pods; by applying the rule, the pod becomes fully isolated:

```
---
apiVersion: networking.k8s.io/v1
kind: NetworkPolicy
metadata:
  name: default-deny-all
spec:
  podSelector: {}
  policyTypes:
  - Egress
  - Ingress
```

Service mesh implementations often rely on looking up service names using a central DNS system. Even that is locked down. You need to start to enable a few controlled scenarios in the platform to remain locked down, but still allow the service mesh to operate. In the following policy, we allow DNS lookup on the legacy conference system, in order for it to locate the Attendee service:

```
---
apiVersion: networking.k8s.io/v1
kind: NetworkPolicy
metadata:
  name: allow-dns
spec:
  podSelector:
    matchLabels:
      app: legacy-conference
  policyTypes:
  - Egress
  egress:
    - ports:
      # allow DNS resolution
      - port: 53
        protocol: UDP
---
```

At this point the service mesh legacy conference service can discover where the attendees are via the sidecar, however the request itself would be blocked. Every routing rule in service mesh needs a corresponding allow rule defined in the network policy adapter. In this final example, we open up the rule for the legacy conference system to communicate with the Attendee service:

```
---
apiVersion: networking.k8s.io/v1
kind: NetworkPolicy
metadata:
  name: allow-conference-egress
spec:
  podSelector:
    matchLabels:
      app: legacy-conference
  policyTypes:
  - Egress
  egress:
  - to:
    - namespaceSelector:
        matchLabels:
          kubernetes.io/metadata.name: attendees
```

For ingress to work, you would also need to add ingress rules from the service mesh gateway through to the target services. In "Application Decisions for Effective Software Releases" on page 142, we outlined application-level decisions for an opinionated platform. Ensuring that the rules and configuration are applied in a consistent manner at release time is another reason to consider an opinionated platform.

By using service mesh and network policies, you have learned how to created a microsegmented architecture. The benefit of this approach is that you can have a scenario whereby security is consistent in a hybrid architecture with both the cloud and environments that were formerly zonal-based. A common pattern that is emerging is using a service mesh to bridge different ("multicluster") networks. This is accomplished via the use of peering service meshes together across the clusters, bringing the on-premises and cloud data plane under the knowledge of a combined control plane.[3] In Figure 9-4 the service mesh is responsible for all routing and can provide a zero trust architecture across networks. The advantage of taking this route is that it leads to a secure evolutionary architecture and homogeneous security environment. By making on-premises work like the cloud, there is now an easy path to evolving the remaining services into the cloud.

---

3 The mechanics of this varies for each service mesh implementation.

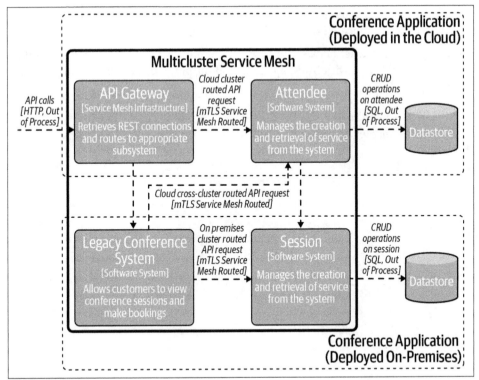

Figure 9-4. Multicluster service mesh peering

Summary

In this chapter you have learned how the use of API infrastructure, such as API gateways, service meshes, and developer portals, can be used to evolve a system when moving to a cloud-based environment:

- There are a number of approaches to evolving or migrating an API-based system toward the cloud, ranging from retain ("do nothing"), to rehost, replatform, repurchase, refactor/re-architect (rewriting to take advantage of cloud infrastructure), and retire.

- When migrating an API application to the cloud, you will often find that the line between north–south (ingress) and east–west (service-to-service) traffic management blurs.

- An API gateway can be used as a tool for migration, as it can encapsulate functionality and act as a facade for multiple backend systems operating from different environments and networks.

- The industry is moving away from zonal network architectures to "zero trust" systems, and service mesh technology can facilitate this move.

- Adopting zero trust allows you to combine both zero trust and zonal architectures, which helps with bridging cloud and on-premises systems during a migration period.

With your journey through the landscape of API architecture almost complete, the next and final chapter wraps up the key concepts and provides a look to the future in this space.

CHAPTER 10

Wrap-up

In the previous nine chapters of this book, you have undertaken a journey covering everything from designing APIs, to implementing, securing, and operating them. The focus has been on architecture, but just as important is how you apply architecture within your organization.

In this final chapter of the book, you will explore emerging API technologies that may play a bigger role in the future and learn how we keep up-to-date with these changing best practices, tools, and platforms.

Case Study: A Look Back on Your Journey

Throughout the book, we have been making evolutionary steps to update and mature the conference system architecture use case that we began with. You can see the starting point in Figure 10-1.

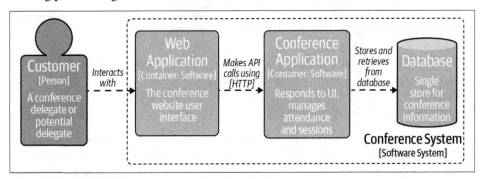

Figure 10-1. Original conference system architecture

Let's look at some of the decisions taken in extracting the Attendee service. As shown in Figure 10-2, and discussed in the Introduction, we made the decision (based on requirements from the conference system stakeholders) to extract the attendees, functionality into an API-based service that would be run as a standalone process external from the legacy conference system.

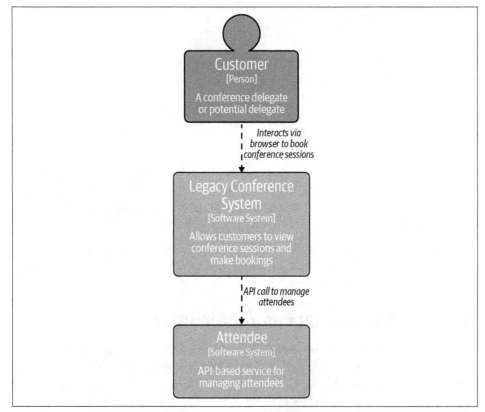

Figure 10-2. Extracting the Attendee service from the conference system

In Chapters 1 and 2, the architecture remained static while we explored how to design and test the Attendee API and service. In Chapter 3 we took our first big evolutionary step, introducing an API gateway between the end-user customer and the existing conference system and new service.

As shown in Figure 10-3, the customer now makes requests to the conference system via the API gateway, which provides an abstraction and single point of entry for traffic bound to either the legacy conference system or the new Attendee service. This step introduced a facade pattern, allowing control over when the legacy service is called versus the modern service.

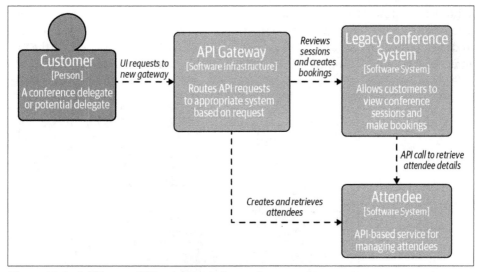

Figure 10-3. Adding an API gateway to the conference system

We took this one step further in Chapter 4, by extracting the conference session functionality from the legacy conference system into a new Session service, and introducing a service mesh to handle the service-to-service API traffic. At this point in the case study, the architecture looked like Figure 10-4.

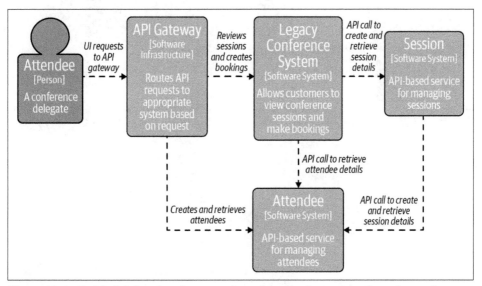

Figure 10-4. C4 Model showing the extraction of the Session service from the conference system

With a focus toward incrementally releasing API-based services in Chapter 5, we created an internal and external version of the Attendee service and used feature flags to determine which service a user's request was routed to. Figure 10-5 shows the two Attendee services side-by-side within the static architecture diagram.

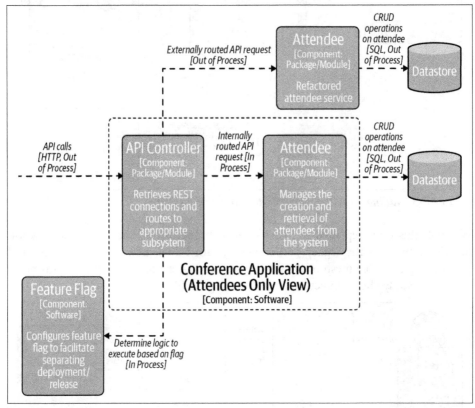

Figure 10-5. C4 model showing two Attendee services being routed to via feature flags

In Chapter 6 we focused on security, and although the architecture remained static, we introduced the concept of a mobile application calling the conference system, as shown in Figure 10-6, in order to provide a realistic scenario to conduct threat modeling.

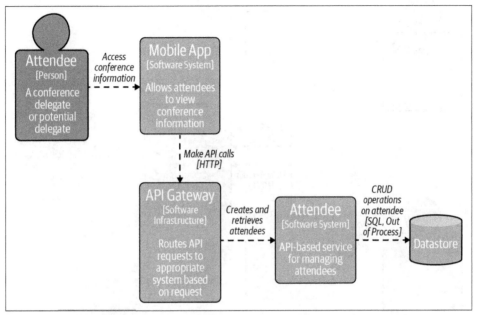

Figure 10-6. *C4 architecture showing a mobile app interacting with the conference system*

Chapter 7 added an external CFP system to the architecture, as shown in Figure 10-7, which required the implementation of external (user-facing) authentication and authorization.

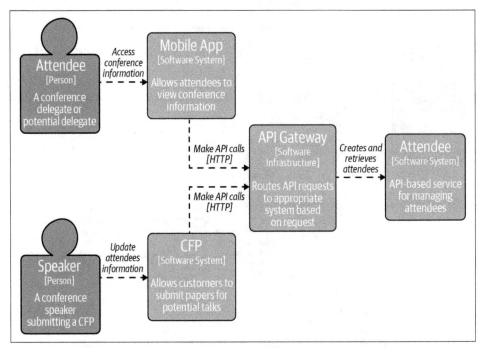

Figure 10-7. External system communicating with the conference system

In Chapter 9 we focused on migrating the Attendee service and API gateway to a cloud platform, which resulted in the architecture shown in Figure 10-8.

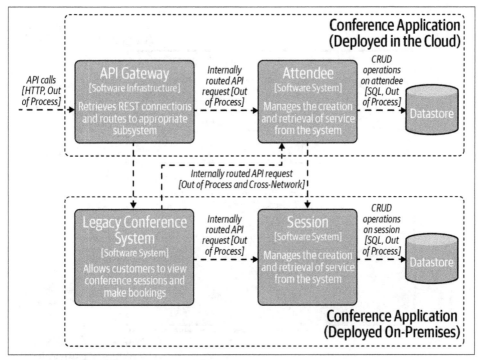

Figure 10-8. Cloud migration to conference system

Finally, in Chapter 9 we provided a potential model for migrating toward a zero trust architecture, with a uniform approach to deployment, routing, and security. In Figure 10-9 there is an option for hybrid architecture while the evolutionary journey continues to the cloud.

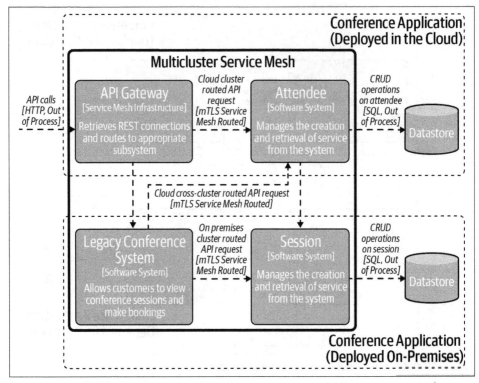

Figure 10-9. Cloud migration to conference system using multicluster service mesh

Throughout the case study, our focus has been on highlighting key decision points that you and your team will have to make as a typical system evolves toward becoming API- or service-based. From the humble beginnings of a single service and database running on premises, as you have journeyed toward a multiservice system running across the cloud and on-premises, you have learned that with the increased flexibility this final implementation offers, there are also trade-offs with architecture and infrastructure complexity.

Although this concludes the evolution of our case study in this book, we encourage you to experiment with creating new requirements, designing new APIs, and extracting additional services.

APIs, Conway's Law, and Your Organization

This is not a book about organizational design, but we wanted to mention the importance of this in relation to designing, building, and running APIs. "Conway's Law" has become famous within the microservice community, and the concept also applies to API architecture:

Any organization that designs a system (defined broadly) will produce a design whose structure is a copy of the organization's communication structure.

—Melvin Conway in *How Do Committees Invent?*

Or, put more succinctly, "if you have four groups working on a compiler, you'll get a 4-pass compiler." We have definitely seen this in the API world—as we like to joke, "if you have four groups working on a microservice system, you'll get four layers of APIs." We couldn't hope to cover the topic of organizational design in the depth it deserves in this book, and so instead we would like to recommend you read the following books:

- *Team Topologies* (*https://oreil.ly/ch1eD*) (IT Revolution Press)
- *Agile IT Organization Design: For Digital Transformation and Continuous Delivery* (*https://oreil.ly/2aeum*) (Addison-Wesley)
- *The Art of Scalability* (*https://oreil.ly/7CX01*) (Addison-Wesley)

If you are looking to undertake a major organizational shift or "digital transformation," we strongly recommend consulting the preceding works. Any API-based system is inherently a socio-technical system, and so you should always factor in the "socio" aspect as much as the "technical."

Understanding Decision Types

Jeff Bezos, the founder of Amazon, is famous for many things, and one of them is his discussion (*https://oreil.ly/7b3Mt*) of Type 1 decisions and Type 2 decisions. Type 1 decisions are not easily reversible, and you have to be very careful making them. Type 2 decisions are easy to change: "like walking through a door—if you don't like the decision, you can always go back." Usually this concept is presented in relation to confusing the two, and using Type 1 processes on Type 2 decisions: "The end result of this is slowness, unthoughtful risk aversion, failure to experiment sufficiently, and consequently diminished invention. We'll have to figure out how to fight that tendency." However, in the majority of cases—especially within a large enterprise context—choosing API-enabling technologies like an API gateway or service mesh is very much a Type 1 decision. Ensure your organization acts accordingly!

Preparing for the Future

When writing a book, we naturally capture experience and knowledge at a fixed point in time. There are always new developments emerging. Following are three topics that we didn't believe yet warranted full sections but are nonetheless worth keeping an eye on for their future impact on API architecture.

Async Communication

Asynchronous APIs are very popular, falling generally into two categories: client-server and client-broker. An example client-server relationship is achieved with technologies such as gRPC, and the client-broker relationship is achieved using intermediate technologies such as Kafka. As you learned about in Chapter 1, OpenAPI Specifications have been critical to consistently describing and specifying REST APIs.

The AsyncAPI (*https://www.asyncapi.com*) is an exciting and developing standard to provide a specification for asynchronous APIs. One challenge with asynchronous-based APIs is supporting the variety of protocol formats and range of technologies. It is definitely one to watch as the popularity of event-driven architectures and the need to define exchanges is a rapidly growing space.

HTTP/3

HTTP/3 (*https://oreil.ly/g7jaE*) is the third major version of the Hypertext Transfer Protocol used to exchange information on the World Wide Web, alongside HTTP/1.1 and HTTP/2. HTTP semantics are consistent across versions: the same request methods, status codes, and message fields are typically applicable to all versions. The differences are in the mapping of these semantics to underlying transport protocols. Both HTTP/1.1 and HTTP/2 use TCP as their transport (as in TCP/IP). HTTP/3 uses QUIC, a transport layer network protocol that uses UDP. The switch to QUIC aims to fix a major problem of HTTP/2 called "head-of-line blocking," which in particular affects websites that require multiple resources to load.

HTTP/3 promised potentially big speed gains, but as the underlying transport protocol has changed, this will require upgrades to ingress proxies and other networking components. The good news is that as of the time of writing, HTTP/3 is already supported by more than 70% of running web browsers.

Platform-based Mesh

As hinted within Chapter 4, many signals are pointing toward service mesh being merged with modern platform offerings. If this trend continues, it may be wise to adopt the mesh integrated within your chosen vendor's technology stack. In much the same way that the majority of organizations adopting a cloud vendor's Kubernetes stack don't replace the container (OCI) or networking (CNI) implementations, it may well be the same in the future with the service-to-service communications. As part of this evolution, we recommend keeping watch on related standards in this space, such as the Service Mesh Interface (SMI) (*https://smi-spec.io*). The emergence and adoption of solid interfaces surely point toward this layer of the communication stack being homogenized.

What's Next: How to Keep Learning About API Architecture

We began this book by mentioning that all three of us started the journey that ultimately led to the creation of this book in February 2020 at the O'Reilly Software Architecture Conference (SACON). We all love learning, and attending events is a big part of our continued approach to gaining new skills and knowledge. One of the most common general questions we get asked relates to how we approach learning and experimenting with new technologies. In this section of the chapter, we'll share with you our practices, insights, and habits.

Continually Honing the Fundamentals

We all believe that it is vitally importantly to constantly revisit the fundamentals of any skill you wish to master. This is especially important in such a fad-driven industry like the software development and operations domains. We'll cover some of the locations of where we search out this kind of knowledge, but we want to stress that when browsing websites, reading books, attending conferences, and the like, we actively seek out the existing and latest coverage of the fundamentals. For example, at many architecture conferences you will find sessions covering topics such as cohesion and coupling, and we have all at times learned and been reminded of concepts that we take back to our offices and apply the next day. As well as reading the latest book on cloud platforms, we also read new takes on traditional topics, such as Gregor Hohpe's "The Architect Elevator: The Transformation Architect."

It's very much a cliche in our industry that "what's old is new," and the cycles of technology that constantly repeat in slightly different forms can be navigated much more effectively by architecture designers who are constantly reminding themselves of the fundamentals.

Keeping Up-to-Date with Industry News

We recommend collating and constantly refining a list of websites and social media sites that provide coverage of the latest news within the architecture and API domains. Reading these once a week will help tune your sense of emerging trends and technologies that you may want to investigate. For example:

- InfoQ
- DZone
- The New Stack
- Software Architecture Reddit (*https://oreil.ly/Ic3K7*)

In addition to these general news sites and aggregators, you will also likely find certain organizations or individuals that write useful blogs on emerging topics. Using an RSS reader, such as Feedly, can allow you to collate these sources and review them on a weekly or monthly basis. Twitter can be a powerful tool for insights and comments on emerging technologies; following individuals who have similar interests and contribute to open source projects is a good way to find out early about new features.

Radars, Quadrants, and Trend Reports

Although you should always perform your own experiments and proof of concept work, we also recommend keeping up-to-date with specific technology trends via analyst sites. This type of content can be especially useful when you are struggling with a problem or have identified a solution and are in need of a specific piece of technology that many vendors offer. We recommend the following sources of information for learning more about the state of the art of technology within the API space:

- ThoughtWorks Technology Radar (*https://oreil.ly/YHlRs*)
- Gartner Magic Quadrant for Full Life Cycle API Management (*https://oreil.ly/HwvO5*)
- Cloud Native Computing Foundation (CNCF) Tech Radar (*https://oreil.ly/G0B7a*)
- InfoQ Trends Reports (*https://oreil.ly/aGY4Y*)

Several organizations and individuals also publish periodic technology comparison spreadsheets, and these can be useful for simple "paper evaluations" in order to shortlist products to experiment with. It should go without saying that you will need to check for bias across these comparisons (vendors frequently sponsor such work) and ensure the publication date is relatively recent.

Learning About Best Practices and Use Cases

We also recommend that you constantly be on the lookout for best practices and use cases related to the work you are doing. Many organizations like to share the why, what, and how of what they are doing. The motivations for this are important to understand, but often it's a mix of altruism, bragging rights, sales awareness, and recruiting. You always have to apply caution when learning about use cases, as most of these do skew toward positive coverage, potentially skipping over the initial failed tries, things that went wrong, or things that are still going wrong. However, the context provided can enable you to pattern match problems and solutions onto your organization and team. Sometimes this can provide confirmation of your chosen technology stack or approach, and on other occasions this can cause you to rethink!

Use cases and best practices can often be found in written and presentation format. Generally we recommend looking for both, and the advantage of conference presentations is that you can chat with the presenters after the talk in order to learn more! Following is a list of conferences that we regularly attend:

- QCon conference series (*https://oreil.ly/YW6pB*)
- CraftConf (*https://oreil.ly/trY4Y*)
- APIDays (*https://oreil.ly/eRSFK*) (API-focused)
- KubeCon (*https://oreil.ly/io6gU*) (platform-specific)
- Devoxx (*https://oreil.ly/ILSss*) / JavaOne (language-specific)
- O'Reilly online events (*https://oreil.ly/rQKIk*)

Learning by Doing

We believe that architects should remain as practicing software engineers. You may not be pushing code to production each day, but we recommend carving out time in your schedule to periodically pair with an engineer on your team or conduct research and experiment with the latest technologies. Without doing this regularly, it is easy for an architect's empathy for developers to fade. Doing this work also enables you to understand new friction points or a toil that may have been introduced by the adoption of new technologies. For example, anecdotally we found that many architects initially misunderstood the impact that container technology would have on developer toolchains. Unless you have experience in building container images and pushing them to a remote registry, it's easy to discount the impact of these actions on your daily workflow of building and maintaining APIs.

Learning by Teaching

As is hopefully evident from this book, we also learn a lot through the act of teaching. Whether this is writing books, teaching courses, or presenting at conferences, nothing beats the experience of assembling the information required to teach a concept. All too often we realize during this process that we don't quite understand a concept, or when asked a question by a student we suddenly appreciate that there is a gap in our understanding.

It is our opinion that another core role of an architect is teaching. Whether it's educating developers about the fundamentals or sharing new best practices, this act of teaching will continually reinforce your skill set and establish your credibility within the larger team.

Best of luck on your journey to mastering API architecture.

Index

About the Authors

James Gough is a Distinguished Engineer at Morgan Stanley working on API architecture and API programs. He is a Java Champion who has sat on the Java Community Process Executive Committee on behalf of the London Java Community and contributed to OpenJDK. James is also coauthor of *Optimizing Java* and enjoys speaking about architecture and low-level Java.

Daniel Bryant is the head of developer relations at Ambassador Labs. When it comes to job roles, he subscribes to the Pokémon philosophy of "gotta catch 'em all," and in previous lives, Daniel has worked as an academic, developer, architect, platform engineer, consultant, and CTO. His technical expertise focuses on DevOps tooling, cloud/container platforms, and microservice implementations. Daniel is a Java Champion and contributes to several open source projects. He also writes for InfoQ, O'Reilly, and The New Stack, and regularly presents at international conferences such as KubeCon, QCon, and Devoxx. In his copious amounts of free time, he enjoys running, reading, and traveling.

Matthew Auburn has worked for Morgan Stanley on a variety of financial systems. Before working at Morgan Stanley, he built a variety of mobile and web applications. Matthew's master's degree primarily focused on security, and this has fed into working in the security space for building APIs.

Colophon

The animal on the cover of *Mastering API Architecture* is an armadillo girdled lizard (*Ouroborus cataphractus*), previously in the genus *Cordylus*.

Armadillo girdled lizards live in the desert on the western coast of south Africa. They are often compared to miniature dragons in appearance: light or dark brown scales and yellow underbellies with black patterns. As far as size, they are typically between 7.5 and 9 centimeters in snout vent length (which does not include the tail).

They live in groups and are active during the day, although most of their active time is spent sunbathing. Their diet consists primarily of small insects (mostly termites), and they brumate (go into partial hibernation) during the winter. Unlike most lizards, which lay eggs, armadillo girdled lizards give birth to live young, one or two at a time about once a year. The females may also feed their young, another unusual behavior for lizards.

Their defense mechanism against predators is to roll into a ball and hold their tails in their mouths. This makes them look like mythical ouroboros, which is a symbol of wholeness or infinity. This unique behavior is the reason for their name, as mammalian armadillos also curl up in a ball.

The conservation status of the armadillo girdled lizard is "near threatened." Many of the animals on O'Reilly covers are endangered; all of them are important to the world.

The cover illustration is by Karen Montgomery, based on a black-and-white engraving from the Museum of Natural History. The cover fonts are Gilroy Semibold and Guardian Sans. The text font is Adobe Minion Pro; the heading font is Adobe Myriad Condensed; and the code font is Dalton Maag's Ubuntu Mono.

O'REILLY®

Learn from experts.
Become one yourself.

Books | Live online courses
Instant Answers | Virtual events
Videos | Interactive learning

Get started at oreilly.com.

Printed in the USA
CPSIA information can be obtained
at www.ICGtesting.com
JSHW051807100624
64551JS00011B/543

9 781492 090632